MOSES
AND THE
DOCTOR

Also by Luke Epplin

Our Team: The Epic Story of Four Men and the World Series That Changed Baseball

MOSES AND THE DOCTOR

TWO MEN, ONE CHAMPIONSHIP, AND THE BIRTH OF MODERN BASKETBALL

LUKE EPPLIN

New York Boston

Cover design by Phil Pascuzzo
Cover photo of Moses Malone by Richard Mackson/Getty Images

Grand Central Publishing
Hachette Book Group
1290 Avenue of the Americas
New York, NY 10104
grandcentralpublishing.com
@grandcentralpub

First Edition: February 2026

Grand Central Publishing is a division of Hachette Book Group, Inc.
The Grand Central Publishing name and logo are registered trademarks of Hachette Book Group, Inc.

Print book interior design by Bart Dawson.

Library of Congress Cataloging-in-Publication Data has been applied for.

ISBNs: 978-0-306-83349-6 (hardcover), 978-0-306-83351-9 (ebook)

Printed in the United States of America

LSC-C

Printing 1, 2025

To Jane and Ava,
my miracles

CONTENTS

PROLOGUE

THE SPEECH

On October 30, 1974, the New York Nets flew to Salt Lake City to face the Utah Stars. It was the Nets' fifth game in six nights, all in different cities. The punishing schedule spoke to the grind of playing in the American Basketball Association, the monthslong blur of predawn wake-ups, airport layovers, and half-full arenas. But that evening promised to be different. Even though the Stars had staged their home opener for the 1974–75 season a week earlier, the franchise had held off on any festivities. The Stars were taking a big risk that year, and the front office recognized that their unprecedented experiment required a blessing from the undeniable face of the league—the MVP, the scoring leader, the defending champion. They were waiting for Dr. J to arrive.

From the moment he'd surfaced on the national stage as a sinewy, scarcely known forward, his Afro flared high and the ABA's distinctive red-white-and-blue ball swallowed up by his enormous hands, Julius Erving appeared a vision of the future, an avatar of a sport that was shifting from the ground to the air. Like compatible puzzle pieces, the ABA and Erving had locked into place at once. One was a fledgling start-up scrambling to disrupt the National Basketball Association's hold on the sport's top talent, the other a leaper from Long Island who'd amassed a cult following on the asphalt courts of New York City. Erving carried that playground sensibility into the ABA, complete with an alter ego, Dr. J, whose balletic moves defied belief.

But few saw them. Because no television network broadcast ABA games nationally, Dr. J remained more rumor than reality, a ghost in the machinery of professional basketball. "I heard the legend of Dr. J, and I said, 'That's bullshit.' Until I saw him in that game," remembered Calvin Murphy, a five-foot-nine dynamo for the Houston Rockets who first competed against Erving in a charity contest during the early 1970s. "When I saw him sit on the rim, take them big hands, and dunk that ball over my whole team, I said, 'Yep, it's for real.'"

Despite possessing the sport's most electrifying player, the ABA struggled to stay solvent. In a league characterized as much by instability as by flamboyance, Erving at times seemed the difference between treading water and sinking. To chip away at the NBA's supremacy, ABA executives threw whatever they could think of against the wall, gimmicks and three-point shots and slam-dunk contests. The Utah Stars went so far as to nab a hoops prodigy straight out of high school.

In the third round of the 1974 draft, the Stars selected a nineteen-year-old center who'd sailed to two state championships at Petersburg High School. For months, college recruiters had camped out in south-central Virginia, promising Moses Malone the world if only he'd sign his name to their commitment letter. While Malone had eventually settled on the University of Maryland, his true desire had been to bypass college altogether. And that was exactly what he ended up doing.

It was a risky, controversial gambit. Detractors charged the Stars with robbing an adolescent of his education; sportswriters questioned whether Malone's gangly frame could withstand the pounding from men many years his senior. To calm skeptics' nerves, cautious Stars officials turned to the ABA's most beloved and distinguished asset.

The night before Halloween in Salt Lake City, a crowd some seven thousand strong hustled to their seats. Like many arenas of the era, the Salt Palace, a cream-colored structure shaped like a snare drum, had minimal pregame entertainment—no loud music, no scoreboard antics, no dance troupes. What they had instead was Erving, clad in the patriotic colors of his Nets warmups, staging a one-man dunking exhibition in the layup line. For audiences not yet weaned on nightly highlight clips, the spectacle would've been as thrilling as the game itself. But then Erving did something unexpected. He strolled to halfcourt and grabbed hold of the public-address microphone.

Even though he was only a half decade older than Malone, Erving, in his fourth season out of the University of Massachusetts Amherst, had already assumed the responsibilities of an elder statesman. A master improviser on the court, he'd learned to deliver what was expected of him off it as well, no matter how peculiar or unconventional, such as praising a competitor in another team's arena. The impromptu speech Erving gave before tipoff was equal parts stirring and comforting, befitting someone whose postgame interviews poured out of him with such fluency that they came across as scripted.

"My high school coach once told me that when you go into the ocean for the first time, you cannot expect to swim right away. First you have to get your feet wet." Erving then turned to Malone. "But, Moses, you have been thrown into the ocean, and you can swim already."

The person least moved by the speech was its subject. The press conferences, the magazine profiles, the highway billboards that heralded his arrival in Salt Lake City, the pregame praise from a renowned competitor—none of that interested Moses Malone.

Basketball was his passion; the public-facing obligations that those who played the sport at the highest level had to fulfill were, for Malone, irritants to be swatted away. He would no more give a follow-up speech thanking Erving than he would strip naked at halfcourt. Wringing words out of the lone teenager in professional basketball already was taxing the most seasoned sportswriters. Malone's approach to his job was as blunt as his demeanor: suit up, sweat and bang, go home.

The philosophical gap between the two individuals off the court manifested in different ways on it. That evening, Malone controlled the paint; Erving managed the flow. Every time a shot went up, Malone broke hard toward the basket, sidestepping defenders, worming through gaps, tipping misses to himself. New York head coach Kevin Loughery watched in disbelief as the Stars rookie grabbed fifteen rebounds, nearly half of what the entire Nets roster pulled down. "You don't expect an eighteen-year-old or whatever he is to come out and play like that," Loughery marveled.

Held to two free throws in the first quarter, Erving exploded for thirty-four points over the next three. Malone kept pace with twenty-eight of his own. At one point, Malone caught a pass inside the foul line, spun around his defender, and, according to Steve Rudman of *The Salt Lake Tribune*, "nearly ripped the basket from its moorings in one of the grandest stuffs ever witnessed, reminiscent, in fact, of the thing that made Erving famous." Erving countered with what Rudman characterized as "aerobatic rushes, vacuum dunks and the neatest rendition of rhapsody in a blur there is in basketball." It was a battle between two equal but opposing forces: smooth and rough, graceful and grinding, ice and fire. In the end, a three-pointer—an ABA invention that the NBA wouldn't implement until 1979—by Erving sealed the game for the Nets.

After his team's 95–91 win, a reporter asked Erving for an assessment of the adolescent whom he'd publicly praised beforehand. "In two words," Erving responded, "I believe."

Over the following eight years, Erving and Malone switched leagues and clubs, won MVPs and shattered records, honed novel styles of play and endured postseason heartbreak. Along the way, the speech bound them together. Whenever they faced each other, Malone would sidle up to Erving and ask, "How's my swimming going?"

Every basketball fan is familiar with the rivalry in the 1980s between Earvin "Magic" Johnson's Los Angeles Lakers and Larry Bird's Boston Celtics. It was, according to legend, the matchup that helped the NBA shed its reputation as a drug-addled, violence-prone league and blossom into a sporting juggernaut whose appeal spanned continents. But this binary between Magic and Bird, the Lakers and the Celtics, has overshadowed other players and teams from this pivotal era that were every bit as instrumental in shaping basketball as a sport, an art form, and a cultural phenomenon. None more so than the two ABA expats who eventually banded together on the Philadelphia 76ers to disrupt the decade-long title swaps between the Lakers and the Celtics.

This is the story of the rambling road that led Moses Malone and Julius Erving to each other. Opposite in temperament and antithetical in approach—one having reimagined the way that basketball was played on the ground, the other in the air—Moses and the Doctor meshed seamlessly, their strengths and weaknesses in perfect counterbalance, establishing a blueprint for future superteam pairings. Together, they set out to accomplish what no other club fronted by stars from the ABA had managed. More than a championship, it was legitimacy they were chasing, not only for Erving's playground-infused style and Malone's unorthodox path but also for a defunct league whose freewheeling, expressive spirit has since come to define basketball across the globe.

PART I

ABA

CHAPTER 1

CALL ME THE DOCTOR

For hoops junkies in the early 1970s, there was no better place to get a fix than at Holcombe Rucker Park, then known as PS 156 Playground, at the corner of West 155th Street and 8th Avenue in Harlem. During the offseason, several of the sport's best players migrated from indoor arenas to the outdoor court that came to be regarded as the Madison Square Garden of playground basketball. Hours before games, at the annual summer tournament, kids staked out spots in the branches of surrounding trees. Faces dotted the windows of nearby housing projects. Spectators jammed bleachers and sidelines, climbed poles and fire escapes, squatted on oil cans and orange crates, and clustered on rooftops and viaducts to glimpse a rare sight: household names like Walt Frazier, Wilt Chamberlain, and Connie Hawkins swapping buckets and talking trash with neighborhood streetball idols. The chance to witness the cream of basketball's named and nameless colliding on asphalt drew crowds that, in sportswriter Peter Vecsey's words, were "thicker than ants at a picnic."

The scene, noisy and exuberant, doubled as a summer block party. Pushcart vendors peddled hot dogs and lemon ices, music blared from transistor radios, shirtless musicians pounded on drums, and horns blared amid snarled traffic from double-parked cars. Everywhere, the smell of sweat, grilled meat, and exhaust saturated the muggy air.

The games lived up to the joyous atmosphere. Letting it all hang out, Rucker competitors punctuated their run-and-gun flurries with behind-the-back passes and chest-thumping dunks. The more dazzling the moves, the more electrified the sidelines. While a drained midrange jumper might draw smattered applause, a twisty reverse layup could whip onlookers into a backslapping frenzy, even if it clanged off the rim. Rather than deflecting blocked shots to their teammates, Rucker defenders spiked balls volleyball-style off the encircling chain-link fence. It was the essence of playground basketball, rhythmic and inventive, theatrical and virtuosic, as much an attitude as a style of play.

In the summer of 1971, a new, mysterious figure emerged on the Rucker scene. He was twenty-one years old, long-limbed and thin as a straw, his Afro adding several inches to his six-foot-seven frame. Rumors circulated of a streetball sensation who could bend and contort his body in confounding ways. Creative and cool-headed, he threw down vicious slams yet seldom flashed a hint of emotion, devastating defenders not by jawing in their ears but by trotting downcourt expressionless.

From the sidelines, a megaphone at his mouth, Rucker emcee Ernest "Plucky" Morris burned through a litany of nicknames. The Claw, Houdini, Little Hawk—each one was inadequate. Finally, during a stoppage in play, the stranger sauntered over to Morris and declared, "Look, if you want to call me something, call me The Doctor."

It was an unveiling, the surfacing of the last American athletic icon whose feats would be more heard about than seen.

Unique to the mainstream sports birthed in the United States, basketball was conceived as an indoor activity. When James Naismith, a physical education instructor, nailed a peach basket to the wall of a YMCA in Springfield, Massachusetts, in 1891, he was, above all, seeking to keep restless young men engaged over the long, cold New England winter. The game's first stars were not the players but the coaches—tactical authority figures who formulated the patterns and strategies on which basketball basics were built. The style of play that developed inside high school and college gymnasiums was plodding and schematic, predicated on principles of teamwork, discipline, and unselfishness: the ball rotating from station to station, the players traversing predetermined routes, the defense reacting and adjusting. Coaches prized the so-called fundamentals of the sport—skillful yet unshowy dribbling, passing, and shooting that minimized error and kept the top-down systems humming efficiently.

There was another, parallel style of basketball that evolved outdoors. It sprouted in ethnically diverse inner-city blocks where the sons and daughters of Irish, Italian, and Jewish laborers lofted rubber balls into milk crates fastened to lampposts and telephone poles. It took equal hold in vacant lots and schoolyards tucked between rowhouses and tenements in segregated neighborhoods like Harlem and North Philadelphia. These became the laboratories where city-dwelling adolescents, lacking access to the grass and open spaces that other games required, organically forged an alternative aesthetic for a sport still in its infancy.

For Black streetballers, whose childhoods often were marred by rampant discrimination, overcrowded housing, and drug-related violence, basketball offered salvation of sorts, an outlet through which they could channel their creative drives. "Just as white college basketball was patterned and regimented like the lives awaiting its players, the Black schoolyard game demanded all the flash, guile, and individual reckless brilliance each man would need in the world facing him," wrote Kareem Abdul-Jabbar, an alumnus of Harlem's competitive blacktop courts.

As much as wins, the playground game rewarded athletic ingenuity. "Our game belonged to us and had varying degrees of difficulty," recalled Chet Walker, a Hall of Fame forward from Benton Harbor, Michigan. "You tried the most wonderful stuff you could think of to score on your friends and make them remember it. It was art, it was survival of the fittest, it was theater." Players who put their personal spin on everything from dribbling to rebounding to blocking shots—ideally while making their opponents look foolish in the process—transformed into urban legends whose idiosyncratic moves sparked chatter across subway lines and brownstone stoops. There was Earl "the Pearl" Monroe twirling around defenders. There was Connie "the Hawk" Hawkins gliding toward the rim, the ball enveloped in his spidery right hand. There was Earl "the Goat" Manigault slamming the ball with his right hand, catching it on the way down with his left, and then ramming it through again. Whenever one of these larger-than-life figures stepped onto an outdoor court, his nickname blew from spectator to spectator like a warm breeze.

In 1950, a generation before streetball legends like Monroe, Hawkins, and Manigault emerged, this novel style of basketball planted its seed when Holcombe Rucker, a Black parks director in New York City, inaugurated a tournament that later bore his name. Over the following decades, the Rucker Tournament in Harlem became the go-to summer scene for professional and playground players alike. Preaching education alongside athletics, Holcombe Rucker made it his mission to funnel striving streetballers into college with scholarships. It didn't take long for outdoor basketball to infiltrate indoor arenas nationwide.

As a child, Julius Erving kept an eye out for traces of it in the games he watched on television. Certain players, like "Jumpin'" Johnny Green of the New York Knicks and Elgin Baylor of the Los Angeles Lakers, captivated him with their artistry. "Elgin taking the rebound and dribbling through traffic is something that I began doing in my feverish daydreams," Erving wrote, adding, "I see [his game] somehow as liberating, the black body moving through white bodies, and the self-sufficiency of the act. For the first time, I have this idea that certain ways of basketball are more beautiful than others."

The innovative on-court style that would whisk Erving to basketball superstardom was rooted in dreams from his childhood. "Back then," Erving recalled, "before I was physically able, I felt these different things within me, certain moves, ways to dunk. I realized all I had to do was be patient and they would come. So I wasn't particularly surprised when they did. They were part of me for so long." On the playground courts of Campbell Park, outside the housing project where he was raised in Hempstead, a town on Long Island near Queens, Erving worked on his game year-round. He dribbled through puddles and around sidewalk cracks until the ball became slick from overuse. In winter, when snow blanketed the ground, Erving shoveled off a rectangle of asphalt so that he could continue launching jumpers at rims frosted with ice. On his way to and from the court, Erving built up his leg strength by hurdling benches cemented to the sidewalk and bounding up dimly lit stairwells.

The game's cerebral demands, too, consumed Erving. Throwing up thousands of shots, he tested assorted spins and release points until he became as skilled with the backboard as a pool shark is with the bumpers, unlocking angles and openings inaccessible to less studious players. "I set no dimensions for my game," Erving explained. "I decided not to limit myself when I found I could do anything that I had ever seen any guy do." Since he had not yet hit a growth spurt, Erving developed the skill set of a guard coupled with the leaping ability of a forward. One of his neighbors spoke of watching Erving practice for hours alone: "Behind his back, between his legs, dunk, and things like that. It would be ten o'clock at night and my mother-in-law couldn't stand the bouncing ball. We'd say, 'Julius, either go home or shoot without bouncing the ball.'"

As uninhibited as Erving was on the court, he craved structure off it. His parents' marriage had been short and stormy, ending when Erving was three. His father died years later from injuries suffered in a car accident. The responsibility of raising Erving and his two siblings fell to his mother, Callie, who supplemented her domestic labor with welfare checks. When Erving turned thirteen, she remarried a sanitation worker more than two decades her senior and uprooted the family to the neighboring town of Roosevelt. "Basketball was my only escape," Erving said of his childhood. "Many times when I was growing up, things would get off on the wrong foot at the house and I'd go down to the park and play ball all day. When I came back, the trouble which had happened at the house was the last thing on my mind. It freed my head."

Filling the father-figure role was Don Ryan, the coach of a Salvation Army team in Hempstead, who plucked a preteen Erving straight off the playground. Piling into station wagons, the club motored into wealthier communities that Erving had little access to, which embedded the idea of basketball providing an avenue into the wider world. Even then, as Erving helped Ryan's squad win back-to-back championships, there was a split between his play and his demeanor. With a basketball in hand, Erving was bold and daring, unafraid to improvise. Without it, he was reserved and pensive. "If someone had said then he would become a Doctor, I'd have said a medical doctor," Ryan reflected. "He was so intense, so serious."

The nickname that would stick into adulthood came from Leon Saunders, an argumentative friend whom Erving dubbed "the Professor." Saunders in turn labeled his dispassionate companion "the Doctor." It was an apt moniker for someone whose placid, clinical bearing had prompted classmates to tease Erving about carrying himself like an old man. On the basketball court it took on a different meaning. Like a doctor, Erving operated, dissected opponents, cut like a scalpel toward the basket.

There was a pattern that recurred at every step along his basketball journey. In a team structure, Erving was eminently coachable, willing to sacrifice his statistics and suppress his instincts for the betterment of the team. But in his free time, he strayed from his coaches' tutelage, devoted to manifesting the athletic artistry he envisioned in his mind. "His talents were evident," remembered Earl Mosley, his junior high coach, "because he used to play with the junk shot, before and after practice. Twisting things, lobs and all kinds of spinning maneuvers." In high school, Erving would sweat through practice and then undertake his own custom-designed drills: shooting right- and left-handed, leaping up to touch the rim, flipping the ball every which way off the backboard. Ray Wilson, his high school coach, used to watch him from afar, impressed by his dedication but dismayed at the effort wasted on shots that would never fly in formal competition. Sometimes he'd pull Erving aside and say, "I don't know why you're throwing that junk up there, son."

Once, during a varsity game, a guard floated a pass to Erving on a fast break. Rather than catching it, collecting himself, and laying the ball softly off the backboard, Erving snatched the ball in the air and flipped it through the hoop in one motion. Wilson was livid at Erving for bringing the outdoor game indoors. "Take that play back to the playground!" he screamed, yanking Erving from the action. It was only later that Wilson realized that, far from chucking up trick shots for their own sake, Erving was pushing the airborne borders of a sport still stubbornly earthbound. "I was putting limitations on him," Wilson recognized. "He needed to get away from structured situations to where he could truly express himself, take the chance of doing things that hadn't been done without the fear of people saying, 'Don't dare to be great.'"

The summer before his senior year, Erving attended a basketball camp in the Adirondack Mountains. Wayne Embry, a ten-year NBA veteran who'd won a championship with the Boston Celtics months earlier, made an appearance. After Embry agreed to go mano a mano with the camp's best player, one of the coaches whispered, "Go get Julius." Not wanting to embarrass the spindly teenager, Embry declared that he wouldn't take any shots from inside the free-throw line. The contest opened with Erving sinking seven straight baskets, after which he sheepishly mumbled, "Mr. Embry, you can play regular basketball against me." So Embry, lowering his shoulder, muscled into the paint. "I am trying to practice my hook, but he was blocking my shot all over the place," Embry remembered. "He totally dominated me."

How could a player capable of beating an NBA star one-on-one escape the attention of many major college basketball programs? Whether because of his still growing frame (Erving peaked at six foot three in high school, sprouting four more inches after graduation), his suspect jump shot, or his muzzled play in formal settings, the recruitment process never reached a fever pitch. One of the schools to dangle a scholarship was the University of Massachusetts Amherst. Erving's high school coach, Ray Wilson, had been a college teammate of Jack Leaman, the head men's basketball coach at UMass. This connection helped persuade Erving to enroll in a state school known more for academics than athletics. Despite being tucked into the same scenic valley as Springfield, the industrial city where James Naismith had birthed the sport, UMass Amherst was a basketball backwater. When Erving enrolled there in 1968, not a single UMass graduate had ever made it to the NBA, and the program had never been nationally ranked. Anonymity was all but guaranteed on a team that seldom crossed paths with the country's top collegiate talent.

George Mumford, a finance major at UMass who later worked as a consultant for several NBA franchises, never forgot the first time he saw his future roommate in action. It was during a pickup game over Labor Day weekend at the start of the fall semester. "I was there with a bunch of freshmen and we were looking to play basketball," Mumford recalled, "and we saw this dude playing in dress shoes, dunking on people." Confined to the freshman squad because of NCAA regulations that prohibited first-year players from participating in varsity competition, Erving did the impossible: his flashy style of play grabbed the attention of a campus in which basketball, as one writer claimed, "created as much enthusiasm as an 8 a.m. lab." It was said that students would show up for the freshman game and then leave before the varsity squad took the floor afterward. Not once that winter did the freshmen suffer a loss. In his downtime, Erving continued to refine his game. "When Julius got to Massachusetts, he couldn't hit a 15-foot jump shot," claimed team captain Ray Ellerbrook. "So every day he'd go out there maybe an hour before practice and stay an hour after practice, shooting, shooting, shooting."

In his varsity debut in 1969, Erving rendered the Amherst crowd "hoarse and hysterical" with a twenty-seven-point outburst. The excitement built game after game. Jack Leaman recalled one contest in which Erving, saddled with four fouls, raced downcourt on a fast break. A guard planted himself in front of the basket, certain to draw the charge that would foul Erving out of the game. Resigned, the UMass head coach glanced down the bench for a substitute. But then a roar echoed across the arena. When Leaman looked up, the guard was still standing in place, waiting for contact that never came. "To this day, I don't know what Julius did," Leaman said. "They tell me he shifted his body in midair to avoid the contact, but if they told me he jumped over the kid, I'd believe that, too."

The bored students who used to amble tardily into Curry Hicks Cage, a musty, barnlike building with a jumble of exposed pipes above the hardwood court, soon swelled to standing-room-only masses. "The games back then used to start at 8 o'clock," said Wally Novak, the ticket manager at UMass. "Well, around 1:30 or 2, the kids would start lining up, four across, outside the Cage. It got so bad, the food service started delivering what they called 'Survival Lunches' because the kids weren't eating. They didn't want to lose their place in line. By 4:30 or 5, I'd open the door and let them in. Within an hour, the place would be full, and then they'd all wait for Julius. We had to turn thousands of kids away back then. I've never seen anything like it." Despite this campus-wide frenzy, the students witnessed a neutered version of Erving. Since college basketball had outlawed dunking in 1967, in part to mitigate Kareem Abdul-Jabbar's (then Lew Alcindor's) dominance at UCLA and in part to stanch the seepage of the playground aesthetic into university settings, Erving found his most potent and crowd-pleasing weapon stripped from his arsenal. Merely touching the rim resulted in a technical foul. "It's a shame we didn't have dunking then," said Leaman. "[Erving would] have built us a new arena."

Erving's years in Amherst were a time of growth and change, with the most life-altering incident occurring away from the court. During his freshman season, his younger brother, Marvin, began complaining about excruciating pain in his joints. Three years apart in age, the two siblings had grown up with mutual admiration for each other despite their opposing interests. Julius was the athlete, Marvin the academic. In high school, Julius became captain of the basketball team while Marvin was elected class president. Marvin revered his older brother for his physical qualities, but Julius revered Marvin equally for his scholarly traits. It was inevitable that Julius's future would involve basketball, yet Marvin's seemed boundless, dependent on wherever his roving intellect steered him.

In February 1969, Marvin was rushed into a New York City hospital. Unaware of the gravity of his brother's condition, Julius closed out the season in Amherst. It was only later, upon receiving a call informing him of his brother's death from lupus, that Julius realized he'd never had a chance to say goodbye.

The pain was overwhelming. Julius lost control, bawling during the drive home to Long Island. For three days he sobbed over Marvin's grave. Then, all at once, a realization hit him: "I was really brought to my knees and made to feel helpless and powerless. I could be gone tomorrow. I felt helpless, but I also became fearless. I felt, 'Well, if I'm going to do something I'm going to let it all hang out.'"

A phenomenon in Massachusetts's Pioneer Valley, Erving remained shrouded in secrecy outside it. A breakout role on the US Olympic Development Team during the summer of 1970, in which he excelled against many of the country's top basketball prospects, earned him respect among his peers but did little to raise his national profile. In 1970–71, his junior season, Erving averaged nearly twenty-seven points and twenty rebounds for a team that routinely squared off against basketball lightweights scattered across New England.

His team's lone moment in the national spotlight came in the National Invitational Tournament at Madison Square Garden. Before UMass's first-round game against North Carolina, sportswriter Peter Gammons rang up a fellow Tar Heels fan to warn him of a springy forward who could give the perennial powerhouse fits.

"Who or what," Gammons's friend responded, "is a Julius Erving? Or for that matter, a UMass?"

The answers were no clearer after the game. Erving fouled out; UMass got trounced, 90–49. It was a deflating end to the season, but there was one final twist. Steve Arnold, a sports agent in New York City, caught wind of the basketball mania sweeping through Amherst. Phoning Erving out of the blue, Arnold posed a straightforward question: "Would you be interested in playing pro basketball, *right away*, if I can line up a team to take you?"

With few exceptions, the NBA had refrained from signing players until they'd finished their four-year college eligibility. The ABA, however, had no such misgivings. Founded in 1967, the ABA, desperate for fans and funds, took a more flexible attitude toward established norms. In its fierce competition for young talent, the ABA went where the NBA wouldn't. The league instituted a "hardship clause" that permitted the drafting of undergraduates with college eligibility remaining if those players could demonstrate financial need—a standard that was malleable enough to encompass nearly everyone.

Spencer Haywood, an Olympic gold medalist in 1968, tested the waters the following year. He became the ABA's first hardship case when he joined the Denver Rockets after his sophomore season at the University of Detroit. The experiment was an unqualified success, with Haywood leading the league in scoring and being awarded the MVP. The next year, he sued the NBA when he attempted to jump leagues. The subsequent lawsuit was settled in Haywood's favor, paving the way for the NBA to adopt its own hardship clause. The ruling opened the floodgates just as Erving was winding down his junior year.

When Jack Leaman caught word that agents were lurking about, he urged Bob Woolf, an attorney in Boston who also represented basketball players, to speak with his star about the decision. Erving's mind, however, already seemed made up. "I don't have anything left to accomplish at Massachusetts," Erving reportedly told Woolf. "I'm tired of playing against teams like Vermont and New Hampshire." By then, Erving had developed a keen sense of his own value. "I know they were charging 50 cents a ticket when I got [to UMass]," he said, "and now it's $3.50."

Because Erving was still largely untested, few professional scouts had him on their draft radars after his junior year. When Arnold approached executives from the Virginia Squires, an ABA franchise that split their home games between several cities across the state, none had seen him play. The grainy black-and-white footage that Arnold sent them showed a long-stemmed forward who could bound from one end of the court to another in only a few strides. It proved intriguing enough to merit a meeting with Erving and his agents at a Philadelphia hotel. There, Al Bianchi, the Squires head coach, took one look at Erving's oversized hands and, in a thick Queens accent, exclaimed, "My god, did you see those meat hooks?" From palm to fingertip, Erving's hands measured twelve inches, 25 percent above average for a man of his height. One writer pointed out that if Erving's height were in proportion to his hands, he'd top out at nine feet tall.

Even though the franchise was terminally strapped, Squires executives swallowed hard and prayed that the half-million dollars they offered Erving wouldn't wreck their payroll. Later, when the press badgered him about why he hadn't stayed in Amherst until graduation, Erving didn't equivocate. "Let's put it this way," he explained, "I have my college degree in basketball."

His college stint over and his pro career yet to begin, Erving spent the summer in between on the playground. Dave Brownbill, a former point guard at Hofstra University, remembered the first time he spotted Erving. Leaping for a rebound, Erving seized the ball with one hand and then took off dribbling the other way, all without using his other hand. There was something comical about the scene: one of the highest-paid basketball players in the country was pounding the asphalt in anonymity on Long Island.

Soon, Erving and Brownbill began tooling around New York City, jonesing for pickup basketball. No longer grounded by NCAA restrictions, Erving's game took flight. Dunking became an artful yet aggressive expression of his newfound liberation, something that Erving claimed he "couldn't get enough of" at first. Sometimes Brownbill had to serve as peacemaker when an Erving slam left humiliated defenders raring to retaliate. "He wouldn't really mean to [embarrass opponents]," Brownbill explained, "but it was just his natural instinct."

Embarrassing opponents in a pickup game was one thing; doing so at Rucker Park was something else entirely. As an amateur athlete on scholarship, Erving had been prohibited from competing in the Harlem Professional Basketball League, an annual round-robin tournament at Rucker from mid-July to early August. In the summer of 1971, having already signed a professional contract, Erving was free to join the Westsiders, a squad cobbled together by Peter Vecsey, a sportswriter for the *New York Daily News*. The roster was rounded out by young standouts like Charlie Scott, Billy Paultz, and Ollie Taylor.

The moves that Erving had dreamed of in childhood now burst forth as if a dam had been breached. "I could see him creating things in real time," George Mumford recalled, adding, "He was unlocked and was able to explore what was possible. He was curious to see how far his talents could take him." Fortified by the thousands of hours he'd logged alone, Erving surrendered to the game's flow. Once, while driving back from a game, Brownbill asked Erving about a dumbfounding move he'd made. Erving had to take a beat to recall it. "It's all on instinct," he said, according to Brownbill's recollection. "I just see what's in front of me and then know how to attack it. And once it's over with, I go on to whatever's next." It was more than just physical expression; improvisation gave Erving a psychological edge, too. "You want to outscore [your opponent] and you also want to freak him out with a big move or a big block," Erving explained. "That way even if the score is tied, you and he both know who's really ahead."

With each passing game, a movement bubbled up, what the *New York Amsterdam News* called "The Julius Erving Cult." Vecsey himself joined it. "Stories of [Erving's] heroics have already grown out of proportion, that is, until you witness his achievements," he wrote. "Immediately, you are converted to a 'believer,' joining the masses already convinced that Erving has all the tools to be the greatest single attraction since the veteran Houdini."

One afternoon, Erving snapped the Rucker Tournament's single-game scoring record by pouring in fifty-four points. On another, a player heaved a halfcourt prayer as the buzzer was about to sound. Erving caught the wayward shot in stride and, as if it were an alley-oop, stuffed the ball through the hoop. In ecstasy, fans spilled onto the court, mobbing Erving through halftime. Ken Buck, the first full-time Black referee in the NBA, who officiated at Rucker in the offseason, found himself at a loss for words. "He shocked me," Buck said. "I never knew he was *that* good." It was a coming-out party, the minting of a new playground idol. An unknown in June, Erving had become by August someone whose rumored presence could pack an outdoor court before he'd even arrived. Once, Erving lent his car to Brownbill. Boos rained down when Brownbill stepped out of the vehicle alone. "Where's the Doctor? What happened? You were supposed to bring the Doctor with you!" the disappointed crowd yelled at him.

Word of Erving's exploits coursed through local basketball circles, up to the highest levels. During one game, Brownbill, chasing a missed shot out of bounds, was stopped cold when an enormous hand lifted the ball off the asphalt. Staring back at him was Connie Hawkins, the foremost NYC playground icon, now a forward for the Phoenix Suns. Throughout the 1960s, Hawkins had reigned over the city's outdoor courts. His delayed entry into professional basketball because of a dubious point-shaving scandal hadn't prevented him from attaining all-star status in both the ABA and the NBA. At Rucker, he was known simply as "the Hawk." At first, spectators had pinned the moniker "Little Hawk" on Erving in homage, but the newcomer made clear that he intended to forge his own identity.

Hawkins and Erving soon joined forces on a squad of NYC stars that squared off against a roster of similarly renowned players from the Baker League, Philadelphia's equivalent of Rucker. Over a pair of home-and-away contests, some of the biggest names in the Northeast battled for bragging rights: Hawkins, Charlie Scott, and Nate "Tiny" Archibald for New York; Earl "the Pearl" Monroe, Archie Clark, and Billy Cunningham for Philadelphia. In the first game, Philadelphia eked out a one-point victory on its home turf, but the tables turned in the second, with New York edging its rivals by five. Fittingly, Hawkins and Erving were named co-MVPs.

That summer, Hawkins turned twenty-nine, close to elderly in the NBA—a mere 16 percent of players were thirty or older that season. With the dawn of the new decade emerged a younger figure around whom urban folklore was already being spun, a near mirror image of Hawkins, with not only the same reedy physique but also the same mythmaking prowess. A king assessing his heir, Hawkins was not yet ready to cede any turf. When asked if he noticed similarities between Erving and himself, Hawkins scoffed. "First of all," he said, "no one compares to me in moves. One thing you can say, though, we are both black."

Even though Erving had yet to log a minute in professional basketball, local reporters wasted no time in casting the twenty-one-year-old as the embodiment of the sport's future, smooth, stylish, and impervious to gravity, someone who, according to the *New York Amsterdam News*, was fashioning a "new type of basketball game. Basketball—Julius Erving style."

Erving wouldn't simply be the next Connie Hawkins. He would be, the *Amsterdam News* concluded, "James Brown, Muhammad Ali, Aretha Franklin, Willie Mays, all in one."

Weeks after the Rucker Tournament concluded, Erving traveled to Newport News for training camp with the Virginia Squires. Minutes into the first full-court scrimmage at Fort Eustis Anderson Fieldhouse, a shot caromed high off the back of the rim. A half dozen outstretched arms vied for the rebound. Rising above them, seemingly out of nowhere, a hand cupped the ball at its apex and then rammed it through the hoop. The dunk, as swift and sudden as a knockout punch, stunned everyone into an edgy silence.

Sharing the court were several invitees who were engaged in a cutthroat competition for end-of-the-bench spots that were often filled by white bruisers who saw limited playing time but appeased fans uncomfortable with the increasing dominance of Black players. Erving's putback slam humiliated them in front of club executives who soon would decide their fates, namely, head coach Al Bianchi and Squires business manager Johnny "Red" Kerr. Sensing the danger, Kerr leaned over to Bianchi and whispered, "Al, we better get him out of there before he gets hurt."

During the Squires' first exhibition contest, against the Kentucky Colonels at Virginia State College in Petersburg, Erving, according to the *New York Amsterdam News*, brought the crowd "out of their seats with a couple of his patented stuff shots and had them screaming with those twisting moves to the basket that became so familiar to those who followed the summer action at the Harlem Pro League." Bianchi couldn't believe his luck. A decade as a guard who'd had to scrape and scuffle to avoid washing out of the NBA had given Bianchi the toughness he needed to survive as a coach in the ABA, where franchises moved at the drop of a hat and talent remained in short supply. Scouts scoured the country for it, combing playgrounds and backwater college programs for anyone who might've gone undetected.

As Bianchi watched Erving pour in thirty points and snag thirteen rebounds against the club that had come within one win of the ABA championship the previous season, he undoubtedly was struck by the same thought that had flashed through his mind the first time he'd seen Erving in action: "Look what we found."

CHAPTER 2

THE PRODIGY

A few miles from the gymnasium in Petersburg where Julius Erving made his professional debut, another sensation was surfacing. Unlike Erving, Moses Malone wouldn't take anyone by surprise. His rise would be one of the most covered sports stories in the nation.

Vic Fulp, a reporter for the *Richmond Times-Dispatch*, wrote the first newspaper profile of the adolescent prodigy in 1972, when Malone was averaging twenty-two points and twenty rebounds per game as a sophomore at Petersburg High School. The interview was tougher than Fulp had anticipated. Through much of their chat, Malone buried his face in his hands, squirming and evading as if he were being interrogated. "I don't ever relax," Malone said. "Like if I know there is a ball around, I'll spend most of the time at the schoolyard playing."

Whatever quotable material Fulp was able to squeeze out of Malone, he printed—with one exception. Midway through, Malone mused, "I don't think I'll go to college. I want to play pro ball when I finish high school." Three years earlier, Spencer Haywood, one of Malone's athletic idols, had jumped to the ABA following his sophomore year of college. Afterward, Malone had jotted down his desire to outdo Haywood by skipping college altogether. He'd then pressed the note between the pages of his family's Bible as a compact between him and God.

Even though others like Erving subsequently turned pro before their college eligibility expired, no player had yet done so straight out of high school. It seemed a fantasy, a daydream of a naive teenager. Fulp left the lines on the cutting-room floor, presumably to spare Malone the embarrassment of not comprehending the enormous disparity between high school and professional basketball.

Malone, however, was dead serious.

On the courts outside the elementary school on Virginia Avenue in Petersburg, the primary objective was to keep the lights on. The losers of the postsundown pickup games had to feed quarters into a coin-operated machine that bought another hour of illumination from nearby streetlights. As a skinny kid whose impoverished upbringing left him with no change to spare, Malone couldn't afford to lose. To stay on the court, he conditioned himself from an early age to be relentless, fanatical, untiring. "About 20 guys would come and go and the games never stopped," Malone recalled. "If I got home at 3 or 4 in the morning, Mama didn't worry. She knew where I was." Sometimes, after everyone had cleared out, Malone would linger there, hoisting unpolished jumpers and chasing down his misses. "Kids in the neighborhood," one store owner recalled, "say Moses slept with his basketball."

Malone dedicated himself to basketball partly to cope with a turbulent childhood. His mother, Mary, separated from his hard-drinking father when Malone was a toddler. The meager paychecks that she brought home from her jobs as a nurse's aide and a grocery bagger at Safeway barely kept the two afloat. They lived in a rundown asphalt-sided frame house with sporadic running water and unmended holes in the walls that let in cold air during winter. It was in the middle of a twenty-five-block, historically segregated section of Petersburg known as the Heights. Johnny Byrd, the owner of a nearby convenience store, manned the cash register with a .38 Special strapped to his hip—a necessary deterrent for the burglars who'd shot at him over the years. "It was a tough neighborhood," one resident remarked. "Guys hanging on the corner, drinking all night. You put a kid there with no father, no brothers or sisters, he's gonna be tested to the max. And Moses was, every day."

It wasn't just Malone. Petersburg tested every Black resident who grew up there. Infamous as the city where bunkered Confederate soldiers resisted defeat in the waning months of the Civil War, Petersburg held tight to its Southern customs. For white residents, the cobblestoned streets and white-columned mansions in the historic district evoked a romanticized antebellum past; for Black residents, the remnants of the downtown slave market served as a reminder of Petersburg's brutal racial history. In 1954, the year before Malone was born, twenty Virginian legislators convened in Petersburg to assert their unyielding opposition to school integration as mandated by the Supreme Court's *Brown v. Board of Education* ruling. Throughout Malone's childhood, segregation, residential as well as educational, remained the norm in Petersburg as school boards stalled through outright defiance or token desegregation. Only in 1970, Malone's freshman year, when a federal court ordered the merger of the town's Black and white high schools, did integration occur at a meaningful level. The opening of the newly constructed Petersburg High School triggered waves of white flight from public to private schools. A month into its first semester, the high school closed for days to deal with white students who were vandalizing stores in protest. Stanley Taylor, an incoming Black student, still bristled decades later at the slurs and stray elbows he stomached while walking the halls between classes.

This racial turmoil stirred up anxiety in Malone. "Before he came to high school, I don't think he'd ever talked to a white person," Bob Kilbourne, Petersburg's athletic director, said of Malone. So withdrawn was Malone that he sometimes slunk outside to eat potato chips during lunch instead of socializing in the cafeteria. When called on in class, he couldn't spit out his answers fast enough. His slender body crowned by a bulbous head prompted classmates to call him Jughead. "He was real quiet then and never had anything to say to anybody," teammate Robert Hanford claimed.

Through basketball, Malone emerged from his shell. Even before high school, he'd built a reputation on playgrounds and in summer youth leagues, where counselors forbade Malone from setting foot in the lane in an attempt to moderate his dominance. Eager to witness the six-foot-six wunderkind in action, Petersburg fans started chanting, "Play Moses!" midway through his freshman season. In his varsity debut, the fourteen-year-old racked up thirty points, albeit more on tenacity than skill. "I can remember when Moses didn't even have a shot," head coach Carl Peal later said. "He would throw the ball up to the boards and score by tapping it in."

Offensive rebounding became Malone's lifeblood, the fuel that would power his game for decades. Nimble, quick, and physical, with an unquenchable thirst for the ball, he was unusually suited for this laborious task. Otis Fulton, a six-foot-eleven center from Thomas Jefferson High School in Richmond, gave up on boxing him out in the traditional back-turned, butt-out manner. Instead, Fulton took to face-guarding Malone, bumping him far from the basket so his smaller teammates could take care of rebounding. "That was the only way that I could at all control him," Fulton said.

From his freshman to his junior year, Malone sprouted an additional four inches. Soon, his per-game averages ballooned to thirty points and twenty rebounds. As the varsity squad muscled into contention for the Virginia state title, the community, Black and white residents alike, responded with an enthusiasm that Petersburg High School couldn't contain. Referees struggled to prevent standing-room-only crowds from spilling onto the court; school officials fretted about the tiny gymnasium turning into a fire hazard. As a result, several Petersburg games shifted across the Appomattox River to the Virginia State College gymnasium, the same one where Julius Erving had debuted on the Squires. Even then, demand for tickets often exceeded the four thousand available seats.

In 1973, Malone's junior year, Petersburg rampaged through the winter undefeated. Against Richmond's John Marshall High School in the sectional final, Malone broke open a tight game by scoring seventeen straight points, helping Petersburg cruise to a 62–43 victory. "Once the Crimson Wave gets the ball inside to Malone, there is virtually no way the soft-spoken junior can be stopped," asserted the *Richmond Times-Dispatch*. Petersburg's subsequent romp through the AAA state tournament in Virginia moved Malone to the front of his recruiting class.

Scouts were already circling. Dave Pritchett, an assistant coach at the University of Maryland known affectionately as "Pit Stop" for his tendency to abandon his rental car outside airport terminals while dashing onto whichever plane would transport him to the next prospect, slipped unnoticed one night into Petersburg, where he watched Malone bolt halfway across the court to wipe out a layup. Upon returning to College Park, Pritchett shut himself in his office and sat there alone, processing what he'd witnessed. Later, he sought out Maryland head coach Charles "Lefty" Driesell. "There's a God in heaven and he's been great to us," Pritchett told him. "One hour and fifteen minutes down the road is the greatest player I've seen in twelve years."

Intrigued, Driesell decided to make the trip to Petersburg himself. On an outdoor court where he'd heard Malone often played, Driesell took stock of a pickup game in progress. Two decades of coaching likely had convinced him that he'd seen it all, yet watching Malone that afternoon, Driesell was struck by a simple, inescapable realization: "That guy is the *truth*."

In the summer of 1973, Malone attended the Five-Star Basketball Camp that Howard Garfinkel organized in Honesdale, Pennsylvania. A basketball fanatic, Garfinkel dedicated himself to helping top-ranked high school players iron out their individual weaknesses. With Malone, however, he didn't know what to do. "Moses Malone is the only player in the history of Five-Star who didn't belong there," Garfinkel later stated. No matter which players Garfinkel teamed him up with, Malone never lost a game. Garfinkel took to yelling, "Whoosh! Whoosh!" whenever Malone swept another rebound off the backboard. The only thing that gave Garfinkel pause was Malone's shyness. Malone, Garfinkel claimed, "didn't say three words the whole time he was in camp."

Malone's senior year, Petersburg High School was untouchable. The team applied a full-court press on defense and ran its offense at a breakneck pace. Stanley Taylor, the team's flashy point guard, fastened silver tassels to his socks and bells to his shorts. A metallic jingle rang through the gymnasium as he sprinted back and forth, tassels aflutter. With their center pulling down twenty-five rebounds a night, Malone's teammates knew that they could jack up shots, and more often than not, Malone would be there to clean up their misses. Lefty Driesell, a frequent visitor to Petersburg that winter, once counted the number of entry passes Malone received during a game. Only four plays were run for him, but he still managed to score fifty-two points, almost exclusively from offensive rebounds.

No club came within thirty points of beating Petersburg High School during the regular season. In one-third of their games, Malone outscored and outrebounded the entire opposing roster on his own. Once, while leaving his feet for a jumper, a rival player glimpsed Malone lunging toward him. Rather than risk having his shot swatted into the bleachers, he spiked the ball to the floor in resignation. Otis Fulton recalled a sequence in which Malone caught a pass near the top of the key, then barreled down the lane. Holding his ground, Fulton drew a charge. On their way downcourt, he joked, "I'm glad you don't have a jump shot." Icily, Malone shot back, "Don't need no jump shot." They were, Fulton recalled, the only words Malone ever spoke to him.

From barbershops to churches, nail salons to street corners, the talk of Petersburg centered on its basketball prodigy. Petersburg High School games became the hottest ticket in Virginia. Sprinkled among the spectators one evening were three head coaches from top-ranked college programs, more than a dozen recruiters, a writer from *Sports Illustrated*, and a camera crew shooting footage for a CBS program called *Eye on Sports*. That winter, the city's post office mailed out its annual holiday cards with the tagline "Greetings from Petersburg, Home of Moses Malone."

Sweeping through to the state finals, Petersburg High School faced its toughest opponent in two seasons. West Springfield, a high school established eight years earlier among the swelling middle-class suburbs of Virginia's Fairfax County, punched above its weight through pick-and-roll basics. Having rarely competed against someone of Malone's height, West Springfield prepared for the championship game by having its shooters launch jumpers over a teammate holding up a broomstick.

On March 3, 1974, chartered buses and packed cars streamed north along Route 64 from Petersburg. At University Hall in Charlottesville, a record-smashing crowd of eight thousand fans watched in dismay as West Springfield clung to a narrow lead through three quarters. The two-pronged strategy of slowing the pace and keeping Malone as far from the offensive boards as possible brought West Springfield to the brink of pulling off perhaps the most shocking upset in Virginia high school basketball.

In desperation, Petersburg coaches scrapped everything and turned to Malone. "Answer the bell!" they urged him during timeouts. Despite contending with a defense that collapsed on him from all sides, Malone managed to snatch nineteen rebounds—one more than the entire West Springfield club—and shovel in a layup that nudged his club ahead for good in the final quarter. As the buzzer sounded, Petersburg escaped with a 50–48 victory, the closest any team had come to beating it over the school's fifty-game win streak. West Springfield had executed its game plan flawlessly, but in the end, it had no answer for Malone, who clinched his second straight state championship.

Weeks later, on March 22, Petersburg celebrated "Moses Malone Day." Limousines shuttled Malone and his teammates to school. At a morning assembly, while the high school band played "He's Got the Whole World in His Hand," administrative officials retired Malone's number. The mayor gave a speech; cheerleaders recited a poem. Afterward, at an outdoor ceremony, college coaches ranging from Maryland's Lefty Driesell to Detroit Mercy's Dick Vitale waited their turn to laud the prospect they prayed would play for them next year. The program was supposed to commence with a sing-along for Malone's upcoming birthday. But when Malone caught wind of this, he marched across the stage and told the woman who was to kick off the festivities that she should skip the song. When she asked why, Malone glared at her. "Because I don't like it."

That afternoon, Malone told a reporter, "A person can ask me anything. If I don't want to talk about it, I just say it's personal... I really don't mind talking with coaches, anybody, as long as they don't get personal." And for Malone, his birthday was personal.

The program was amended. No song was sung.

Over the following months, hundreds of recruiters, from Maine to Hawaii and everywhere in between, descended on Petersburg. "I'd walk out of my house in the morning and they'd be there, looking for Moses," remembered Robinette "Pro" Hayes, an assistant coach at Petersburg High School. "I'd get to school and they'd be there. I'd come home at night and they'd be there." More than a quarter of all college basketball programs nationwide seduced Malone with offers of scholarships, perks, clothes, women, bribes—whatever it took to lure the surest thing in basketball since Wilt Chamberlain to their campus. One abandoned a new car with the keys on the dashboard in front of his house; another slipped Malone's uncle an envelope stuffed with cash. A thriving grift soon took hold in Petersburg, with hustlers guaranteeing recruiters access to Malone in exchange for under-the-table payments. An assistant coach from the University of New Mexico set up camp at Howard Johnson's in Petersburg for two straight months to show his dedication. The press tracked the ins and outs so closely that, as one journalist put it, the Malone saga shared "front-page headlines in Washington with the final days of Watergate." A television news anchor in Richmond went so far as to read an open letter on air that urged Malone to stay loyal to Virginia.

The intrusion of so many recruiters and reporters into his private world put the shy and introverted Malone on edge. After school, he often sneaked into his house through a back window to avoid the swarm of cameras out front. In the dark, he'd hide under his bed so that no one peeking through the windows could catch a glimpse of him. Columnist Sam Lacy claimed in the *Baltimore Afro-American* that Malone's telephone "took more punishment than the gong in the ring at Madison Square Garden." Changing the number, which Malone did twice, did little to stanch the calls. Day and night the doorbell rang, with one recruiter arriving as soon as another left. Those who scored an audience with Malone struggled to crack his sphinxlike demeanor, to extract anything out of him beyond curt responses in a voice so deep that, in one reporter's words, "it sounds as if his vocal cords are in his legs." Malone developed a code for friends: if someone knocked on the front door four times, paused, knocked three more times, paused again, and then knocked twice, the Malone family would let them in. To everyone else, access remained restricted. "All this stuff is fine, I suppose, but you know, most of the time I just want to be left alone," Malone told the *Richmond Times-Dispatch*, which characterized the adolescent as "Garbo-ish."

His last months of high school sped by in a blur: banquets, interviews, alumni pitches, backslaps, handshakes, and tutoring sessions to raise his grades to the C average needed to earn a college scholarship. In between, Malone was on the road. "The recruiters dragged me to about twenty-five schools," he recalled. "Sometimes they brought me in to meet the president of the university, who talked to me like he wanted to be my father. That made me laugh. They fixed me up with dates. Then when I got home those girls called me long distance and pretended they were in love with me. What kind of stuff is that?" The frenetic pace put a strain on his family. His mother, Mary, developed painful ulcers, which Oral Roberts, the famed televangelist, offered to heal should her son choose to play basketball at the university that bore his name.

By June, a front-runner had emerged. Since he'd first laid eyes on Malone, Lefty Driesell had sensed that signing a prospect of this caliber would power the University of Maryland to a national championship. Over the next year, Driesell put thousands of miles on his Lincoln Continental, driving back and forth from College Park to Petersburg. As affable as he was dogged, Driesell leaned on decades of salesmanship to outmaneuver the mob. He never panicked when Malone dodged his presence. "To tell you the truth, I rarely talked to Moses," Driesell remembered decades later, adding, "He didn't sit down and let me recruit him. He was always leaving." Instead, he worked on gaining Mary's trust, intuiting that no one had more influence on Malone than his mother. For one of Malone's visits to the campus, Driesell, having learned of the teenager's love for cars, rented a Mercedes-Benz and dispatched assistant coach Howard White to Petersburg in it with simple instructions: chat with Malone about cars, then transition to his intentions for next year. Malone, however, foiled the plan by closing his eyes as soon as he climbed into the Mercedes. During the subsequent three-hour drive to College Park, Malone pretended to sleep, and not a word passed between the two.

Eventually, Driesell's tricks and persuasion, along with Mary's desire for her son to stick nearby, won out. After Malone verbally committed to Maryland over the phone, Driesell and assistant coach Dave Pritchett dashed down to Petersburg with the formal paperwork. So paranoid was Pritchett about Malone changing his mind that he insisted that he and Driesell sleep in their car outside Malone's house. Driesell refused. When they showed up along with Pro Hayes at 6:30 in the morning on June 20, 1974, Chuck Noe, the head coach of Virginia Commonwealth University, was already at the door. "I *told* you!" Pritchett yelled in a panic.

After Noe's last-ditch pleas fell short, Mary Malone invited Driesell, Pritchett, and Hayes inside. Moses was fast asleep upstairs. Late for work already, Mary and Hayes climbed the stairs to wake Moses. Bleary-eyed, he rolled over, snatched the commitment letter from Hayes's hands, signed it, and then fell back to sleep.

When Hayes charged downstairs with the completed document in hand, he claimed that Driesell "leaped about three feet in the air."

Two months earlier, in April 1974, the Utah Stars of the ABA had thrown an unexpected curve into the country's wildest recruiting saga by picking Malone in the third round of the amateur draft. The selection wasn't unprecedented—the Philadelphia Warriors had drafted Wilt Chamberlain out of high school in 1954, and the Detroit Pistons had tapped Reggie Harding in 1962 after he'd run into college eligibility issues. But neither player had risen directly to the pros. Malone hadn't entered his name in the draft or given any public indication that college wouldn't be his next step. When someone informed Malone of the Stars' selection, he'd blown it off as a joke: "Don't give me that. They're not gonna take no player out of *high* school." But then, while driving home, he heard a radio report confirming the news.

The idea of Malone skipping college dismayed his inner circle. Bob Kilbourne, the athletic director at Petersburg High School, had fought off scouts from the Virginia Squires, who'd found it impossible to ignore the in-state phenom whose high school games sometimes outdrew their own. When the Utah Stars pulled the trigger instead, Kilbourne's response was equal parts paternal and patronizing: "I know it's a big temptation for a boy from St. Matthew Street, but pro basketball will be there later and he needs to get an education first."

Perhaps if Utah Stars representatives had pursued Malone as vigorously as college recruiters did, he would never have committed to Maryland. But in the first few months after the draft, the Stars made no concerted effort to sign their third-round pick. The reasons had little to do with Malone. During the four years that Malone had attended high school, the Stars had won more games than any other ABA franchise. In 1970, fresh from having relocated to Salt Lake City from Los Angeles, the Stars had shocked the league by storming to their first championship. Three straight division titles followed, culminating in 1974 with another trip to the ABA Finals, where they lost to the New York Nets. Despite this on-court success, Bill Daniels, the owner of the Stars, struggled to stay one step ahead of bill collectors. Half of the twelve thousand seats at the Salt Palace remained vacant during home games, well below the ticket sales needed for the Stars to break even. Fed up with unremitting red ink, Daniels unloaded the club to a syndicate headed by a local businessman named James Collier in August 1974.

Aware that drastic measures were needed to turn a profit, Collier trained his sights on the Stars' unsigned third-round pick. He tasked general manager Arnie Ferrin with an unconventional opening assignment: finding out if Malone's heart was set on playing for Maryland. In his first phone conversation with Malone, Ferrin emphasized that if it was an education Malone was after, the Stars wouldn't stand in his way. Malone, however, equivocated just enough for Ferrin, Collier, and Morris "Bucky" Buckwalter, the Stars' incoming head coach, to drop everything and fly to Virginia.

They holed up at a Holiday Inn outside Petersburg. The fall semester would commence on August 28, leaving them with mere days before Malone attended his first class in College Park. Buckwalter understood that convincing Malone to back out of his commitment to Maryland would require a visual demonstration of all he stood to gain from professional basketball. So on August 25, across the orange crate that served as the family's coffee table, Buckwalter stacked $5,000 in hundreds, money that Malone could walk away with the moment he signed the six-figure contract also presented to him. Buckwalter then whipped out a photo of a green Lincoln Continental Mark IV, claiming that it, too, would be Malone's. Without missing a beat, Malone asked if the car came with a built-in phone, which Buckwalter agreed to with a laugh. It had been the most words he'd gotten out of Malone, whose inscrutable reaction to each sales pitch consisted of nodding and making a guttural "Mmmm" sound that resembled a push lawn mower after an insufficient pull of the ripcord. Decades later, during a basketball-related trip to China that Malone and Buckwalter took together, the two reminisced over a glass of wine. To Buckwalter's astonishment, Malone recited minute details from those initial conversations, underscoring that his caginess in no way meant that he didn't comprehend the situation.

The one thing that Malone insisted on was transparency with the University of Maryland. Lefty Driesell claimed that Mary Malone called afterward to inform him of the meeting with Buckwalter. In a panic, Driesell asked to speak to her son. "Moses," Driesell told him, "you ain't signing nothing for less than a million dollars cash." Then he climbed into his car and sped south to Petersburg.

Even though Driesell couldn't offer the same monetary rewards, he was adamant that attending college was in Malone's financial interests. "The publicity he's going to get in his first year at the University of Maryland may be worth a million bucks," Driesell told reporters. "Tell me something: how many times will the Utah Stars be on television next season? Maryland will be on national TV six times and on regional TV 11 times.... It just makes sense for him to wait." Driesell might've been more accepting if Malone were to jump directly to the NBA, a league that, though only a quarter century old, had established itself as the gold standard of professional basketball. But the ABA, in Driesell's mind, was nothing but a "beachball league," chock-full of "bandits and outlaws." The ABA, he claimed, "was giving these wild contracts to people, and the money ended up not being as much as they told players it was going to be." Driesell could scarcely contain his contempt for Stars executives, who he thought were preying on his prized recruit: "I tell you what they're doing: they're trying to take advantage of this kid because they know he's poor."

Certain that Malone was being ripped off, Driesell contacted Donald Dell and Lee Fentress, a pair of lawyers in Washington, DC. "He called us," Fentress remembered, "and said, 'I know you guys have done a few basketball contracts for your clients. Would you look at this contract and advise Moses?'" Sure enough, it turned out that the contract that Buckwalter had offered was a team-friendly four-year deal with twelve one-year options that were terminable at the Stars' discretion. Both Fentress and Dell instructed Malone not to sign it. Fentress assumed that Malone would rededicate himself to the University of Maryland; instead, Malone confided in Fentress about the note he'd pressed into a Bible that sketched out his dream of skipping straight to the pros.

Seeing which way Malone was leaning, Fentress called Driesell to state that he and Dell couldn't represent the Maryland head coach and Malone at the same time. If Malone's heart was set on turning professional, then they intended to work on securing a fairer contract for him. Though his strategy to dissuade Moses from joining the ABA had backfired, Driesell took the long view. "I was just looking out for Moses," he said decades later. "I was trying to get him not to sign. But I also wanted him to get the best deal he could because he deserved it."

Over the next two days, Buckwalter, Ferrin, and Collier tore across the state's toll roads at a frantic pace, burning through nearly a hundred quarters in their journeys to Malone's house and his new agents' offices. Not wanting to draw the attention of the press, they'd park their rental car atop a nearby hill in Petersburg and descend only when the coast was clear. Once, when reporters showed up unannounced, Ferrin, Collier, and Buckwalter had to crawl on their stomachs across Malone's lawn to escape, fending off stray dogs that nipped at their clothes.

Fentress and Dell got to work stripping the contract of any contingency language. Mary Malone was the lone holdout, uneasy with her son missing out on a college education. "All that money the pros offered—he can get it later," she told sportswriter Rick Telander. "His education is only four more years. We can make it. We've slept on couches a long time. I told 'em my child wasn't gonna play no pro ball." So in their talks with the Stars, Fentress and Dell wrote Mary into the contract, adding a monthly stipend and a housing allowance for her. "That inducement to his mother became very important to Moses," Dell remembered. Eventually her skepticism waned, and the two sides settled on a five-year deal worth close to $1 million, all guaranteed. Even though Dell was no stranger to brokering deals for athletes, cutting a landmark contract for a teenager left him plagued with fears of having become a "flesh-peddler."

On August 27, Malone lingered in bed until noon, then kept everyone guessing by taking off with his mother for College Park. Officials at the University of Maryland were so encouraged by his presence that they convened a snap press conference. But Malone and Mary didn't attend; instead, they circled back to Washington, DC. In his lawyers' offices, where Dell claimed that Malone and Driesell had "had a strong disagreement about Moses's decision to go pro," Malone made up his mind. Around 11 p.m., Malone, Dell, and Fentress piled into a car and drove across the Francis Scott Key Bridge to Virginia, since the legal age to sign a contract there was eighteen, as opposed to twenty-one in DC. At a nondescript Ramada Inn in Rosslyn, just over the state line, Malone ended the drama with his signature.

Back in Petersburg on August 28, Malone stepped outside clad in a T-shirt, red pants, and a straw sombrero. Trailing him was a scrum of reporters and TV cameras. Malone had no interest in giving them what they wanted. A newly minted millionaire at nineteen, he ignored their requests with the confidence of a man twice his age.

"If you are going over to the school [playground] to play, can we shoot some film on you?" one Richmond correspondent asked.

"I don't think so," Malone answered. "More I think about it, it's too hot to go shoot."

"How about lifting up the hat so we can see your face?" a cameraman begged.

"No, I don't think I can do that, either," Malone said. "I like it just the way it is."

That day, Malone caught a flight to New York City, where he attended a press conference to announce his signing. Mary appeared relieved that the interminable recruiting saga was finally over. "Tonight," she said, "may be the first in two years that I'll get eight hours sleep."

The sporting establishment, fearful that the move would weaken a college basketball industry that had grown fat off the labor of unpaid athletes, reacted with defensive fury. "The signing is reprehensible, unbelievable," fumed University of Maryland athletic director Jim Kehoe. "What will Malone do if he doesn't make it? What will he do with the rest of his life?" *New York Daily News* columnist Carl Rowan concurred: "The overriding factor is that in playing for the Stars, Malone will not gain the education, the self-assurance, the ability to cope in all situations—things he needs far more desperately than a pocketful of money."

Even in the Black press, contentious arguments broke out. A. S. "Doc" Young, a longtime columnist for *The Chicago Defender*, the most significant African American newspaper of the mid-twentieth century, criticized Malone for being a bad role model whose decision would spur less talented prospects to forgo their college degrees: "In an era when disadvantaged people desperately need all the education they can get, the black athlete who gives education the finger must be included with the worst examples impressionable kids will ever see." Sam Lacy of the *Baltimore Afro-American* saw things differently. He took particular issue with "whites who have never been black, who don't understand what it means to be black, who cannot—despite their protestations to the contrary—even hope to comprehend the stature of a poor black from a poor environment in a rich America." As a result, Lacy contended that "whenever a black kid from a black ghetto finds himself offered a million dollars he should grab it and run like hell."

Malone, for his part, brushed off the doubters. "It don't make no difference how old I am," he later explained, "because I still think I can bust y'all."

CHAPTER 3

THE RED, WHITE, AND BLUE

Since its inaugural season of 1967–68, the ABA, the league that Moses Malone was soon to join, had remade professional basketball as both a game and a business. It had been the brainchild of a ragtag group of businessmen eager to capitalize on a sport whose popularity was expected to spike over the following decade. To endow the new league with legitimacy, the original ABA franchise owners tapped a basketball legend as the commissioner: George Mikan, the bespectacled big man who'd been the first superstar of the NBA in the late 1940s and early '50s. His most lasting contribution as ABA commissioner was to change the shade of the ball from the conventional orange to red, white, and blue—garish stripes of color that swirled together like a pinwheel each time a shot was launched. It was an apt symbol for a vibrant athletic enterprise bent on scrambling traditions.

Like many fledgling leagues, the ABA teetered terminally on insolvency. Clubs moved and floundered, rebranded and folded. Each season opened with at least one new or rebooted team. Only two franchises—the Indiana Pacers and the Kentucky Colonels—straggled into the mid-1970s with their original names and locations intact. A television contract would've stabilized league finances, but networks already grappling with anemic viewership for televised NBA games never took the bait. To boost their bottom lines, ABA executives instead staged whichever stunts and sideshows might persuade locals to spend an evening in drafty, smoke-wreathed gymnasiums rooting for teams that might not exist by season's end. To basketball purists, the ABA smacked of the big top, with on-court novelties like three-point shots seeming no different from halftime gimmickry featuring milking cows and Playboy bunnies. Even the ABA's multihued basketball looked to critics like something that belonged on the nose of a seal. "I thought they were making a mockery of the game," wrote center Wayne Embry, summing up a sentiment common among NBA chauvinists.

With talent at a premium, competition between the two leagues was fierce, which resulted in novel ways of drafting and signing players. In addition to inventing the "hardship clause" to beat the NBA to the punch on the country's top prospects, the ABA doled out exorbitant six- and seven-figure sums through a financial scheme known as the Dolgoff Plan, which enabled owners to pay a portion of a player's contract and then to defer the rest largely by bundling it in annuities that could be spread out over decades. Salaries soon skyrocketed not only in the ABA but also in the NBA, where stars like Rick Barry and Billy Cunningham jumped leagues or threatened to do so in order to negotiate fatter paychecks with tightfisted owners who no longer enjoyed a monopoly on the game's professional ranks. It was an advantage relished by players who'd chafed under the restrictions of the reserve clause, which bound them to the team that had drafted them and prevented them from becoming free agents after their contracts expired. When a proposed merger between the two leagues was floated in 1970, Oscar Robertson, the president of the National Basketball Players Association, went so far as to file an antitrust suit to block it so that members of his union could preserve their newfound financial leverage.

Life in the ABA seemed an unbroken string of red-eye flights and airport layovers. Often, players scrambled to catch multiple connections on puddle-jumping planes en route to midtier cities like Louisville, San Antonio, and Indianapolis. "I can remember when we had to [fly] from Virginia to Memphis," New York Nets guard Bill Melchionni said. "It would take almost five hours with all the switches you had to make. You can almost drive there that fast." Wali Jones, a guard who'd signed with the Utah Stars in 1974 after a decade in the NBA, told teammate Gerald Govan that the excessive commercial travel made his one season in the ABA feel like two in the NBA. Once, while stranded at an airport, Jones muttered, "Govan, you played eight years in *this* league?" Even for referees, some of whom the ABA poached for higher pay, the strain of the long season drove them to a breaking point. "As I went along and I saw all these dumpy little arenas and the ragged type of play and the horseshit travel and all the rest of it—teams folding and players getting traded seemingly in the middle of games—I just couldn't take it," wrote referee Earl Strom, who begged the NBA to take him back. It was unglamorous, uncomfortable, and, in the eyes of many in the basketball establishment, undignified.

For others, however, the ABA spelled freedom. With fewer dominant centers than in the NBA to clog the lane and with the three-point line pulling defenders to the perimeter, the spacing was more open in the ABA. Shoot-first athletic guards and forwards flourished. Often in too much of a hurry to settle into orderly patterns, they attacked the basket at will, figuring out how to score in the moment. ABA games were fast, loose, defensively slack, and spontaneous—a product tailor-made for the color televisions that were fast supplanting black-and-white models, even if networks never capitalized on it.

Julius Erving felt right at home. At last, he'd found a formal setting that complemented his personal style, a league where his imagination could run wild. It was in the ABA that he injected the playground into the bloodstream of professional basketball. More than anyone, Erving lifted the action above the hardwood into the air, the last uncharted realm of the court. The ball cupped in one hand, his body contorted yet controlled, he spun in physics-defying shots that NBA legend Bill Russell deemed "beautiful in the same way that an ice skater's leap is beautiful—or even in the same way that a painting is beautiful." Willie Wise, an all-star forward for the Utah Stars, likened Erving's fluid play to ballet. "At times out there," Wise admitted, "he's so beautiful that I find myself watching him rather than guarding him." Erving himself often spoke of his style more in artistic than in athletic terms. "My overall goal," he later stated, "is to give people the feeling they are being entertained by an artist—and to win. You know, the playground game, refined."

During warmups, Erving intimidated rivals by slamming in ways that few had seen: over his head, off the backboard, across his body. "If you paid and just saw the pregame layup drill, you'd have gotten your money's worth," writer Mike Littwin said. Once, a Virginia Squires teammate asked Erving how he'd come up with an especially creative dunk. "Last night," Erving replied, "I had a dream and saw myself doing it. I never tried it until today."

Though Erving's impact was immediate, few witnessed it firsthand. Because the Squires split their home games among four cities across Virginia—Norfolk, Hampton, Richmond, and Roanoke—Erving quipped that they were the only club that had to fly to home games. Squires fans could expect to catch no more than one-third of the club's in-state games in the two seasons that Erving suited up for them. With few televised games to bring him to the masses, Erving was unseen in a way that enabled his legend to take hold. Somewhere in the wilds of the ABA, fans whispered, was a shaggy-haired virtuoso for whom no feat was impossible.

Rumors of his exploits circulated through word of mouth, each retelling adding more spring to his jumps, more twists to his moves. A columnist for the *Los Angeles Times* gave voice to the outlandish oral mythology that unspooled about Dr. J: "It is said that the good doctor was not born, he sprang full-blown when somebody rubbed his hand across a lamp.... He can hang in the air so long on a jump shot, they say, he could jump out of a one-story building and take an hour to hit the ground. If he jumped off the Empire State building, he'd hover indefinitely."

The style of basketball that Erving and the ABA showcased—kinetic and expressive, brisk and brash, ripped straight from inner-city playgrounds—soon became branded as uniquely Black in nature, an athletic equivalent to the nascent hip-hop beats bubbling up in the Bronx. The team focus tilted from the collective to the individual, from set plays choreographed by coaches to extemporaneous moves conjured up from within players. A feedback loop developed between pros unveiling the free-flowing shots they'd honed on outdoor courts and inner-city youths emulating them on playgrounds. Audacious and unapologetic on the court, the players were equally outspoken and self-assured off it. They sparred with owners over contracts and fought to assume greater control of their brief careers. Many also courted the spotlight by becoming fashion icons. Ditching suits and ties, they helped set the template for what would be known as "soul style," complete with dashikis, turtlenecks, medallions, shades, and vibrant leisure suits.

The 1970s began with team rosters in both leagues evenly split between white and Black players; by the end, more than 70 percent of players were Black. For decades, NBA executives had abided by an unwritten quota system that filled out rosters with white benchwarmers and limited the number of Black players on the court at any given moment. The ABA had no such historical baggage. It wasn't unusual for its games to feature majority-Black lineups trading three-point bombs and in-your-face dunks, the trash talk echoing through the arena. Little by little, a backlash built among ticket buyers, who were predominantly white. Rather than celebrating the evolution of the sport, many griped in racially coded language about disorganized play and selfish stars. One anonymous basketball executive later groused to *Sports Illustrated*, "The question is: Are [Black players] promotable? People see them dissipating their money, playing without discipline. How can you sell a black sport to a white public?"

Aware of this challenge, Erving obsessed over the image he strove to project. "I wanted to learn the whole game—interview sessions, the media, making time, being available, trying to say something that was representative of how I truly felt," he said of his first years as a pro. After games he sometimes lingered for hours, catering to the needs of whoever crossed his path, no matter if it was beat reporters fishing for soundbites or kids begging for autographs. Erving asked friends to sit with him during interviews and then critique his performance, pointing out every misstep and verbal tic. His eloquence deserted him only when asked to describe a move he'd made up in the moment. "Did Beethoven have to explain how he wrote the Ninth Symphony?" he once snapped in frustration.

Erving thought deeply about his role not just as an athlete but specifically as a Black athlete. "A lot of stereotypes of black athletes used to bother me when I was growing up. So I wanted to rectify some of that. I was influenced by Jackie Robinson, Joe Louis, the things happening to Arthur Ashe. Bill Russell," he told *Philadelphia Magazine*, adding, "When I got a platform, a stage, I didn't need to get up there to be Mr. Bojangles. It was important to me to be Julius Erving, not Dr. J. On the court I could don the cape and fly and soar and play, but when I stepped off I needed to be a person, a person that commanded a certain type of respect." This duality between Dr. J and Julius Erving, between a bold and fearless athlete on the court and a dignified and accessible ambassador for the ABA off it, allowed him to break into the American mainstream more smoothly than other Black stars of the era.

Still, there were bumps along Erving's road to stardom. After averaging twenty-seven points and nearly sixteen rebounds per game his rookie year, Erving grew disillusioned with the Squires. Upon finding out that the agent who'd convinced him to leave the University of Massachusetts Amherst had been on the ABA's payroll, Erving demanded that his contract be renegotiated. When the Squires refused, Erving took matters into his own hands, signing a four-year contract with the NBA's Atlanta Hawks. Shortly thereafter, the Milwaukee Bucks selected him in the first round of the 1972 NBA draft. Three clubs now laid claim to Erving. Lawsuits piled up all summer. Making his intentions clear, Erving headed to Atlanta, where he planned to pair up with "Pistol" Pete Maravich on the Hawks. Just two games into the following preseason, however, a judge ordered Erving back to Virginia to play out the remainder of his rookie contract. Rather than resisting, Erving returned to the Squires and went on to lead the ABA in scoring in 1972–73.

Not far from where Erving had grown up, Roy Boe, the majority owner of the New York Nets, took stock of the thousands of families who jammed the Long Island Railroad and choked the parkways to Uniondale each time the Squires came to town. At season's end, Boe sank the Nets' fortunes in one player, forking over more than a million bucks to settle the three-team dispute over Erving's rights. He then locked Erving down with an eight-year deal for just shy of $3 million. Erving got out of Virginia, but the yearlong dispute marred his reputation. In the summer of 1973, a joke made the rounds: "Did you hear about the new Julius Erving doll? Wind it up and it signs another contract."

Through it all, Erving never abandoned his roots. As soon as each season ended, the playground beckoned. Rolling up to an outdoor court in New York City in his white-on-blue Avanti, Erving would stroll languidly through the crowd, ducking any outstretched hands so as not to mess up his fastidiously coiffed Afro. He was a sight to behold, unflappable and self-contained, cool on the sidelines and hot on the blacktop, a snapshot of '70s chic. Around him, every tree, lamppost, and fire escape would be covered with people. "I played year-round," Erving said. "I wasn't distracted by other things. All I wanted was to be the best I could be. Off the court, I was reserved, almost to the point of being shy, but on the court I was wide open, at high intensity, with a take-no-prisoners approach." His buzzy, heady vitality pulled in hangers-on from across the city, presenting him with opportunities his roving eye couldn't resist. For a while, Erving later revealed, he experimented with sleeping with a different woman every night.

It didn't take long for Roy Boe's seven-figure gamble to pay off. With Erving on board, the Nets' turnaround was instantaneous, from twenty-four games below .500 in 1972–73 to twenty-six above in 1973–74. Erving led the league in scoring, ran away with the MVP, and spurred the Nets to an unlikely championship. Skeptics who'd questioned whether Erving's playground-infused style could translate to success in the ABA now had their answer.

Despite the league's grim financial landscape, the ABA possessed an asset the NBA coveted. As long as Erving, the most exciting player in the sport, plied his trade with a tricolored basketball, the NBA couldn't dismiss its rival as a second-rate operation unworthy of its attention.

Though the ABA teemed with stars—from bruisers such as Artis Gilmore and George McGinnis to scorers like Dan Issel and George Gervin—some believed that the player who might someday overtake Erving as the face of the league was a teenager who'd crashed the league cold in 1974. Shortly after the Utah Stars signed Moses Malone, one anonymous league insider proclaimed, "I am not exaggerating when I say that Moses may ultimately mean the salvation, and the making, of the American Basketball Association."

In the runup to training camp, billboards across Salt Lake City swapped their usual advertisements for a stark white background overlaid with a single sentence: "Moses Will Lead Us." What seemed a message of hope was tinged with desperation: a franchise unable to turn a profit was wagering that a nineteen-year-old rookie could rescue professional basketball in Utah.

The Stars kicked off the 1974–75 season on October 18 in Uniondale. Rising amid the shingled houses and low-slung shops was Nassau Coliseum, an ovular, state-of-the-art arena that had opened two years earlier at the exorbitant cost of $32 million. The Nets had landed in Long Island after a half decade of itinerant wanderings through armories in New Jersey and gymnasiums in New York so chilly that bench players had to bundle in winter coats. Five months earlier at Nassau Coliseum, the Nets had defeated the Stars for the franchise's first title in its seven-year existence. But the fans now flocking there had more on their minds than an ABA Finals rematch. "I was sitting in the stands," said Rod Thorn, an assistant coach on the Nets, "and I overheard lots of people saying they came to the game for only one reason: Moses Malone."

Curiosity about how well an adolescent would fare against grown men helped the Nets surpass the five-figure mark in attendance on Opening Day for the first time in franchise history. Breaking the suspense early, Malone scored on a rolling layup a mere fourteen seconds into the first quarter. The next trip down the floor, Malone tipped in a missed shot. Not even being switched onto Julius Erving defensively shook Malone's confidence. Testing the rookie, Erving tried to sneak a pair of shots past him; Malone swatted both into the stands.

Even though the Nets ran away with a 105–89 win, all anyone wanted to talk about afterward was Malone's nineteen-point, eleven-rebound debut. Erving in particular was bombarded with questions. "With all the talent [Malone] has, I didn't think he would have trouble or choke because it's something he's been doing all his life," Erving said before adding a perceptive note of caution: "I figured that his biggest problems would be off the court, dealing with people and putting up with the press and media."

In the visitors locker room, engulfed by notepads and microphones, Malone slumped on a trainer's table. His elbows on his knees and his eyes cast downward, Malone looked like he'd rather tread barefoot across broken glass than submit to postgame questioning.

"What are your thoughts? How do you feel after your first game?" one reporter asked.

"I feel about the same as when I was in high school," Malone muttered. "No change."

"What's the difference between high school and pro ball?" another probed.

"The difference? People get old. In high school they are young."

Malone's first week exposed him to the ruthless churn of the ABA. From Long Island, the Stars flew to Hampton, Virginia, and then to St. Louis for three road games in three consecutive nights, all losses. When the team returned to Salt Lake City to face the Denver Nuggets, Stars executives held off on staging a welcoming reception despite the promotional blitz that had heralded Malone's arrival. The real Opening Night was when Dr. J came to town.

On October 30, the New York Nets rolled into Salt Lake City in the midst of a brutal stretch that saw them playing six games in a week, including four on the road. Undoubtedly exhausted, Erving nonetheless grabbed the public-address microphone before tipoff and made his fateful speech about Malone being thrown into the ocean and being able to swim already. Erving proceeded to strip off his warmups and pile up thirty-six points while leading the Nets to another win over the Stars. Even so, fans filed out of the Salt Palace happy. They'd heard Erving give his blessing for the Stars' experiment. Then they'd seen Malone pour in twenty-eight points and snatch fifteen rebounds, affirming that Erving's speech hadn't been empty praise.

Malone, it seemed, could swim just fine on his own.

Everything about Julius Erving was commercial. For the youngest player in the ABA, the opposite was true.

Following his decision to turn professional, Malone had flown to Salt Lake City. Greeting him in the terminal had been a cluster of microphones. Even though reporters from across the state had converged on the capital, Malone, decked out in a florid Hawaiian shirt, had brushed past them without uttering a word. No matter how much team officials begged him to reconsider, Malone had refused to speak to the press. It wouldn't be the last time.

Two sides of Malone became immediately evident. With his teammates, some of whom were more than a decade his senior, Malone settled into an easygoing rapport, jokey and garrulous. Getting Malone to shut up in private, Stars trainer Bill Bean claimed, was sometimes harder than getting him to talk in public. But as soon as a stranger penetrated the team bubble, the dynamics flipped. Malone turned monosyllabic, blank-faced, detached. "Look how alive he seems, how open he is," one unnamed teammate said of Malone during a shootaround. "You [a reporter] go up and introduce yourself, though, and, click, he turns it off, won't even look at you sometimes."

To sportswriters, he spoke fast and low, his Southern drawl mushing his clipped words together so incomprehensibly that one Utah disc jockey dubbed him "Mumbles Malone," a nickname that would cause the self-conscious Malone to retreat further into himself. Even players struggled to understand his diction. New York Nets guard Bill Melchionni remembered when Malone once came into the Nets locker room to chat with players whom he'd gotten to know. "Moses," forward Rich Jones reportedly told him, "next time you come in here, you better bring an interpreter."

Often, Malone sported a pair of headphones to drown out questions from reporters and deflect requests from radio announcers. "Trying to interview Malone these days," one writer claimed, "is about as productive as chatting with your favorite light socket." After Malone refused to talk with a writer from *Sports Illustrated* who'd come to Utah for a feature, the owner of the Stars pleaded with his players to change Malone's mind. At one point, a correspondent for Walter Cronkite's *CBS Evening News* flew to Salt Lake City to do a TV segment on the rookie. "When he found out we were here," the reporter said, "Malone put his warmup on inside out so we couldn't see his name. I guess he figured we wouldn't recognize him. I'll tell you, I've interviewed all those Watergate guys—Dean, Mitchell, Erlichmann—and Moses Malone is harder."

Time and again, beat writers disappointed readers itching for insights into the Stars' mysterious teenager. Months of snubs emboldened them to resort to irregular tactics. Steve Rudman, who covered the Stars for *The Salt Lake Tribune*, hatched a plan that involved salvaging the unused snapshots of Malone that his newspaper's photographer took during games. Following an afternoon shootaround, Rudman spread several photos, including one blown up to poster size, on a trainer's table. Marching over to Rudman, Malone pointed at the pictures and declared, "You're gonna give me those." Rudman agreed, but they wouldn't come free: Malone would have to sit for an exclusive interview.

Later, Rudman knocked on the door of the suite at the Tri-Arc TraveLodge where Malone had set up residence. Instead of the glowering figure he'd come to know in the Stars locker room, Rudman encountered a shy yet obliging participant who recounted his life story without embellishment, even volunteering more details than Rudman asked for. At times, Malone reversed the conversation, inquiring about Rudman's own background. By the end, Malone felt secure enough to open up about his isolation in Salt Lake City, a still unfamiliar place that he didn't feel comfortable navigating unless in the company of a teammate. No longer was Rudman a nameless member of the swarming media hordes. From then on, Malone took time, albeit briefly, to answer Rudman's questions after practices and games. If he was in a good mood, Malone would jokingly pester Rudman for photos. Years later, after Malone had moved on to Texas, Rudman showed up once in the Houston Rockets locker room, and Malone, without missing a beat, asked, "You got any more pictures?"

What many mistook for surliness was rooted in self-protection, in not letting others in until Malone had vetted them. "The people who call Malone aloof and arrogant don't understand him," claimed Pro Hayes, one of his coaches in Petersburg, adding, "Ever since high school, he's had people grabbing at him. Do this, do that, sign here. Most of them are just out to take advantage. . . . Moses keeps people at arm's length now, at least until he has time to size them up. If he likes them, they're his friend for life. If he finds he can't trust them, forget it. He'll drop 'em like flies."

On a deeper level, race factored into Malone's chilly relationship with the media. The mostly white reporters who covered professional basketball in the 1970s had trouble relating to the stresses of being a six-foot-ten Black man in a state that was more than 97 percent white. A transplant with no cultural bearings in the region, Malone could scarcely blend in with his surroundings during an era when the Church of Jesus Christ of Latter-day Saints opposed interracial marriage and forbade individuals of Black African descent from holding leadership positions. Entrusting his narrative to journalists ungrounded in the racial snubs and slights that afflicted him must've seemed unappealing and unwise, especially when many of the same journalists intimated that Malone was unintelligent and inarticulate.

In reality, Malone had been attuned to racial matters since he'd started making waves in high school. About his four years at Petersburg High School, he groused, "We won fifty straight games and two state championships, yet the baseball team is treated better and I don't know when they last won a game.... But we have a black coach and black players, and even at the banquet all I got was a certificate, no most valuable award or anything." The ensuing debate about Malone's decision to skip college was laced with paternalistic condescension that cast Malone as a mindless vessel batted about by white authority figures. "Sports and society have this Malone kid all wacked up," Marquette head coach Al McGuire asserted. "I think anyone who can get to this kid for a day or two can convince him to go to Mars."

What McGuire and others failed to grasp was that Malone, far from being manipulated, was making choices that were wholly rational under his circumstances. Months after signing with the Stars, Malone helped his mother move into a three-bedroom ranch-style house in Ettrick, a suburb of Petersburg. For once, she wouldn't have to spend the winter huddled for warmth beside an oil stove. Her relief at no longer having to scrape by prompted some skeptics to reconsider. "I used to tell Moses he had done the wrong thing. But I was wrong," admitted Pro Hayes, adding, "Now he's happy all the time because [his mother] is happy. That was more important to him than a college education."

Malone faced an equally steep learning curve in broadening his game. Superior offensive rebounding had stunted the development of his jumper and post-up moves in high school. As a result, Malone's offensive arsenal, according to one sportswriter, consisted of "left-side garbage and right-side garbage." A three-foot putback in the lane was considered an outside shot for Malone. Del Harris, an assistant coach for the Stars, summed up Malone's game as "meat and potatoes. He just rebounded and scored what he grabbed."

Tom Nissalke sensed the promises and the pitfalls of Malone's play when he replaced Bucky Buckwalter as head coach of the Stars two-thirds of the way through the 1974–75 season. On February 12, in a contest against the Memphis Sounds, Malone recorded the kind of triple double that players didn't brag about: twenty-five points, fifteen rebounds, and eleven turnovers. "I heard he could do this and that," Nissalke said, "but after seeing Moses, I was appalled. There had been no effort to coach him." A disciplinarian whose relationship to his players was strictly business, Nissalke rode Malone hard in drills and scrimmages. During huddles, Nissalke demanded that Malone look him in the eye rather than staring at the floor. "[Malone] simply had never learned the basic skills which any pro center has got to possess," Nissalke later stated. "But by the end of [his rookie] year, he was a completely different player. He went from a very indifferent player to a player who was very attentive. He went from a very poor practice player to a player who would almost sweat blood in practice."

What tripped up Nissalke and others was that Malone's on-court demeanor could be deceptive. He would saunter down the floor blank-faced, ostensibly detached from the unfolding play. But then, as soon as a shot went up, he'd dart to the basket, weaving around bodies until he lodged himself in a spot that gave him a chance to get a hand on the rebound. While Malone could hold his own with the league's leapers—it was said that he could touch his head to the rim with a standing vertical jump—he relied more on tenacity than height. Thanks to lightning-quick second and third jumps, Malone would tap missed shots volleyball-style to himself with the confidence that no defender could beat him to the ball. The second his shoes landed on the hardwood, he would spring back in the air as if on a pogo stick. Bill Sharman, who'd won four championships with the Boston Celtics decades earlier while playing alongside such legends as Bill Russell and Bob Cousy, detected Malone's potential for greatness on the spot. "I know he's young," Sharman told Steve Rudman, "but he's the best damn offensive rebounder I've ever seen—and I've seen everybody."

Bullying from bigger players didn't bother Malone. He'd arrived in Utah as slender as an antenna but unafraid to mix it up. Gerald Govan, a thirty-two-year-old forward who was one of the few players to have competed in every ABA season since the league's inception, adopted a protective posture toward the unrefined rookie, mentoring him on the ins and outs of being a professional athlete. One thing was immediately apparent: Malone got a perverse kick out of roughhousing beneath the boards, which Govan learned the hard way when he took an elbow to the face during practice, shattering his nose. "He didn't quit," Govan said of Malone. "They knocked him down, they bent him because he was skinny. And I thought, 'They're gonna hurt him.' But he didn't have no quit in him at all. Knock him down, knock him around, you didn't have to worry. He's coming."

By season's end, Malone had competed in every game but one. He logged nearly forty minutes per contest while scoring just shy of nineteen points and pulling down nearly fifteen rebounds. He led the ABA in offensive boards and finished among the top ten in overall rebounds, blocks, minutes, free throws, field-goal percentage, and win shares. The question was no longer whether the rookie belonged. It was how terrifying Malone was going to be once his offensive game rounded out.

Even so, there was a nagging sense that Malone hadn't lived up to the hype of his entry into the ABA. No matter how much he improved, his rugged style was never going to be as aesthetically pleasing as Erving's. What's more, Malone's aversion to everything promotional hadn't boosted the Stars' box office as much as anticipated. Malone the player had a boundless ceiling; Malone the performer seemed unlikely to develop.

As Harvey Kirkpatrick, the public information director for the Utah Stars, said of Malone: "Having a superstar you can't publicize is like finding a gold mine on somebody else's land."

CHAPTER 4

DISSOLUTION

To Moses Malone's relief, the summer of 1975 was uncommonly tranquil. "I'm going home to the schoolyard and play basketball," he said of his offseason plans. "I feel good. Basketball is my rest, my vacation." The media circus that had swirled about him for three straight years finally disbanded.

His rookie season had been successful enough for the NBA to suppress its high-minded ideals. Whatever qualms the league felt about depriving teenagers of higher education were trumped by its unwillingness to lose out on the next prep-to-pro superstar. "I must have scouted at least 50 high school players last winter as a result," said Jack McMahon, an assistant coach for the Philadelphia 76ers. Two of the first twenty picks in the 1975 NBA draft hailed from high school: Darryl Dawkins, selected fifth by the 76ers, and Bill Willoughby, selected nineteenth by the Atlanta Hawks. It was a seismic shift for a league that mere years earlier had fought all the way to the Supreme Court to preserve its rule that players must be four years removed from high school before they suited up in the NBA, and a seemingly irreversible disruption to basketball apprenticeships brought about by Malone's pathbreaking season.

When Malone, with less fanfare but more poise, returned to Utah for his second year with the Stars, his ascendance was interrupted by an injury. On September 25, minutes into the first full-game scrimmage of the Stars' training camp at Highland High School in Salt Lake City, Malone hauled in a rebound in heavy traffic. It was a routine play, no different from the more than twelve hundred rebounds he'd accumulated the previous year. This time, however, his right foot landed awkwardly on backup center Randy Denton's sneakers. Staggering over to Stars trainer Bill Bean, Malone asserted, "Foot broke." Since nothing in Malone's expression suggested that it was anything more than a sprained ankle, Bean didn't take him seriously. But Malone kept repeating, "Foot broke."

Subsequent X-rays showing a hairline fracture confirmed Malone's intuition. A player unused to sitting on the bench would miss at least a month of action.

Even with Malone on the shelf, the ABA remained loaded with talent. That preseason, in head-to-head exhibition matchups between the two leagues, ABA teams beat their NBA counterparts in thirty of forty-eight games. The NBA shrugged off the results as meaningless, unrepresentative of how things would shake out if the contests carried actual weight. Not everyone shared that view. "We can't cop a plea. If we play the ABA, we give up the psychological edge, and we have to get up ourselves or get beat," said Pete Newell, the general manager of the Los Angeles Lakers, who declined to schedule games against ABA teams partly for fear of being embarrassed.

What the ABA lacked, as always, were customers and capital. At the start of the 1975–76 season, the Baltimore Claws, a franchise that had relocated from Memphis in the offseason, folded without playing a single regular-season game. Weeks later, the San Diego Sails, a recently rebranded team, cut their losses before their per-game attendance dwindled to three figures. The Virginia Squires were lurching toward the same fate. "We have a crisis every two weeks when they have to meet payroll," an anonymous Squires employee said of the team's owners. At the same time, the league's strongest clubs, the Denver Nuggets and the New York Nets, tried to make a break for it, petitioning the NBA for admittance, which ultimately became snarled by legal roadblocks. Bit by bit, the ABA was stumbling toward extinction.

The domino-like toppling of teams soon wended its way to Utah. There, while Malone convalesced in a walking cast, Stars owner Bill Daniels scrambled to save his franchise. Since moving the Stars from Los Angeles to Salt Lake City, Daniels had seen the fortune he'd amassed as a cable television magnate dwindle through a series of dicey investments. In 1974, he'd poured $1 million into his failed campaign to become governor of Colorado. The next year, he bankrolled boxer Ron Lyle's rise to the heavyweight title bout, which Lyle lost in eleven rounds to an aging Muhammad Ali. Strapped for cash, Daniels tried three times to sell the team, each time unsuccessfully. Businessman James Collier assumed control of the Stars in 1974, during the time Malone was signed, but his failure to deliver on promised payments soon returned the club to Daniels. With the addition of Malone and the subtraction of popular players like Zelmo Beaty and Willie Wise because of money problems canceling each other out, ticket sales stayed flat. Weeks into the new season, Daniels was barely able to pay his players.

On November 29, 1975, the Stars cruised to a thirty-six-point victory over the Spirits of St. Louis, another club beset by box-office woes. Unbeknownst to the players, executives from both clubs were engaged in backroom efforts to merge the impoverished franchises. When those talks broke down, it became clear that basketball in Salt Lake City couldn't be saved. At the start of December, according to forward Steve Green's recollection, Daniels showed up in the locker room clutching a bottle of Johnnie Walker Blue Label. With tears running down his face, he announced the dissolution of the Stars. "It's a shame that a six-year investment has come to this," Daniels told the press.

Dismayed at his sudden unemployment, trainer Bill Bean threw open the Stars equipment room and invited the players to take what they wanted. While his teammates grabbed all they could carry, Malone limped off to retrieve a cart, which he stuffed with basketballs, shirts, and shampoo. It was a telling scene: the twenty-year-old with a seven-figure contract wasn't too far removed from the child in the Heights who'd worried about keeping the streetlights on. Denton recalled that when team officials used to dole out meal money on the road, Malone mostly dined on cheap fast food, then pocketed the change, stashing away every last penny.

With the Stars disbanded, the Spirits of St. Louis scavenged their roster, picking up Malone and three of his teammates. A year after his unprecedented passage from Petersburg to Salt Lake City, Malone was on the move again. He embarked on this new journey stoically, buffeted by a truism that his upbringing had ingrained in him: "Everybody go down. Everybody go up."

The truism pertained equally to Julius Erving, who came into that uncertain season with something to prove. After he'd glided to the championship in his first year with the New York Nets, his title defense had been cut short the following year by the very club that Malone was now joining.

In 1974–75, the Spirits of St. Louis, despite sporting an array of explosive individual talent—spectacular scorers like Marvin Barnes, Freddie Lewis, and James "Fly" Williams—had struggled to jell into a cohesive unit. They'd ended the regular season twenty games below .500, sneaking into the playoffs only because the ABA's three-round postseason required the participation of eight of the league's ten teams. Like a stick of dynamite with a finicky fuse, the Spirits finally ignited in the first round. After losing the first game, they swept four straight games from the shell-shocked Nets.

For once, Erving had been upstaged. Marvin Barnes was a player who possessed as much talent as anyone in professional basketball. Apathy and scandal, which stuck him with the nickname "Bad News," hindered him from deploying it consistently. But in that series, at least, Barnes dethroned the Nets by pouring in thirty points and grabbing fifteen rebounds, besting Erving's per-game averages of twenty-seven and ten.

Eight months later, as the league contracted from ten teams to seven, it was clear that Erving would have limited time to avenge the loss. Whether the ABA could even survive to the playoffs was an open question. By midseason, there were hardly enough players left to stock two all-star teams. Resourceful to the end, ABA officials leaned into what they did best: they improvised. A hastily arranged new format for the All-Star Game was put in place, calling for the team that boasted the best record in the season's first half—in this case, the Denver Nuggets—to square off against a lineup of star players culled from the six other ABA franchises. It was the first—and only—time that an All-Star Game would feature the full roster of an existing club. Since the game would take place at McNichols Sports Arena in Denver, where the Nuggets played, it also was the only time that it doubled as a home game.

As a way of showcasing the league's vitality amid mounting fears of collapse, a sellout was required. Fortuitously, the ABA's most passionate fan base resided in Denver. That season, Nuggets games drew a shade below thirteen thousand spectators. Only two NBA franchises, the Los Angeles Lakers and the New York

Knicks, raked in more money than the Nuggets. Still, taking no chances, organizers dropped $45,000 on a pregame concert featuring Charlie Rich and Glen Campbell, country-music luminaries with ample draw in a Western town like Denver.

Not yet satisfied, ABA executives racked their brains to come up with a similarly appealing basketball-related showcase. Inspired by the arm-wrestling competitions between National Football League players that ran at halftime of televised games during the 1975 NFL season, they recognized that what strength was to football, jumping ability was to basketball. Already, hoops buffs gathered to gawk at ABA players showboating during pregame warmups, so why not pit the most creative of these leapers against one another to determine the league's best dunker? Out of desperation was thus born what *Sports Illustrated* would dub "the greatest halftime invention since the restroom."

Like everyone else, Erving had never taken part in a formal slam-dunk contest. The closest he'd come was during clinics for Converse, the shoe that sponsored him. At the conclusion of these clinics, after having unleashed a few crowd-pleasing jams, Erving would bring down the house by running full speed downcourt, soaring from the free-throw line for a one-handed stuff, then sprinting toward the exits, never looking back. Erving didn't even know what he was capable of. Junior Bridgeman, a guard for the University of Louisville, claimed that during his senior year, the New York Nets, in town to play the Kentucky Colonels, once took the floor at Freedom Hall just as his college squad was wrapping up practice. Bridgeman overheard a reporter tell Erving that he knew of only two players who could spin around completely in the air before dunking. Not yet warmed up, Erving grabbed a basketball, charged toward the hoop, and executed a flawless 360-degree dunk. "Now there's three," he said nonchalantly. Despite his considerable abilities, getting graded on dunks as if they were gymnastic routines was so novel that Erving spent fifteen minutes in the locker room before the All-Star Game pantomiming the moves that he planned to unveil.

On January 27, 1976, a sellout crowd at McNichols Sports Arena tapped their feet to Glen Campbell's "Rhinestone Cowboy," then watched the Nuggets battle the ABA all-stars to a near draw through two quarters. When the halftime horn sounded, players and fans stayed put to witness an experiment that featured five competitors executing five dunks while a panel of judges assessed each on artistry, originality, and crowd response. From the start, enduring dunk-contest archetypes materialized. There was the hulking center who relied more on force than finesse (Artis Gilmore), the superstar who seemed to come down with the jitters (George Gervin), and the wild card capable of upsetting the favorites (Larry Kenon). Those were the opening acts; the main draw promised to be a faceoff between two of the league's most mesmerizing players.

All week long, David Thompson, a rookie for the Nuggets whose nickname, "Skywalker" (pre–*Star Wars*), spoke for itself, had prepared by testing out a variety of dunks during practice and soliciting his teammates' advice on polishing his act. His final dunk that evening—a double-pump slam from the baseline in which he spun 360 degrees in midair—elicited a roar that echoed like thunder across the arena. "Doc's in trouble," Artis Gilmore murmured from the sidelines.

Unruffled, Erving grasped two multicolored basketballs. As he walked toward the basket, according to Nets coach Kevin Loughery, "all the other players moved out onto the floor to get a closer look and sat down, like, okay, now it's The Doctor's turn." Clad in a blue all-star jersey, with striped socks pulled up nearly to his knee braces, Erving dunked both balls backward at the same time from the standing position.

Before his next attempt, he shooed aside the all-stars sitting cross-legged at halfcourt. Planting his right foot inches behind the free-throw line, Erving turned around and loped to the opposite free-throw line in seven long strides. It was a theatrical prelude—a long jumper calculating his steps, a seasoned showman building suspense. He paused long enough for fans to rise to their feet. As they realized what he was attempting to do, the arena lapsed into silence. Dunking from the foul line seemed a fantasy, so unrealistic that Doug Moe, a crusty assistant coach with the Denver Nuggets, placed a substantial bet beforehand that Erving would fall short.

The basketball palmed in his right hand, Erving streaked downcourt. A step inside the free-throw line, he elevated. His back arched, his sinewy body elongated, the red-white-and-blue ball clutched high above his bountiful Afro, Erving appeared, in that split second suspended in air, the incarnation of the playground game, a full-on revolution in short shorts. At once wholly individual and universal, he seemed a picture-perfect representation of the direction his sport was heading.

By the time Moses Malone arrived in Missouri, the ABA was barely afloat and the Spirits of St. Louis were in shambles. The team's best player, Marvin Barnes, had missed several games during the 1975–76 season due to a lawsuit brought by a college teammate who claimed that Barnes had smashed him across the face with a tire iron. "When you got Marvin Barnes on your team," forward Steve Green said, "you're already going to have trouble listening to the coach or following his orders. Man, we were just a bunch of misfits." Ron Boone, an eight-year veteran who'd kept a watchful eye over Malone in Utah and then trailed him to Missouri, sensed that nothing good would come of their new situation.

"Moses didn't need that environment in St. Louis," he said. "It didn't help him at all."

Just as Boone feared, the dysfunction of the Spirits rubbed off on Malone. After his broken foot healed, he appeared to be a different player on the court. His production slumped; his effort slackened; even his attitude toward the coaches regressed. Before one game, while Spirits head coach Joe Mullaney was outlining plays on a chalkboard, Malone walked away. When Mullaney asked where he was going, Malone grunted, "Peeing."

Late in the season, Philadelphia 76ers assistant coach Jack McMahon scouted the Spirits in anticipation of a merger between the NBA and the ABA. He left unimpressed. "When you'd watch Malone, you come away thinking, 'How could they give a million dollars to that guy?'" Fan support in St. Louis mirrored the players' attitude. On some nights, it seemed possible to hand-count the spectators in the stands. "For Moses, as young as he was, it was like a lost year," Stars assistant coach Del Harris concluded.

It was shaping up to be a lost year for the league, too. "I knew that it was going bad in the ABA because we played the same team like three times a week," recalled Randy Denton. "It was getting kind of ridiculous." As their professional world shrank, a sense of beleaguered solidarity bonded those who remained. Green claimed that when games concluded, opposing players sometimes hashed out dinner plans before leaving the court. "We were all friendly among ourselves because we knew, I think, that this thing's going down, this whole league."

Still, it wasn't hopeless. Any league with Dr. J in it had value. The NBA, whose franchises were similarly mired in red ink, salivated over the box-office and television-ratings boosts that importing a free-throw-line dunker would provide. "There are athletes who are known as 'the franchise,'" said Dave DeBusschere, who'd become the ABA commissioner in 1975, shortly after his playing career with the New York Knicks had wrapped up. "Well, Julius isn't the franchise. He's the *league*." Because of that, Erving received treatment not afforded to others. Once, during a game against the San Antonio Spurs, forward Mark Olberding was guarding Erving too physically for Kevin Loughery's tastes. "Hey, look, the guy's killing Doc," the Nets head coach griped to the referees, "and you know if Doc gets hurt we can all pack it in and start looking for jobs. If anything happens to the Doctor, the league goes down the tube."

The ABA staggered on till the playoffs. Midway through, the Virginia Squires went bust, leaving little doubt that this postseason would be the league's last. Malone played no part in it. The Spirits of St. Louis, true to their underachieving nature, failed to qualify. Erving, in contrast, assumed the role of protagonist. Withstanding a second-round scare, his New York Nets advanced to the Finals, where the Denver Nuggets awaited. Before the opening game, Coloradans swept up so many tickets that Nuggets employees scrambled to install nearly four hundred extra seats in McNichols Sports Arena. On May 1, 1976, the largest crowd to attend an ABA game—more than nineteen thousand strong, two thousand above capacity—spilled into standing-room-only sections.

Even though New York had dropped eleven consecutive games in Denver, the players came out unintimidated by the boisterous fans and unaffected by the thin mountain air. For twenty-four minutes, the Nets and the Nuggets battled to a standstill. In the second half, each team grabbed the lead, then surrendered it just as fast. Sensing that his teammates were flagging, Erving took matters into his own hands. Down the stretch, he scored eighteen of the Nets' final twenty-four points, including the two that mattered most.

With four seconds left and the score knotted at 118, Erving caught a pass near the three-point line, dribbled into the right corner, and launched a fifteen-foot fadeaway over the outstretched arms of Bobby Jones, the Nuggets' defensive specialist. "I was all over him," Jones remembered. "I was probably a half inch from blocking his shot. But he just made a better play than I did." The essence of the ABA was embedded in that sequence: the athleticism to pull the shot off, the stripes of color blending together in a hypnotic swirl as the ball rotated through the air, the unjaded joy of teammates mobbing Erving afterward. "I want this championship more than any other because it might be the last year of the ABA," Erving said. "The intensity of these games requires a serious pose. This is serious business."

Before the second game, Nuggets coach Larry Brown, desperate for solutions, urged Jones to deny Erving the ball wherever he was. "So I did," Jones said, "but he ended up bringing the ball up the court." Wearing Jones down, Erving racked up forty-eight points, twenty-five in the fourth quarter alone, snapping an almost three-decade record in professional basketball for most points in a quarter. Erving would go on to score thirty-one in Game Three, thirty-four in Game Four, and thirty-seven in Game Five. "We all knew that he was the guy who drove the bus," Nets guard Al Skinner said of Erving in the Finals. "He'd been given the keys and just told the rest of us, 'Come ride with me.'" The Nuggets, despite having a more balanced offensive attack, wound up in a 3–2 hole, which, Pat Putnam of *Sports Illustrated* wrote, "is what can happen when humans go five-on-one with a helicopter."

Back on Long Island the night before Game Six, one victory shy of the championship, Erving paced around his bedroom, sleepless and fidgety. "He kept the heat turned up and kept looking out the drapes, waiting for the sun. He was going over [the upcoming game] in his mind and it was doing things to him," remembered his wife, Turquoise, whom Erving had married in 1974. "When I finally got up, the temperature was over 90. He was trying to burn us up."

On May 13, the Nets fell behind by twenty before the dread of returning to Denver for a winner-take-all seventh game sparked a furious rally. Erving poured in thirteen quick points, the Nets' pressing defense forced one turnover after another, and the Nuggets' seemingly insuperable lead vanished. When Nets forward Rich Jones banked in a layup that put the Nets up 112–106 with three seconds remaining, hundreds of fans poured onto the court at Nassau Coliseum. Unable to restore order, the referees gave up. The final game in ABA history never officially came to completion.

Days earlier, the championship trophy, a silver bowl, had been swiped from the back seat of Dave DeBusschere's rental car in Denver. Panicked, the commissioner's office had asked Nets owner Roy Boe about the whereabouts of the silver bowl the Nets had received upon winning the 1974 championship. In a gesture that encapsulated the financially fraught season, that evening the Nets were awarded a championship trophy they already owned.

Hours afterward, Erving sat alone in a corner of the Nets locker room, crushed paper cups and drained champagne bottles strewn before him. Most of the celebrants had already departed, but Erving, his uniform stained with sweat and alcohol, lingered for a beat longer, not yet ready to let go of the league that he'd shaped and been shaped by. "If this was the last ABA game," he stated, a touch of mist in his voice, "at least we went out in high style."

CHAPTER 5

THE START OF THE ODYSSEY

For Julius Erving, so accustomed to soaring above it all, the only direction to go was down.

His dominance in the ABA Finals reinforced what the NBA had to gain from a merger. When it finally occurred on June 17, 1976, preparations for the next leg of Erving's odyssey began in earnest. CBS, which held the broadcasting rights for the NBA, revised its scheduling for the upcoming 1976–77 season. The New York Nets would now feature twelve times in CBS's first eighteen weeks of programming, including the season opener against the Golden State Warriors.

Behind the scenes, however, the Nets were buckling. The ABA-NBA merger came at a cost. Two ABA franchises—the Spirits of St. Louis and the Kentucky Colonels—folded altogether. The remaining four clubs—the New York Nets, the San Antonio Spurs, the Indiana Pacers, and the Denver Nuggets—were forced to cough up an imposing $3.2 million fee for entry into the NBA, along with a $150,000 settlement paid to the disbanded clubs. The Nets incurred an additional $4.8 million indemnity for encroaching on the New York Knicks' territory. Their upcoming ubiquity on CBS wouldn't help the Nets' bottom line, since the onerous terms of the merger prevented ABA clubs from sharing in television revenue until they'd been part of the NBA for three years. Scraping together funds to cover these astronomical expenses stretched Nets owner Roy Boe thin. But his monetary woes soon seemed trivial in comparison to the phone call that would haunt the franchise for decades.

It came from Irwin Weiner, a gruff, redheaded huckster out of New York City's Garment District. Over the past decade, he'd ridden the wave of escalating salaries spurred on by competing leagues to become one of the sport's foremost agents. Before the launch of the ABA, few basketball players had employed agents; certain executives, such as Red Auerbach of the Boston Celtics, had refused to negotiate with them. Now, owners and general managers hoping to keep superstars happy had to contend with the likes of Weiner, who once declared, "I live by the code that you can't be too greedy." So when Weiner called Boe to inform him that his client Julius Erving would sit out training camp until his contract was renegotiated, the Nets owner wasn't surprised. "Weiner comes every year to renegotiate *every* contract," Boe said with a sigh.

Weiner claimed that three seasons earlier, when Erving had signed his eight-year contract with the Nets, there had been an unwritten agreement that the deal would be sweetened midway through. Boe, however, was in no position to do so—not even for his team's prime moneymaker. Privately, Boe assured Weiner that he'd reward Erving as soon as the Nets' finances stabilized. Weiner demanded a written statement to that effect. Boe declined. A stalemate ensued. As training camp opened, Erving hunkered down in his seventeen-room mansion in northwestern Long Island, growing increasingly anxious. "All I asked for was a letter of intent spelling out what 'something' means," he said in reference to the unspecified bonus that Boe had promised.

Twice in five years, a contract dispute had delayed Erving's start to a season. The first had failed to put a permanent dent in his popularity, but this time, sharper barbs were hurled his way. "The Doctor is guilty of malpractice," sportswriter Dave Anderson groused. "He showed that at heart he is a mercenary, that more money was more important to him than his role as the Nets' symbol." His lone appearance in a Nets uniform that autumn came on the cover of *Sports Illustrated*, where he posed alongside Celtics center Dave Cowens, orange NBA basketballs tucked under their arms.

Sensing that Erving wouldn't be available, CBS pulled its opening-night broadcast of the Nets versus the Warriors. Without Erving, executives claimed, "it would be just another game." What should have been a period of ascension—when Dr. J, shrouded in legend, became fully seen—turned into one of division.

In the fall of 1976, Moses Malone drifted through the wreckage left in the merger's wake, searching for safe harbor. The Spirits of St. Louis were no longer. Along with other newly teamless ABA players, Malone was placed in a dispersal draft. The Chicago Bulls, whose abysmal 24–58 record the previous season had granted them first crack at the choicest talent, coveted Artis Gilmore, a colossal center tailor-made for the NBA, a league that valued size above all. It was expected that the Atlanta Hawks would nab Malone second, but perceptions about Malone's supposedly sour attitude and "brittle bones" prompted the Hawks to trade the pick to the Portland Trail Blazers. Holder of two of the first five selections, Portland used both on players whose positions and skill sets overlapped: Maurice Lucas and Moses Malone. It was an early sign that Malone's ongoing odyssey through the basketball hinterlands wouldn't conclude in the Pacific Northwest.

The Trail Blazers, a franchise that hadn't advanced to the playoffs since its founding in 1970, sought to reverse its fortunes by stocking up on height. In addition to Bill Walton, an exceptional center who was also exceptionally prone to injury, the roster boasted six forwards, too many to give significant minutes to. Malone, for all his potential, wasn't a snug fit in Portland. The Blazers were fronted by head coach Dr. Jack Ramsay, a balding tactician whose gaudy polyester suits stood in stark contrast to his meticulous playbook. The recipient of a doctorate in education from the University of Pennsylvania, Ramsay took pride in the "Dr." before his name. Fittingly, his approach to basketball was intellectual, grounded in airtight systems that emphasized selflessness, ball movement, fast breaking, and pressure defense. From the moment Malone arrived, there were doubts about whether someone who'd missed out on college tutelage possessed the basketball know-how to slot into Ramsay's heady schemes. Equally important, Malone's $350,000 purchase price and exorbitant contract rendered him expendable given the cheaper options on hand.

In the days before training camp opened for the 1976–77 season, Ramsay all but hung a For Sale sign around Malone's neck. Malone, Ramsay said, "has a contract and he's our property, so to speak, but he is a duplication of the talent we already have." In contrast, Ramsay gushed about Maurice Lucas's sunny future in overcast Portland, making it clear that the agile forward was "exempt from any dealing." The message wasn't lost on Malone. Before heading out west, he knew not to overpack. "I only took half my clothes," Malone admitted.

The first thing he heard upon landing in Portland was a local radio DJ speculating about where Malone would be shipped next. Adjusting to a new league was difficult enough, but Malone was grappling with something entirely foreign to his basketball life: being unwanted, disposable, a trade chip stuck in limbo.

While Blazers executives haggled with other clubs over his rights, Malone busted his tail in practice, then slunk away mutely afterward. Paring his vocabulary down to the bare minimum,

Malone uttered "foot" or "wrist" when he needed attention from the trainer. The press took their usual shots at him. "Malone should like Portland," one writer asserted, "because there aren't a lot of people there, and all the rain will give him an excuse to stay home and avoid the ones who are there." Amid the gloom, his talent shone through, raw and unpolished though it was. It was most readily apparent during an exhibition game against the Blazers' regional rival, the Seattle Supersonics, on October 17, 1976. Subbed in midway through the second quarter, Malone single-handedly willed his club to victory by amassing twenty-four points and twelve rebounds in only twenty-six minutes. When asked if he was surprised by Malone's star turn, Bill Walton shook his head. "[Moses] didn't do anything tonight that he hasn't been doing in practice." Even Ramsay, who'd toed the company line about unloading Malone, wavered: "We'll have to give Moses some more thought, no question about that."

It was too late. Days afterward, for a first-round draft pick and some cash, the Blazers shipped Malone to Buffalo, the pro basketball equivalent of Siberia. Reporters who phoned for his reaction were greeted with a gruff "No comment."

The Buffalo Braves were Malone's fourth team in ten months. He'd journeyed from the Rockies to the heartland, from the Pacific Northwest and now to the Rust Belt. "I'm sure those years left a scar on Mo," his former coach Tom Nissalke later said. "He learned early on that you're just a piece of luggage in this business."

Malone already knew how to pack for short stints. "Half a suitcase," Malone said of what he brought with him to Buffalo.

As the postmerger season began, Julius Erving was nowhere to be seen.

Pat Williams, the bespectacled general manager of the Philadelphia 76ers, monitored the tribulations of the New York Nets with curiosity. A former minor-league catcher, Williams had started his front-office career by soliciting advice from Bill Veeck, a maverick baseball owner notorious for outrageous gimmicks and antiestablishment tendencies. Transitioning into basketball in 1968, Williams married a showman's ingenuity with an evangelical Christian's conviction. He was just as likely to book wrestling bears at halftime as he was to drop Bible pamphlets in the men's room. He knew that Dr. J, a spectacle unto himself, could far outstrip the magnitude of his promotional efforts. With nothing to lose, he phoned Bill Melchionni, the former Nets point guard who'd transitioned into the club's front office, to let him know that if the Nets failed to scrounge up the cash necessary to placate Erving, the 76ers would welcome a crack at it. "It was kind of like saying to Raquel Welch's mother, 'Hey, if she ever needs a date, here's my phone number,'" Williams later wrote.

Melchionni brushed him off. But as the exhibition games dwindled and Erving showed no sign of caving, panic set in. Slowly it dawned on Melchionni that the franchise was in worse financial shape than he could've imagined. "We had a significant number of minority owners," Melchionni remembered, "and if it had been laid out to them properly about what the long-term benefits were to keep Doc, they might have done it. But Roy Boe owned 25 or 30 percent of the team, and he just didn't have the money to pay all the fees to enter the league and to the Knicks." It was rumored that Boe had dangled Erving to the Knicks in exchange for canceling the pricey indemnity, but the deal never got off the ground. So on October 11, 1976, Melchionni called Williams back. He was blunt about what he needed: not players, not draft picks, just money—$3 million for the Nets and another $3 million going to Erving.

Days later, Williams boarded the Metroliner to New York City to feel out Melchionni in person. Satisfied, he arranged a meeting with Fitz Dixon Jr., the owner of the 76ers and one of the wealthiest individuals in Philadelphia. Dixon's great-grandfather Peter A. B. Widener had built a transportation empire by laying streetcar and trolley lines in cities from Chicago to Baltimore. Heir to the family's nine-figure fortune, Dixon led a life of philanthropy and leisure, ferrying between seasonal homes in Florida and Maine on private planes and yachts. Most of his time otherwise was spent at Erdenheim Farm, a five-hundred-acre manor outside Philadelphia whose grounds teemed with Black Angus cattle, racehorses, and exotic flowers that were reportedly valued at $1 million.

Dixon had stumbled into sports for the same reason as many blue-blooded barons with cash to burn. "I always wanted to own a pro team in Philadelphia," he told *The Philadelphia Inquirer*, adding, "I guess I bought the basketball team because I hate soccer and this was all that was left. . . . Frankly, my background in [basketball] is zilch." Dixon's ignorance of the NBA hadn't stopped him from plunking down roughly $8 million for the Sixers in May 1976. Because the promising club he'd inherited came with several young stars, notably George McGinnis and Doug Collins, Dixon's first offseason as owner hadn't yielded massive changes to the roster—until Williams showed up at his farm four days before Opening Night with an emergency proposition.

Cutting right to the chase, Williams told Dixon, "Fitz, we have a chance to get Julius Erving." The statement failed to register, so Williams put it in terms his boss would better understand: "He's the Babe Ruth of basketball."

Intrigued, Dixon asked what it would take to land Erving. Sheepish about quoting a price for a single player that bordered on the total sum the new owner had paid months earlier for the franchise, Williams answered softly, almost in a whisper, "Three million to sign him. Three million to acquire him."

Dixon paused. He asked if Williams was recommending the transaction. Williams nodded. Without hesitation, Dixon replied, "Then go get it done." The meeting lasted no more than five minutes.

The following days unfurled at breakneck speed. Williams and a battery of lawyers bolted to New York. Half the attorneys huddled with Nets executives, the other half with Erving's agent. Negotiations stretched through the night and into the morning. Meanwhile, Dixon paid a visit to his banker to take out a loan. "Not even me," he quipped, "buys something like [Erving] on petty cash."

By October 20, two days before the start of the season, a tentative deal was whisked to the NBA commissioner's office. In anticipation of its approval, the Sixers front office installed twelve new phone lines. Even then, when Williams tried to get through, the switchboard was overloaded with fans and reporters inquiring if the rumors were true. Williams had to call the Flyers, Philadelphia's professional hockey team, and ask an operator there to pass along the good news to Sixers employees.

Erving's sale stunned a league already shaken up by the merger. CBS tore up its TV schedule on the spot. In Philadelphia, the reaction verged on ecstasy. Sixers center Caldwell Jones fell to his knees and wept, while guard Doug Collins burst out laughing. Pat Williams spun so joyously in his office swivel chair that it snapped in two. "With Julius, George McGinnis, and Doug Collins, every game is going to be a combination of Mardi Gras and a Fourth of July picnic," Williams gushed to the press. "I don't know if I'm going too far, but I think this has the potential to be the most exciting, breathtaking team in the history of sports in this country."

A few dissenting voices seeped through. Notably, 76ers head coach Gene Shue believed that the addition of Erving, brilliant though he was, could upset the balance of a roster already strong enough to vie for the championship. Ultimately, fearful of Erving joining a competitor, Shue set aside his doubts and gave the deal his lukewarm blessing. All at once, the weight of expectations fell squarely on his shoulders. "Am I allowed to lose one [game]?" he mused aloud, his voice quivering with awe and anxiety.

Sixers employees who arrived early to the team offices on October 21 glimpsed scores of eager customers lining up around the block. Inside, the phone lines lit up like a Christmas tree. "We sold $48,000 in season tickets alone today," team publicist Harvey Pollack remarked. Cash-strapped Philadelphians tried to bribe ticket vendors with everything from color televisions to pounds of filet mignon. The surge in sales extended to clubs across the country. One fan in Michigan plopped his paycheck in front of a Detroit Pistons representative and said, "Give me all the tickets to Dr. J that this will buy."

The day the deal was announced, Erving endured a three-hour medical checkup, then raced down to Pennsylvania for a press conference at the South Philadelphia Hilton. Lit up by flashbulbs and floodlights, Erving spoke for the first time since his holdout had begun a month earlier. The scrum of microphone-wielding reporters expecting typical sports platitudes were taken aback when a slightly dazed Erving trained his rhetorical fire on Roy Boe, whom he again accused of reneging on the unwritten pact forged between them. "This is not slavery," Erving asserted. "No one can drag a player on the court."

In Long Island, Erving had forged a home for himself. It was the place where he'd grown up, where he'd clinched a pair of championships. He and his wife, Turquoise, were raising two kids there, with another child on the way. "I've stated during the holdout period that my first preference was to play for the Nets," Erving insisted. But now he was transitioning to a franchise he had no ties to. He'd never played a professional game in Philadelphia, had never practiced with the Sixers, had never even met some of his new teammates. He was starting from scratch in a league and in a city where he'd have to prove himself anew and rebuild all he was leaving behind in New York.

There was no time for introductions as Erving rolled into the Spectrum on October 22, hours before tipoff on Opening Night. So many media members jammed into the Sixers clubhouse that Erving had to escape to the bathroom for sanctuary. "It was," Pat Williams said, "like President [Gerald] Ford was in the locker room." Several players wormed through the masses to welcome him, including George McGinnis, a broad-shouldered forward built like a tank. Two years earlier, Erving and McGinnis had split the MVP award in the ABA. Afterward, McGinnis had decamped for the NBA, becoming the face of the Sixers youth movement. "By George, We've Got It," billboards across Philadelphia had proclaimed. It was McGinnis's team that Erving was joining, so much so that the Sixers front office had sought McGinnis's approval to ensure that he could coexist with someone whose star shone brighter than his own. "George," Erving told him after McGinnis had endorsed the signing, "we're gonna do a number."

Erving emerged on the court clad in a uniform he'd never worn before. His presence lent a dreamlike aura to the pregame activities, an overall disbelief that a player whom everyone in the audience knew about but few had seen had somehow landed in Philadelphia. That feeling climaxed during player introductions when Dave Zinkoff, the Sixers' public-address announcer, called his name. As Erving jogged to the foul circle, the sellout crowd, eschewing the hard-bitten cynicism often associated with Philly fans, welcomed him with a two-minute standing ovation.

Spinning to face all corners, a spotlight on his face, Erving held aloft one fist, then the other. Steve Solms, a real estate executive who was a sidelines fixture at Sixers games, dashed onto the court and handed him a black leather physician's satchel with "Erving" emblazoned in gold across the side.

Dr. J now had all he needed to set up his practice in the NBA.

There was only one problem: the 76ers lost.

The game opened with Erving on the bench, boning up on unfamiliar offensive and defensive schemes. The first time he touched a non-red-white-and-blue ball in a regular-season game, early in the second quarter, Erving threw a pass to the other team. While he racked up seventeen points in sixteen minutes, he also bricked eight free throws and committed five fouls. Rusty, tentative, and out of shape, he was nowhere near the explosive force fans had expected. "My mind felt I could do anything, but my body wasn't ready," Erving admitted.

The San Antonio Spurs, an ABA transplant making their NBA debut, hung tight with the Sixers in the first half, then inched ahead in the second for a 121–118 win. The outcome seemed understandable amid the whirlwind events of the past days. "We were all so happy to have Julius that we went out and played like horseshit," McGinnis said.

The Sixers caught a sunrise flight the next morning to Buffalo, where they were to face the Braves. It'd been two years since the first Julius Erving–Moses Malone matchup had generated national headlines, but now everything was different. Both were on rosters they'd crashed after training camp had concluded; both had been on their respective teams for only three days.

Their first encounter in the NBA proved anticlimactic, a stark depiction of their unsettledness. Erving scratched out thirteen points in fifteen minutes. Malone had nothing to show for the two minutes he played: no points, no blocked shots, no fouls even. Neither player pulled down a single rebound—the only time in a professional game that Malone had failed to do so. With the Sixers again suffering a three-point defeat, Gene Shue's contrarian intuition that the addition of Erving might upend the club's delicate harmony started to seem prescient.

Afterward, Malone grumbled about his playing time to Braves assistant coach Charlie Harrison, who relayed the complaint to head coach Tates Locke. Unmoved, Locke didn't mince words: "We told [Malone] that he had only been here a few days and we couldn't just play him immediately over our players. I wasn't going to placate this kid."

Behind the scenes, Malone's agent, Lee Fentress, was locked in tense negotiations with the Braves front office. Upon Malone's arrival in Buffalo, Fentress had asked for a new three-year deal for $300,000 annually; the Braves had countered with a five-year pact for less. The talks dragged on. After Malone logged a measly six minutes in two games, Fentress raised the issue of playing time. Braves co-owner Paul Snyder took to the media to claim that Fentress had demanded a clause in Malone's contract that guaranteed him twenty-four to thirty minutes per game, which Fentress vehemently denied. Soon, it became clear that Malone, whom some had hailed as the Braves' potential savior a week earlier, was as unwanted in Buffalo as he'd been in Portland.

If he'd taken the traditional route, Malone would've been starting his junior season at the University of Maryland. Instead, he found himself being tossed about between coasts without a city to call home. "[Moses] was happy happy in Utah," his mother, Mary, said. "He hasn't been happy happy since."

Tom Nissalke sensed Malone's discontent from afar. After the Utah Stars had folded, Nissalke had drifted to Puerto Rico to front its national basketball team in the 1976 Olympics, then crossed over to the NBA, becoming the head coach of the Houston Rockets. From their time in Utah, Nissalke recognized how sensitive Malone was, how prone he could be to spiraling into wordless funks when discouraged. "I knew he was in a bad way," he said of Malone in Buffalo. Believing that safe ground was necessary before Malone sank too deep into himself, Nissalke urged Ray Patterson, the Rockets general manager, to snag Malone while his stock was in decline.

On October 24, 1976, the day after the Braves beat the Sixers, Patterson phoned Snyder and told him that "he could be a hero immediately if he would let us take Moses off his hands. He would be saving his franchise a whale of money, he would be getting rid of a player who wasn't playing, and so on." Snyder wavered, but Patterson insisted that they either make the deal right away or call it off. Ultimately, Snyder surrendered Malone to the Rockets for two first-round draft choices and cash.

En route to Houston, Malone reflected on the odyssey that had shuttled him to five teams in less than a year. If he'd harbored any doubts about whether he needed only a half a suitcase in southeastern Texas as well, they were assuaged as soon as his plane landed at Houston Intercontinental Airport. Waiting for Malone in the terminal were Nissalke and his assistant, Del Harris. Nissalke greeted the orphaned twenty-one-year-old with the words he'd been waiting to hear since leaving Utah.

"Mo, now you're home."

PART II
NBA

CHAPTER 6

THE PHILADELPHIA MONSTER

On the morning of October 26, 1976, Jim Foley, the public relations director for the Houston Rockets, arrived at work to find a novel occurrence: a rush for tickets.

Ever since the Rockets had relocated to Houston in 1971 after four undistinguished seasons in San Diego, professional basketball struggled to get a toehold in Texas, a football state through and through. During their first year there, the Rockets split their home games between Houston, San Antonio, Waco, and El Paso, sometimes in arenas unsuited to the sport. Before one contest in El Paso, a fierce windstorm swept through town, covering the floor with dust and sand. Because players couldn't change direction without sliding, referees had to suspend traveling violations. The Rockets, sportswriter Tommy Bonk remembered, "were really like a little traveling band, putting up tent posts and playing underneath that."

Even once the organization anchored itself in Houston, its arena was said to be the loneliest place in town whenever the Rockets were playing. In 1974, three years into their Houston tenure, a shade over two thousand spectators attended the Rockets home opener. General manager Ray Patterson once was pulled over for speeding. When the police officer inquired about what he did for a living, Patterson said that he worked for the Houston Rockets. "Oh, you mean like over at NASA?" the cop asked. Rockets players who appeared at community events occasionally were mistaken for very tall astronauts. In the absence of fans, traditions, and winning seasons, the Rockets flirted with collapse amid ownership churn and financial woes severe enough for players to fret about their paychecks bouncing.

So the line now forming outside the box office must've seemed fantastical to Foley. Moses Malone was to make his Rockets debut the following evening, but that wasn't the reason that vendors burned through ten thousand tickets by midafternoon. It turned out that Houstonians, their tepid support of professional basketball notwithstanding, were just as susceptible as the rest of the country to the temptation of seeing Dr. J in person.

Hours before the game the following evening, more than three thousand fans crashed the gates at the Summit. Since the Rockets had never sold out their home arena, these ticketless hopefuls were shocked at being turned away. It was the largest crowd ever to attend a professional basketball game in Texas. Erving tied the frenzy to the oral mythology that had accrued over the years: "A lot of the reason why people are coming out is because they are skeptical of the ABA players, particularly myself," he said. "They want to see if what they heard is true."

For that game, at least, it was. Looking nothing like the cautious, winded figure who'd labored through the Sixers' opening contests, Erving unleashed his high-flying act for the first time in the NBA. In thirty minutes, he tallied twenty-seven points, thirteen rebounds, and nine assists. Seven of his ten field goals were dunks. At one point, Erving slashed across the baseline, drifted airborne behind the basket, and then extended his right arm far enough inbounds to flick a one-handed shot off the backboard on the other side. "Just another move," Erving told reporters in the locker room. "I just shot a layup. You just figure if you play up in the air, sooner or later you've got to come down." Equally encouraging, his costar, George McGinnis, matched Erving's point total, helping the Sixers blitz the slow-footed Rockets 116–94.

Because Moses Malone had worked out only once with his new teammates since arriving in Houston, Tom Nissalke had planned to ease him incrementally into the Rockets' rotation. But once the Sixers' lead became insurmountable, Nissalke saw little harm in asking Malone to remove his warmups. Until then, no one had made Erving think twice about barreling into traffic. Malone, however, changed the calculation when he swatted one of Erving's layups into the stands, which drew a roar from a crowd that had been waiting all night long for someone to do exactly that.

Afterward, the word most frequently bandied about the locker rooms was "potential"—the heights that each club might ascend to after their respective stars settled in. "[The 76ers] aren't polished yet, but neither are we," said Rockets forward John Johnson. "I think if we could have had Moses for the entire game tonight, we might have beaten them by twenty instead of vice versa."

Rockets guard Calvin Murphy wasn't so certain. "Once [Erving] gets the feel of his teammates," he said, "the world's in trouble."

A decade had passed since the Philadelphia 76ers had last clinched an NBA title, their first and only one in 1967. No dynasty had ensued. Wilt Chamberlain, the Philadelphia native who'd powered the championship run, had demanded a trade after the following season. Stripped of their dominant center, the Sixers had slid into mediocrity and beyond, finishing last in the Atlantic Division for three straight seasons starting in 1972–73.

Little by little, the organization rearmed itself with a host of brash and colorful young players: Darryl Dawkins, Joe Bryant, Doug Collins, and Lloyd Free, among others. But it was George

McGinnis's decision to ditch the ABA for the City of Brotherly Love in 1975 that spurred Philadelphians to dream big again. Until then, McGinnis's career had traversed uninterruptedly from peak to peak: Mr. Basketball in Indiana in high school, All-American in college, MVP in the ABA. He was an awesome presence, a football linebacker masquerading as a basketball big man, someone whose combination of strength and speed struck defenders as unfair. Broadcaster Neil Funk believed that had McGinnis developed a work ethic, "he might have gone down as the greatest power forward ever to play."

But he never did. The floppy painter's cap that McGinnis frequently donned at Sixers shootarounds spoke to his commitment. He appeared to invest more energy at practice in sneaking puffs of cigarettes and sips of Coke than he did in refining his idiosyncratic one-handed jumper that he heaved like a shot put toward the hoop. "He was never a hard worker," Pat Williams said. "Given a choice between paying the price and cutting a corner, George would always cut the corner."

His influence rubbed off on his younger teammates. Darryl Dawkins, another quick, brawny big man, had arrived unmolded in 1975 from Maynard Evans High School in Orlando. Sixers backup center Harvey Catchings remembered the moment he first laid eyes on the eighteen-year-old: "When Darryl walked into the locker room, we had never seen a body like his. He was six eleven and chiseled. He was young and arrogant and flamboyant." Since Gene Shue preferred playing veterans over rookies, Dawkins stuck mostly to the bench. Not yet able to distinguish himself on the court, he worked on fashioning an image off it. He wore multiple gold chains around his neck during games and colorful outfits like red sweatpants held up by black suspenders at practice. The bad habits Dawkins formed while watching players like McGinnis loaf in practice altered the trajectory of a career that should've bloomed into stardom. "I'd come into the locker room at halftime," Dawkins recalled, "and one guy would be smoking a cigarette and another would be drinking a beer. I just did the same thing."

Jamming Julius Erving into this outrageous, maddening mix ignited a mania that swamped the squad everywhere they traveled, from airports to hotels to arenas. Sixteen of the 76ers' first eighteen road games were played before packed houses. "I thought I was on tour with Mick Jagger," Sixers assistant coach Chuck Daly said. During an era when rock-star stadium tours were coming into their own, the 76ers were staging their own aerial version, complete with pyrotechnics in the form of a pregame dunking exhibition in the layup line. "We're an experience," Erving declared. "There never has been a team like this one. No one was ever willing to pay the bucks to get a team like this."

Seeing the Sixers live promised drama, tension, volatility—the spectacle of so much dazzling yet discordant talent trying and often failing to mesh their individual gifts into a cohesive whole, let alone to share the ball among themselves. Critics cast the team as everything wrong with professional sports: mercenary stars, gluttonous owners, free-form play. To some, they were all lead guitar with no rhythm or bass, a five-man rotation of dueling solo artists that could bury an opponent one night, then squabble their way to a loss the next. "The Philadelphia Monster has been born into this world, big and ugly and dumb," Leigh Montville of *The Boston Globe* wrote the week that Erving was signed. "It is like all monsters, partly terrifying, partly ridiculous, totally awesome and hateable. It is a team without reason, a team without design, just gobs and gobs of talent lumped together in this one throbbing mass."

Erving and McGinnis, far from forming a potent one-two punch, struggled to distill their considerable talents into a common purpose. Both were ball-dominant improvisers with erratic jump shots who favored breaking down defenders one-on-one. As a result, the two often played in parallel rather than in tandem. When one had the ball, the other stood statuesque on the opposite side. A local journalist characterized the Sixers offense as "a line at a delicatessen. You took a number and waited your turn at the counter. Every so often, somebody would take all the numbers and four other hungry stomachs would go home growling." Once, McGinnis asked head coach Gene Shue why Caldwell Jones, the most selfless player on the Sixers, wasn't more involved in the offense. The next game opened with Shue calling two post-up plays for the center; both times, his teammates neglected to pass to Jones. It didn't help that McGinnis expressed frustration at being overshadowed by Dr. J. "I always felt I never got my due in the ABA," McGinnis said weeks after Erving joined the Sixers. "It was always Julius's league. So does this become Julius's team?"

Sensitive to being perceived as an interloper, Erving muffled Dr. J during the season's first half. General manager Pat Williams had explained to him that on a team larded with shoot-first scorers with sizable egos, it would be best for team harmony if no one scored thirty points a game. "What I could bring wasn't truly needed," Erving later stated, "so it was discussed that less would be more." Rather than insisting that the ball come to him, Erving sacrificed his own offense to keep his teammates involved and satisfied. Flickers of playground-inspired brilliance seeped through, but mostly he appeared deferential, passive, tentative. In the halfcourt, defenders sagged off him, encouraging Erving to hoist midrange jumpers. Even when Erving wanted to take over a game, the Sixers' peculiar dynamics thwarted him from doing so. "Here I was that first week playing tough and going all out, playing my game," Erving recalled, "when [Sixers guard] Fred Carter said, 'Hey, easy man, you're working too hard.' Then I found out what he meant. In Philly when a man got hot and, you know, made three or four in a row, the defense didn't have to adjust to stop him because our own offense made an adjustment to stop him. By not giving him the ball." Though CBS had loaded its national schedule with Sixers games, expectant viewers often had trouble telling what all the fuss had been about. It felt like vindication for NBA loyalists who'd never had a kind word for Erving's former stomping grounds. "The ABA was a minor league," Boston Celtics president Red Auerbach declared. "Over here Erving is just another small forward."

In early January 1977, the Sixers faced the Nets on Long Island for the first time since Erving left. Greeting him at Nassau Coliseum were signs that read "Juda$." Still, coming back home put Erving in a nostalgic mood. "New York was my first preference," he said after scoring eighteen points in a winning effort. "That's where I wanted to be. I still think about what it would be like if I were still with the Nets. I'd be happier there than I am now." It wasn't just the Nets that he pined for. He missed the camaraderie of his former league, the freedom it offered him. "The ABA was one for all," he said decades later. "We were the upstart league, the survival league, so there was a lot of fun associated with the ABA. I missed that."

Prioritizing money over happiness upended his personal life, too. Between games, Erving would speed 150 miles north to spend time with Turquoise and their newborn son. When he couldn't make the trip, he lived first in a hotel in Philadelphia near the Spectrum, then in an apartment in the city's Society Hill neighborhood. It was a lonely period, with long stretches on the road or in the air, in hotels or rentals, far from home. "If I were with the Nets, there would be less division in my life," Erving remarked in February 1977, adding, "Being traded to Philadelphia was a situation I'll never celebrate or cheer about. But you have to be realistic. Life goes on."

Erving's play perked up in the season's second half, especially after he was named MVP of the All-Star Game, but the Sixers' turmoil showed little sign of abating. Bench players who could've started on other teams put up so many shots in the minutes they were granted that they became known as the "Bomb Squad." Starters looked askance at the trigger-happy second unit; the reserves seethed at taking a back seat to the starting five. Never shy about airing their grievances, players began to duke it out in public. "All I do is sit on the bench," Darryl Dawkins griped. "Sit on the bench and get fat. I'll go somewhere else and lose the fat." Joe "Jellybean" Bryant, whose son, Kobe, would follow him into the NBA decades later, dreamed about Erving fracturing his leg so that Bryant could soak up more playing time. Lloyd Free, who later changed his name to World B. Free, once bricked so many of his patented high-arching jumpers that his teammates suggested that passing might be something he should consider. Free was in no mood to hear it. "I'm tired of being insulted," he fumed. "I'm doing the things I can do, but [Gene Shue] is making me feel like a yo-yo, pulling me up and down. I've got one year left on my contract and somehow I'm gonna get out."

Besieged and embattled, the Sixers head coach shrugged. A dozen years removed from an all-star playing career, Gene Shue had become a hands-off coach who didn't believe that his duties entailed scolding adults who never seemed inclined to listen anyway. It hardly mattered to him whether players popped off to reporters or twirled basketballs on their fingers while he spoke. "Players being unhappy doesn't make me unhappy," Shue stated. "A player can say what he wants. I don't give a damn." By March, however, the situation had deteriorated to such an extent that Shue was forced to implement a new policy: any player who publicly demanded a trade would incur a $500 fine for the first instance, $1,000 for the second. Even then, the sniping continued, sometimes from unexpected sources. Turquoise Erving, who ran as hot as her husband ran cool, published a blistering article in *The New*

York Times that asserted, "No one here respects Gene Shue. How many guys want to win one for Shue? Not one. And sometimes not even for themselves."

Despite it all—the trade demands, the infighting, the inconsistency, the ceaseless drama that defined their season—the 76ers possessed too much talent to sink. When they performed at the breakneck tempo they preferred, they looked unbeatable, frightening even. But true to a team that, according to Sixers guard Henry Bibby, had "an attention span of about 10 seconds," they'd drift, they'd fool around, they'd bicker, and soon, double-digit leads would evaporate. Even so, the Sixers hung tight in enough games to rack up fifty wins, tops in their division and second only to the Los Angeles Lakers in the NBA.

They weren't invincible and they weren't the greatest team the league had ever known, but neither had the Sixers imploded. Now, heading into the playoffs, the hope was that the short-series format would benefit a club rich in potential but deficient in focus. "We've been like a wagonload of gold moving cross-country," George McGinnis said. "Everybody waited in ambush to get their piece. Now we have arrived. Intact."

The trade that saved professional basketball in Houston had been made in the dark. Before it'd happened, Rockets general manager Ray Patterson had seen only photos of Moses Malone. There'd been no college or ABA games to review, nothing from the few moments Malone had logged with the Buffalo Braves. Patterson had had to place his trust in head coach Tom Nissalke, who'd assured him that Malone was a towering behemoth who soon would rack up twenty points and twenty rebounds per game. So Patterson was dismayed, according to his son Steve, when "Moses showed up and he's only about six foot nine inches, with the smallest hands you've ever seen, like he couldn't even palm a basketball. Ray freaked out, because Moses is standing there in the office and he'd expected someone like Kareem [Abdul-Jabbar]." The question that flashed through Patterson's mind as he gazed at the player for whom the Rockets had mortgaged their future was "Oh my God, what have I done?"

No one, not even Nissalke, could've predicted that five months later, the Rockets would wind up one win short of matching the Philadelphia 76ers' record. It all started with Malone's winding recovery from being unwanted. When Malone arrived in Houston, Nissalke could tell something was wrong. Malone's confidence was shot, and he didn't play with the same "spark of intensity" that the head coach remembered from their time together in Utah. To Rockets center Kevin Kunnert, Malone's flaws seemed mechanical. He had, Kunnert noticed, questionable footwork and a tendency to get thrown off balance when bumped. Before practice, Kunnert and other Rockets big men logged so many hours helping Malone refine his fundamentals that Kunnert complained about sore feet from the extra work. The attention paid off. Within a month, the Rockets reliably could pencil in double digits in points and rebounds from Malone.

Slow, steady, and unspectacular characterized the Rockets' brand of basketball. Outrunning opponents or getting caught up in an on-court beauty contest held no interest to them. Instead, the Rockets stuck to what they did best: rebounding, locking down opponents on defense, setting screens, and moving the ball until one of their sharpshooters—Mike Newlin, Calvin Murphy, or Rudy Tomjanovich—had an open jumper. According to Washington Bullets head coach Dick Motta, the Rockets "defy a lot of percentages, because, after all, that's what you want them to do, shooting from the perimeter. But they do it because they have that one equalizer in the middle—Moses Malone. If they miss, Malone has at least a 30 percent chance of getting the ball, of keeping it alive."

A franchise-best forty-nine wins and a second-round victory over the Bullets in the playoffs barely raised their profile. It wasn't until their clash with the Sixers in the Eastern Conference Finals that the national spotlight shone on the Rockets. It was an intriguing matchup between two teams that, despite their near-identical records, couldn't have been more different. The 76ers ran clubs off the court; the Rockets ground them into the floor. The Sixers abided by the playground ethos of "Whoever got it shot it"; Rockets scrimmages sometimes operated under the restriction that no one could shoot until four passes had been made. The Sixers were as ubiquitous as the Rockets were underground. Beat writers claimed that they could toss their notebooks into the Sixers locker room and within minutes, the pages would be jammed with quotes. Malone hadn't spoken enough words to fill a single page the entire season. One Philadelphia writer summed up the Sixers-Rockets series as "your basic fight for survival featuring the cheetah and the water buffalo.... Not on his best day is the water buffalo ever going to chase down the cheetah. The only chance the Rockets have in this thing is if the games are played in tall grass."

Malone did all he could to bog down the Sixers in the opening game, racking up twenty-two points by halftime while grabbing seven offensive rebounds. "One would've thought Moses Malone was Farrah Fawcett the way he attracted everyone's attention," beat writer Tommy Bonk noted. But the fleet-footed Sixers, in full-on attack mode, sprinted ahead by seventeen after three quarters, then cruised to a 128–117 win.

The differences between the teams' stars were on display afterward. Courteous and approachable, Erving showered Malone with praise: "The improvement is phenomenal. The control is phenomenal. I'd seen him develop a short jumper. I knew he had quickness and overall coordination. He used to spin and run over guys, charge them. Now he's got control of all that." Malone, huddled in a far corner of the clubhouse, growled at anyone who drew near: "I have no comment, nothing to say about nothing." Finally, he agreed to talk. When one reporter asked how switching teams three times had affected his season, Malone snapped, "I'm not going to talk about the past," which shut off any further questions.

The following day, Nissalke cracked down hard in practice, punishing his players with wind sprints and repetitive drills. The session got so heated that two Rockets players nearly came to blows. The Sixers, in contrast, leafed through newspapers, laughed with reporters, put up a few free throws, and cleared out within thirty minutes. Their lackadaisical attitude didn't hurt them in Game Two, a 106–97 romp for the 76ers. For Philadelphians, who considered the Rockets "the warm bodies the 76ers were running over on their way to the NBA Finals," the series seemed such an afterthought that the Spectrum hadn't even sold out. The following day, when the club landed at Houston's Intercontinental Airport, Sixers trainer Al Domenico amused the players by riding the luggage conveyor belt in a full circle.

Feeling slighted, the Rockets laid the Sixers out flat in the third game. Malone muscled in thirty points while pulling down twenty-five rebounds, only nine fewer than the entire Sixers lineup. "Sweep my ass!" guard Calvin Murphy yelled as the Rockets closed out a 118–94 drubbing. Anger coursed through the Rockets locker room afterward. "[The 76ers] won one more than we did during the season," Nissalke fumed. "Only one more, with the best talent in basketball. I can't figure that out. And all the writers were saying we were bums and shouldn't be here."

Unworried, the 76ers pushed the Rockets to the brink of elimination by clamping down on Malone in the fourth game, a 107–95 win. "Can't shoot if you ain't got the ball," Malone muttered when asked about his five-point performance. One victory short of advancing to the NBA Finals, the Sixers jeopardized their momentum by running their mouths. "[Malone] doesn't play anybody. He only concentrates on rebounds," Philadelphia forward Steve Mix stated. "We've gone at him a lot and we've been successful. He's such a bad defensive player, we were moving everything through him. He's terrible."

Before the fifth game, Malone and point guard John Lucas sat down for breakfast in downtown Philadelphia. Seething with anger, Malone declared that the Rockets were going to sweep the rest of the series. It was such an assured prediction that Lucas took it as truth. "If Mo says we're going to win three games, we're gonna win three games. I'm not going to argue with Moses Malone."

Erving nearly spoiled Malone's prophecy by exploding for twenty-seven points in the first half of Game Five, propelling the Sixers to a four-point lead. But then, a familiar pattern emerged: they eased up, they settled for jumpers, they lost focus. "We screwed around and screwed around and screwed around and screwed around and let 'em back into it," George McGinnis said. The Philadelphia crowd grew hushed as the lead vanished in the final quarter. After Houston pulled off a 118–115 shocker, reporters clamored into the Rockets locker room upon catching word that Malone, who'd capped his seventeen-point, nineteen-rebound night by nailing the shot that had put his club ahead for good, had lathered himself up into a word-spilling rage. "[Steve] Mix, he don't know what he's talking about. . . . Mix probably had something to drink when he said that," Malone thundered, adding, "How does he know about defense? He be on the bench."

Later that evening, hundreds of fans mobbed the Rockets players when they landed in Houston, pounding their backs and showering them with confetti. "They threw that stuff right in my mouth," Malone griped. Outside the Summit, locals unfolded lawn chairs, switched on handheld radios, and settled in for the night. When the ticket office opened at 10 the next morning, a crush of people waving dollar bills charged forward. Police hollered into bullhorns for order. Unable to turn back, those who'd scored tickets took to climbing the sides of the booth, belly-flopping into the crowd, and surfing to safety across outstretched hands. The scene, one reporter noted, "looked like fall registration at the University of Texas or perhaps the world premiere of *Jaws*." Five years after the Rockets' arrival in Houston, it seemed that professional basketball had a future in Texas after all.

On the sidelines of Game Six was a plastic buffalo—a motivator for a team written off by Philadelphia scribes before the series had even begun. That evening, the contrasting cheetah and buffalo styles neutralized themselves. The Rockets never pulled ahead by more than seven, the Sixers by more than three. Erving put up thirty-four points; Malone pulled down sixteen rebounds. In the final quarter, the Sixers offense slowed to a crawl, became timid, indecisive. It was up to Erving to rescue them. He scored or assisted on seven of the club's final nine points. "They went from fast break demons, a bunch of cheetahs in the first game, to a team running a lot of set plays, then looking around for help," Tom Nissalke observed. "They'd get down there, and then start looking for Julius. I'd have to say that they looked a little like water buffaloes."

In the end, the series hinged on a single play. With eight seconds remaining and the Sixers ahead by two, Rockets point guard John Lucas hurtled into the lane, spun around, and then crashed into Sixers guard Doug Collins. Sent sprawling on contact, Lucas instinctively flipped the ball toward the basket. It settled into the net as referee Jake O'Donnell whistled a foul. A noted contrarian unafraid to rule against the home team, O'Donnell waved off the game-tying bucket, thrusting out his arm in a charging motion. Nissalke hurled his clipboard halfway across the court. A barrage of paper cups and coins rained down from the furious crowd. Bombarded by loose change, Erving tucked a quarter and a penny into his sock as mementos. The officials eventually cleared the court, but the final seconds were immaterial. O'Donnell's call against Lucas effectively ended the series.

Rockets guard Calvin Murphy, though peeved at the outcome, could hardly blame the ref. "We had a timeout, and we told John [Lucas] that Doug Collins was guarding him and Doug Collins was the master of the flop," Murphy remembered, adding, "So what does [Lucas] do? He dropped his shoulder and he drove. And what did Doug do? Took the charge, which was not a charge, but [Lucas] had no business going to the basket in the first place. We told him, 'Don't do it.'"

Even if the call had gone the Rockets' way, they still would've needed one more win to advance to the NBA Finals. But decades later, members of that team had no doubt that, with the Sixers' mystique punctured, the series would've been theirs to take. "I don't ever say we got screwed in any game except that one," Rockets guard Mike Newlin stated. "We knew we would've gone back to Philly and beaten them. We knew we would've."

Years afterward, Malone would refer to that call as the low point of his career. "I felt completely empty after that game because we were so close to making the Finals. We probably would've gone on to beat Portland, and I'd be wearing that ring right now."

CHAPTER 7

INDIVIDUAL VERSUS TEAM

Shortly before noon on May 21, the day before the 1977 NBA Finals began, the Philadelphia 76ers sauntered into practice loose and relaxed, looking no more troubled than if prepping to face a pedestrian opponent at midseason. Their outfits were as dissimilar as their personalities, a wash of styles and colors. Making it to basketball's biggest stage hadn't changed them. They warmed up as they always had: by lofting balls skyward from halfcourt. "We've been consistent all season. Consistently unpredictable," Julius Erving explained. "We are not a blackboard team. I don't know whether we could have gotten this far if we were. We've never believed in orderly practices or doing things by the book."

Their opponents, the Portland Trail Blazers, had just wrapped up a workout that had unfolded with the precision of a symphony orchestra. In the eyes of Bill Livingston, a sportswriter for *The Philadelphia Inquirer*, Blazers practices were an "incredible study in intensity and enthusiasm." Head coach Jack Ramsay, a whistle dangling around his neck, fronted the opening calisthenics himself—a conductor warming up his talent. When the whistle blew, Ramsay demanded absolute attention: no dribbling, no shooting, no ball spinning. Brooking little dissent, he placed his utmost faith in the painstakingly composed offensive and defensive schemes that he expected his squad to execute with minimal deviation.

"The players," Ramsay insisted, "are the medium through which the coach expresses his philosophy. The artist must be in control of his medium, and a coach must prepare his players for their performance." Blazers guard Lionel Hollins said the team "ran the system so well that it became part of our DNA. We practiced and practiced and went over the same things. Jack [Ramsay] was so detail-oriented. He taught us that details matter."

Basketball fundamentalists who were uncomfortable with the creeping influence of streetball viewed the Finals matchup as a morality play that pitted two distinct styles against each other: playground versus playbook, freelance versus structure, individual versus team. The Sixers were painted as outlaws, a stormy band of malcontents slapped together by an owner with bottomless coffers and capable of overpowering opponents with extraordinary one-on-one talent. *Philadelphia Inquirer* columnist Bill Lyon later characterized them as "a non-team for whom passes were something you reserved for your friends at the guest gate." The Trail Blazers, in contrast, were hailed as purists, selfless practitioners of patterned play and off-the-ball movement. "Teamwork," Hollins said, "is preached so much that when one of us turns an ankle, we all limp." For some, the stakes were existential. "Basketball will be set back fifty years if the 76ers ever win," one unnamed fan declared.

Bleeding through it all was another binary: Black versus white. Race had been baked into mainstream coverage of the 76ers all season long. Rather than lauding the faster, freer, more expressive brand of basketball that had propelled the Sixers into the championship round, the press pathologized it in terms that white Americans often ascribed to the Black inner city: disorderly, brash, unruly, authority-averse. Articles about the club oozed with racially tinged condescension. The cure for the squabbling Sixers, a writer for *The Sporting News* declared, was "teamwork, character, and a little humility"—in other words, less playground, more deference. The 76ers were an object of both fascination and derision, at once an unmissable spectacle and an emblem of a troubled league that had gotten too Black too fast for its fans' taste. Reporters fixated on markers of the players' wealth—their Mercedes and colorful clothes and six-figure contracts—as a means of calling out their lack of hustle, their perceived unwillingness to sully their hands with the dirty work that wins titles. "All season, we've been the millionaires in our tuxedoes out there and the other team was carrying its lunch pails," said Doug Collins, the team's lone white starter. George McGinnis put it more bluntly: "I think most of white America thought of us as a bunch of bigmouth, cocky, high-priced n****rs."

At the heart of it was Julius Erving—or Dr. J, depending on how the narrative was framed. The gap between Erving and Dr. J had never been wider. More than anyone, Erving had deviated from the Sixers' me-first ideology, curbing his creative instincts—he averaged eight fewer points than in his final season in the ABA—to such an extent that at one point he'd mused, "When are you going to see the old Dr. J? Maybe never." Somewhat echoing the media's criticisms, he spoke frankly of his club's helter-skelter approach. "Lots of times we run up and down and I don't know what's accomplished," Erving said during the playoffs. "That's how we play in games. As far as execution goes, we don't work on it. That's why our execution suffers. We're a fast break team. We create as we go along. You can't practice that."

At the same time, there was an alternative narrative that centered on Dr. J in the abstract, the spiky-haired, slickly outfitted leader of the league's foremost Black club. In this telling, Dr. J had abandoned his home out of greed and latched onto a superteam that closely resembled the outlaw league he'd hailed from. As a result, the stigma of the ABA along with its accompanying racial baggage clung to Erving like an unshakable odor, no matter how much he modeled the team-oriented approach that critics claimed the Sixers lacked.

Erving's superstar counterpart on the Trail Blazers, Bill Walton, headed into the Finals saddled with baggage of his own. His, however, was spun in wholly different ways. Walton was two people at once: a fundamentally flawless center whose pair of immaculate seasons at UCLA in the early 1970s had thrust him into the national spotlight and a long-haired, tie-dye-clad, left-leaning vegetarian who used to answer his phone "Impeach Nixon," had been hauled off to jail at an antiwar protest, and had once faced questioning from the FBI about associating with someone connected to the kidnapping of heiress Patty Hearst. "If a black player ever tried any of that stuff, he would've been banished from the league," wrote Darryl Dawkins, cutting to the core of a double standard that cast aspersions on Black players for speaking their minds while affording white players wide latitude.

By 1976–77, his third season in the NBA, Walton had learned to clam up about his off-court endeavors, which garnered him positive profiles of personal growth as he led the league in rebounds and blocked shots. He was a player of such exceptional instincts and vision that he could boost his team without ever putting the ball in the hoop. When Walton was healthy, the Trail Blazers were the best team in the NBA; when he was hurt, they were the second worst.

To his credit, Walton swatted away efforts to portray him as the sport's "Great White Hope." But that didn't stop the media from trying. Too much was on the line to quibble with Walton's past. In the first postmerger Finals, after the mass injection of ABA talent had scrambled the rhythm and complexion of NBA games, the best shot at reassuring aggravated fans and executives that white team basketball could still triumph over Black expressive individualism flowed through Walton's club.

Before the start of the opening game on May 22, 1977, Sixers fans welcomed the Trail Blazers to Philadelphia by pelting the players with paper cups—a gesture consistent with a city whose fabled brotherly love had never extended to sporting events. The tipoff heralded what was to come. Sixers center Caldwell Jones batted the ball to George McGinnis, who whipped it downcourt to Julius Erving for a one-handed jam. It was the exact sort of crowd-igniting play that the Blazers had been hoping to prevent. Nearly every time Erving caught the ball, three defenders swarmed him. That didn't stop Erving from exploding for thirty-three points.

In the end, the Blazers netted more rebounds and assists, but the Sixers fired up more shots, which put them over the top, 107–101. Basking in the victory, Erving lobbed some veiled shots at his critics. "I don't have anything to prove to anyone," he asserted, adding, "I was trying to be steady, trying to be a factor, not only with my scoring, trying to have a total consciousness of how I could do the best for my team."

No game more fully captured the beauty and the bedlam of the Sixers than Game Two. For twenty-four minutes, they flew up and down the court with the speed and brute force of a locomotive. By the time the halftime buzzer sounded, the Blazers found themselves down by eighteen. Even though the lead held in the second half, the drama that had destabilized the Sixers all season once again reared its head. Midway through the fourth quarter, Darryl Dawkins tossed Blazers forward Bob Gross to the floor while the two tussled for a rebound. Popping back up, Gross stomped toward him as if to retaliate, and Dawkins threw a wild left hook that missed Gross but nicked his own teammate Doug Collins above the right eye. Maurice Lucas, the Blazers' self-appointed enforcer, charged across the court and clocked Dawkins on the back of his neck. Taken by surprise, Dawkins whirled around and put up his dukes like a bare-knuckled boxer. Around them, spectators vaulted railings and poured onto the hardwood. Referees pulled the two fighters apart while security guards chased after Philadelphia fans eager to incite a rumble. In the eye of the storm, Erving plopped down at center court, resting his elbows across his knees, waiting for the familiar gust of anarchy to breeze by.

Ejected from the contest, Dawkins stormed into the locker room, incensed not at Gross, Lucas, or the referees but at his teammates for insufficiently jumping to his defense. Awash in rage, Dawkins toppled two floor-to-ceiling lockers, tore apart a metal fan, bent several folding chairs, and ripped a toilet off its concrete base, spraying water all over. Loose shoes were floating across the floor by the time the game ended. As George McGinnis put it, the locker room looked "like a hurricane had hit a junkyard."

Clad in a fedora and a cream-colored suit, a carnation peeking from the front pocket, Dawkins ranted to reporters about his perceived betrayal. When Pat Williams attempted to calm him down, Dawkins shoved the Sixers general manager. Decades later, Dawkins was still sore. "What was Doc doing when the tussle started?" he asked. "Sitting his ass down on the court and being an eyewitness." It was an image that resonated almost as much as the scuffle itself. "When Doc sat at halfcourt, it sent a message: 'I am part of this team, but I'm not going to get involved in something like this.' I think that it would've been a better look if he'd come over and put a hand on Darryl and tried to break it up," Sixers backup center Harvey Catchings said, adding, "Once that incident happened, it changed the whole dynamic. The fact that your leading guy stepped away and sat down... We're supposed to be a team, and whether you step in or not, you're part of the visual. That hurt us."

Whatever good spirits should have trailed the team to Portland dissolved into dysfunction and backbiting. Following the

Sixers' humiliating 129–107 loss in Game Three, Steve Mix and Joe Bryant jawed at each other about playing time in the locker room, then filled the next day's newspapers with quotes about their feud. Everything fell flat in the fourth game. The Sixers' slam-dunk extravaganza played to silence during warmups; their vaunted breakneck offense sputtered. They fell behind 19–4 in the first quarter and never recovered. Abandoning his seat with minutes to play and his team down thirty, Sixers owner Fitz Dixon muttered, "A disaster, isn't it?"

Desperate for a reset, head coach Gene Shue convened a team meeting at a hotel in Cherry Hill, New Jersey. Over beers and cheese, they reviewed film of their back-to-back losses. "I looked around," Erving later said, "saw a lot of things going in one ear and out the other. Saw guys' (minds) wandering. Saw guys going to sleep." Those were the least of the Sixers' problems. Steve Mix was nursing a severely sprained ankle, Lloyd Free a cracked rib that had collapsed one of his lungs. Hampered by a painful groin pull, George McGinnis was receiving regular injections of cortisone and xylocaine, which numbed his left leg. He fell into such a dire shooting slump that his teammates had taken to yelling "Brick!" whenever he chucked a jumper during shootarounds. Shue was forced to close his practices to the press to avoid embarrassing comparisons to his opponents' sessions.

For the first time since he'd dragged the New York Nets to the ABA championship the previous season, Erving took matters into his own hands. He sensed that if the Sixers were to regain the momentum, he would need to take "Dr. J out of the closet." Erving's command to his teammates was uncharacteristically forceful: "Unless somebody else is going well, here's where the ball should come." Over the next two contests, he hoisted a full 30 percent of the Sixers' shots, piling up thirty-seven points in the fifth game, forty in the sixth. So fervently did Erving attempt to will

Philadelphia to the title that one writer claimed he "resembled a guy pulling a locomotive with his teeth."

In one memorable sequence, Erving fielded an inbounds pass, dribbled through four Blazers defenders, then threw down a vicious one-handed slam over Bill Walton. Before heading back, Erving flicked the ball off Walton's back—a small playground gesture of one-upmanship. It was Dr. J's long-awaited national unveiling, the moment when the oral mythology turned visual, putting to bed any remaining uncertainties about whether Erving's alter ego had been a smoke-and-mirrors apparition, born of a defunct bush league in which "defense" had been a dirty word.

But it wasn't enough. Exhausted, Erving sucked air on defense, unable to keep pace with Blazers forward Bob Gross. The Blazers swung the ball around the perimeter until Gross, running Erving through multiple screens, shook free for open jumpers. An eleven-point scorer in the regular season, Gross poured in forty-nine total points in the final two contests, both wins for the Blazers. "Who the hell is Bobby Gross?" broadcaster Neil Funk asked Sixers assistant coach Jack McMahon after the Blazers clinched the championship in six games.

"He's the guy that just kicked our ass," McMahon retorted.

In reality, it was a group effort. Consistent with Jack Ramsay's philosophy of sacrificing individual accolades for the collective good, the Trail Blazers reached near parity on offense—all five starters averaged double digits for the series, with none scoring more than twenty points per game. Erving, at thirty per contest, bested the next closest Sixer by eleven points. "What went wrong with the Sixers," Bill Walton proclaimed amid the celebration, "was we're the better team." A fan-made banner draped across the upper reaches of Portland's Memorial Coliseum had summed it up neatly: "The Blazers fly United. The Sixers use four planes." Basketball executives breathed a sigh of relief.

Symbolically, at least, the NBA had staved off one final challenge from the ABA.

In the hours after George McGinnis—whose shooting touch had deserted him so fully that he likened himself on the court to "a blind man searching for the men's room"—had missed a tying shot at the end of Game Six, sealing the Sixers' 109–107 loss, Erving sprawled out across the locker-room floor, an ice bag perched on each knee. Over and over, reporters took turns asking variations of the same question: what happened? Doug Collins marveled at Erving's patience and self-control in those circumstances, at his willingness to respond to each query without snapping, "You dumbass, I just answered that question." Even amid the sting of defeat, Erving managed to puncture the argument that playground basketball had unraveled under pressure, that this was the last the league would see of the attitude and the approach that the ABA had ushered into the NBA. "If we won, you would all be saying that our style is the wave of the future in the NBA. The old Boston Celtics team concept would be a thing of the past," Erving said. "Now, because we lost, tradition has been upheld and we're just a bunch of outcasts. One shot in the final minute could have changed that."

Finally, after every notebook and recorder was full, Erving brushed off the ice bags, slung his gym bag over his shoulder, and shuffled toward the exit. Just then, a reporter for a local Oregon newspaper dashed in with apologies for being late. "It's OK," Erving murmured as he dropped his bag to the floor, prolonging the worst night of his professional career out of duty and etiquette.

Fury gripped Philadelphia in the days after the 76ers fell to the Trail Blazers. Everywhere, residents groused about how a club swollen with talent had bickered among themselves while a championship had sifted through their fingers like sand.

For decades, Philadelphia's professional sports teams had made a habit of frittering away playoff berths and championships, often in excruciating fashion. The Phillies of Major League Baseball would go nearly a century before winning a World Series. In 1964, they held a six-and-a-half-game lead in the National League with twelve games remaining before ten straight losses cost them the pennant. Similarly, the Eagles of the National Football League were in the midst of a title drought that would stretch for more than five decades. Even though the Flyers of the National Hockey League were coming off back-to-back Stanley Cups, they, too, were entering a fallow championship period that persists as of this writing. So when the Sixers dashed out to a 2–0 advantage against Portland, Philadelphians braced themselves not for victory but collapse. In Philadelphia, journalist Jere Longman said, "victory is only defeat that hasn't happened yet."

Jerry Selber, a self-professed "basketball freak," sensed the anger at Norris Square Park in North Philadelphia, where college players and even some ex-pros clashed in sharp-elbowed pickup games. "The prevailing feeling was, this was in our grasp and we got robbed. How the hell did that happen?" Selber remembered.

By day, Selber labored on the creative end of Sonder, Levitt & Sagorsky, the agency that handled the Philadelphia 76ers' advertising. In the summer of 1977, Selber and his colleague Victor Sonder racked their brains to figure out how to reflect in an advertising campaign the city's emotional response to blowing the NBA Finals. They settled on the slogan "We Owe You One." In four words, it conveyed two distinct messages: an apology for the previous season and a promise for the upcoming one. It validated Philadelphians' gripes while also suggesting that this club somehow was immune to the city's hard-luck history. The subtext, Selber explained, was that "you fans have a right to a title, and dammit, we're gonna give it to you."

Erving harbored misgivings not only about guaranteeing a championship in a fickle profession but also about having to continue fielding questions about losing the last one. When asked if Philadelphians deserved a title, he scoffed, "Are you kidding? Where did we screw up last year? I thought we had the potential to win a championship. We didn't win a championship, what happened happened. We had a hell of a year. We just didn't win the championship." Nonetheless, ever the company man, Erving reluctantly agreed to appear in the television commercial for the campaign.

Toward the end of summer, right before training camp, a film crew set up in the locker room at the Physical Fitness Center at Hofstra University, close to Erving's house on Long Island. As they began rolling, Erving stared straight into the camera, extended his elongated index finger, and, enunciating each word unhurriedly, uttered the line that would hang like a millstone around his neck into the following decade: "We . . . owe . . . you . . . one."

CHAPTER 8

RISE AND DRIFT

The seeds of Moses Malone's superstardom were sown at Fonde Recreation Center in downtown Houston. Built in 1960, Fonde first gained prominence as the summer workout site for the University of Houston men's basketball team. It was Malone who bolstered Fonde's status as the go-to venue for pickup basketball in Houston, the Rucker Park of the Lone Star State. In the offseason, Malone banged there weekly with dentists and college prospects, accountants and streetball sensations, those on their way somewhere in basketball and those who never gave up the dream. "You went down to Fonde to make a rep or to protect your rep," said Houston Rockets guard Calvin Murphy. "You're playing against people that never had a chance to make it in the pros, and they're trying to prove something. You had to bring your A game so you didn't get embarrassed." The parking lot reflected the diversity of talent, with luxury vehicles lined up next to tarnished jalopies. The rules were old-school: shirts versus skins, first to fifteen won, the winners held court, the losers retreated to the back of the line. "There was no 'I'm just going to show up and run up and down,'" Rockets forward Major Jones stated. "If you didn't win, you'd be on the sidelines for a while."

Fonde became Malone's home gym during the summer. When his team got on a roll there, losing players slipped off their shoes, aware that their day was done. Kids from the nearby Allen Parkway housing projects, unable to afford tickets to the Summit, flocked to Fonde to watch, but Malone had little interest in putting on a show for them. Unlike Erving, Malone approached pickup games as he did anything else basketball related: concretely, single-mindedly, as part of a day's work. Robert Reid, a Texas native who joined the Rockets in 1977, noticed that Malone used Fonde as a staging ground for moves that he aspired to add to his offensive arsenal. "On Monday, [Malone] would do only layups—run the floor and do layups right-handed, then left-handed," Reid remembered. "On Wednesday, he would do everything drop-step—on the left side, on the right side. Next week, it was everything off the glass—a short jumper, a hook. Moses didn't just come to play. He worked on what he had to do, to make it perfect.... So now, when the season started, he had his whole game intact."

Malone's dedication to Fonde attested to his downtime priorities. He didn't have much appetite for leveraging his burgeoning athletic fame into moneymaking ventures. He made no effort to become a commercial pitchman, even less to build a brand. Whenever business opportunities came up in conversation, whether with corporations hoping to collaborate or venues seeking personal appearances, Malone shut it down with three words: "Talk to Lee"—his agent, Lee Fentress, who would deflect the requests more tactfully. For Malone, basketball wasn't a springboard to something bigger. It was enough on its own. "Moses loves to [play] more than anything," Rockets general manager Ray Patterson said. "Julius [Erving] is the same way, but basketball's not *everything* in his life." As Malone himself put it, "All I do is play basketball. It's like a doctor's a doctor and a lawyer's a lawyer. I'm a basketball player, that's my profession."

For Erving, being a star came coupled with off-court duties and obligations that couldn't simply be waved away. He took it upon himself to serve as an ambassador for a sport whose professional iteration had never matched the popularity of college basketball. Erving believed that it was important for Black athletes in particular to take heed of public perception, to think about whether their speech and manner were contributing to long-standing stereotypes. "I measure my words," Erving said. "It goes back to growing up, watching interviews on television. Some athlete would come on and say, 'Uh, I do what I feel like out there.' I just didn't want to sound like some dumb black guy." If someone wasn't living up to this standard, Erving sometimes let his diplomatic facade slip. When asked in 1977 whether he would rather team up with Darryl Dawkins or Moses Malone, Erving naturally chose his fellow Sixer. But his reasons for doing so were atypically blunt: "I would take Darryl over Moses. Darryl has more range, he's stronger, and he's quicker mentally. He has the ability to talk, communicate, understand what's going on. All that good stuff."

Erving's response trafficked in a widespread assumption about Malone: that he said little because he had little to say, that his lack of verbal polish derived, at least partly, from an overall lack of mental acuity. When Malone did talk, reporters continued to sneer at him for not speaking clearly. Perhaps the defining characteristic of Malone's public persona was that hardly anyone could make head or tail of his rapid-fire, Southern-tinged dialect. Even referees were stumped. "You can't understand him, but he's always grumbling," one unnamed ref stated. "You'll give him a technical once in a while, but you're just guessing." Not everyone considered Malone's infrequent, incomprehensible speech to be a liability. Letting his own bias slip, Tom Nissalke found it a welcome relief from the many outspoken Black players of the period. "Moses will be like Bill Russell," Nissalke asserted, "except that he won't talk as much, which will be great."

What his critics missed was that Malone's lack of interest in giving the overwhelmingly white power structures in and around the NBA what they wanted was, above all, an assertion of his own autonomy. Choosing when to talk gave Malone an edge in the give-and-take between reporters and players. He tilted the playing field in his favor by making it clear to the press that he was available on his terms, not theirs. Unlike Erving, Malone rarely lingered in the locker room doling out print-ready nuggets for the next morning's editions. Keeping them at arm's length, Malone referred to the beat writers for the *Houston Chronicle* and the *Houston Post* not by their names but as "Chronicle" and "Post." Behind their backs, Malone called reporters "janitors," broom-wielding busybodies scrounging for dirt. Tommy Bonk, who covered the Rockets for the *Houston Post*, recalled a standard conversation with Malone:

Malone: *I don't talk on Tuesdays.*
Bonk: *Moses, it's Wednesday.*
Malone: *I don't talk on Wednesdays.*

Rockets executives suggested that Malone enroll in speech classes, but he blew them off. "I don't think I have to change my whole way of talking and acting when I'm happy with myself," Malone asserted. "I've always been happy with Moses Malone, the person."

As long as reporters steered clear of personal matters and stuck to basketball, Malone, when inclined, spoke perceptively and fluently about his approach to his craft. "You play with teammates long enough, you learn how they shoot, where they like to shoot from, what their shot does while it's in the air. And you learn if he more likely will miss long or short. Right there, you have a real advantage in going for the offensive rebound," Malone told *Houston Chronicle* sportswriter George White, adding, "On our team, for example, I know Rudy [Tomjanovich] shoots a flat shot that probably will bounce back in the direction it came if he misses. Murf [Calvin Murphy] and Mike [Newlin] shoot with big arches. I play the ball to come off the rim to the opposite side." Even his more typically truncated answers were laced with homespun wisdom and humor. When asked to expound on his approach to defense, Malone shot back, "You can't talk defense, you have to play it." After a reporter suggested that his smallish hands prevented him from being an even better rebounder than he was, Malone wouldn't hear it. "I think I have great hands," he insisted. "I think the *ball* is too big."

In many ways, southeastern Texas was the ideal spot for someone of Malone's temperament. A former boom-or-bust town, Houston was growing by leaps and bounds in the 1970s. Stretching across its horizon was a swelling sprawl of minimally zoned neighborhoods connected by miles of zigzagging freeways. Football was part of the social glue that bound together longtime residents and the diverse migrants surging into the city. Professional basketball was secondary at best, which suited Malone just fine. Houston was far enough away from the country's media capitals for Malone to ascend into the NBA's upper echelon with minimal buzz and scant appearances on national television. As a result, he was able to wander the city's streets with little concern about being harassed or badgered. He claimed that he could even sneak undetected into open-air pickup games across the city, introducing himself as Mike Wynn. "People would think I was just some old guy they could take care of," Malone said, somewhat improbably, considering his height and size. By the time he left, having wreaked havoc on the playground, that alias would be permanently seared into the minds of those who had no idea of what had just hit them.

By his midtwenties, Malone had become a paradox: at once the NBA's dominant force and its best-kept secret. Sizable numbers of basketball fans would have been hard-pressed to pick his face out of a lineup. He had no signature moves, no alter egos, no easily packaged highlights. Rebounding was his obsession, the building block of his bruising style. It was rugged and unglamorous, more an expression of will than beauty, the sort of gritty task that, while necessary, seldom appealed to advertisers or casual fans. "Anybody can shoot a jump shot," Malone sneered. What he did, in contrast, required fanatical resolve, austerity, a blue-collar work ethic that rendered him more laborer than entertainer. "Basketball at this level can't be fun when you're on the court with guys who are professionals," Malone told George White. "You don't have time to have fun. If someone pays money to see you, you are at work."

If audiences were slow to pick up on Malone's mastery, opposing players were not. "It's very rare that you go into a game knowing that if you don't block out one man, you're not going to win," said Steve Hawes, a center for the Atlanta Hawks. Malone's unorthodox methods gave New York Knicks center Bill Cartwright fits. Malone, he claimed, often shot the ball on the way up, unworried about accuracy because of his propensity for recovering his own misses. "That second jump was so fast," Cartwright recalled. "You couldn't really do anything about it because he just had that ability to get up and down really, really quickly." A tad undersized as a center, Malone wore down taller men with a motor that never stopped whirring. "He spends every single second fighting you for position," Darryl Dawkins said. "You have to fight him and bump him and go to the boards and try to outjump him. You feel like you're trying to box out an octopus." On nights when Detroit Pistons center Bob Lanier faced Malone, he prepared solemnly, sitting alone in the whirlpool, staring for long stretches at the ground, telling his coach to have the backup center ready. Malone, Lanier knew, was "going after every rebound like it's his last meal."

Through single-minded focus and thousands of summer hours logged at Fonde and various outdoor courts, Malone transformed from a player who, according to his first professional coach, Bucky Buckwalter, "couldn't shoot a lick" into one with reliable, if limited, post-up moves and an array of short hooks and jumpers. Over three NBA seasons, he raised his scoring average from 13.2 to 24.8 points per game. But it was with rebounding that Malone fundamentally altered what was possible in the sport. In 1978–79, Malone shattered the record for offensive rebounds in a season, pulling down an astounding 587, almost twice as many as the next closest player. In the four decades since, no one in the NBA has come within fifty rebounds of matching that number. It cemented his place as a singular counterweight to the ascendant playground-inspired artistry that stars like Erving were professionalizing—defiantly unpretentious yet punishingly effective. "Moses didn't play basketball," Rockets guard Mike Newlin claimed. "He played Moses. I'm not saying that disparagingly at all. I'm simply saying that somewhere along the way, his understanding of basketball was truncated, but his understanding of hustle and grit and determination wasn't."

In 1979, after leading the league in minutes and offensive and defensive rebounds, Malone was named the MVP in the NBA. At the ceremony to collect his award, Malone gave customarily short remarks that showcased the closed-door wit that his teammates had become familiar with. "I couldn't have done it," Malone said, "without the Calvin Murphys, Rick Barrys, Rudy Tomjanoviches, and Mike Newlins. They did a lot of missin'."

In the two seasons after the 76ers had squandered a championship, the club defaulted twice on its debt to Philadelphia. "We owe you one" turned into "We owe you two" and counting. During those years, Julius Erving was a physical wreck, hampered by an excruciating groin pull that made it difficult for him to walk, let alone jump. Balky braces hugged each of his crotchety, arthritic knees. Erving, Darryl Dawkins later wrote, had "as much lateral movement as a fire hydrant." The physical toll of bounding across asphalt courts had caught up to him.

No longer able to overwhelm opponents with sheer athletic ability, Erving had reached a crossroads. "For the first time," he reflected, "I wasn't enjoying myself playing. I was really looking at the game as a job." This might've been enough for someone like Moses Malone, but for Erving, whose game fed off flow and invention and wonder, it was stifling, joyless. His scoring average plummeted from 29.3 points per game during his last season in the ABA to 20.6 in 1977–78. In a twist that few would have predicted at the time of the merger, Malone became the first ex-ABA player to win an MVP in the NBA during the same season that Erving failed to secure a single MVP vote. Prominent publications like *Sports Illustrated* ran stories with headlines like "Hey, What's Up with the Doc?" Thoughts of retirement flickered through Erving's mind. "There was an emptiness inside of me," he said.

His home life, too, was in disarray. Erving had married Turquoise Brown in 1974, during his first season with the New York Nets, but he admitted to engaging in extramarital affairs over the following years. That made him no different from many other professional athletes. Nine months of living out of suitcases, hopscotching the country for short stays in cities they had no bearings in, infused players' lives with loneliness. Temptations beckoned at every hotel and arena. Some indulged their desires openly—Dawkins, for example, tooled around in a van that had the words "Gettin' Room" painted on one of its sides. Newspaper columnist Mark Whicker recalled that Dawkins once asked him to mail twenty different envelopes addressed to twenty different women in twenty different cities.

After Los Angeles Lakers games in the 1980s, players and celebrities flocked to the Forum Club, an exclusive nightclub in the arena where the Lakers played, which gave ample free passes to single women.

Others, like Erving, were more discreet. In the late 1970s, Erving carried on an affair with Samantha Stevenson, a sportswriter who sometimes covered the Sixers. It resulted in her pregnancy. A hush-hush deal was hammered out in which Erving would provide financial support for the child while the ordeal remained under wraps, keeping his carefully curated image intact. It would be decades before the public found out and even longer before Erving met Alexandra Stevenson, his daughter. In the meantime, the adultery strained a marriage already burdened by absence and distance.

Philadelphia still hadn't become home—and not just because Erving continued to commute there from Long Island. The city had yet to embrace this iteration of the Sixers unreservedly. There was a sense among certain fans that the "best team that money can buy" cut against Philadelphia's civic identity—the blue-collar ethos that the city's sports franchises were expected to embody. It was an identity forged through centuries of loss and ridicule. Once the financial, artistic, and political capital of the country, Philadelphia had lost its primacy little by little to New York and Washington, DC, the two East Coast powerhouses it was sandwiched between. By the 1970s, Philadelphia had morphed into a punch line. It was said that comedians could open their sets with a guaranteed laugh simply by mentioning that they were from Philly. The city's put-upon identity became so ingrained that a local marketing firm erected a billboard along the Schuylkill Expressway that read "Philadelphia isn't as bad as Philadelphians say it is." A chip perpetually on their shoulders, Philadelphians took to valorizing underdogs and brawlers who were unafraid of standing up to flashier, more well-heeled opponents.

The team that captured Philadelphia's heart during this era was the Flyers, a boisterous, scuffling hockey club whose hard-nosed ways had earned them the moniker "Broad Street Bullies." The players punched the clock, sacrificed their bodies, then drank together at unpretentious watering holes. Starting in their Stanley Cup championship season of 1974 and stretching into the following decade, the Flyers performed to sold-out crowds at the Spectrum, a marked contrast to the basketball franchise that shared the same arena. The Sixers seemed to exemplify the opposite of what many locals prized in the Flyers: disunity, greed, egoism, an aversion to practice. "The Flyers were the working man's team when they rose to supremacy," Bill Livingston wrote in *The Philadelphia Inquirer.* "The most laborious thing [the Sixers] do," he continued, "is cart their checks, which are big enough to fund your average banana republic, to the bank every couple of weeks."

In many ways, the two teams were proxies for the larger developments that had polarized the city along racial lines. By the late 1970s, deindustrialization had begun to rot Philadelphia's urban core from the inside out. Manufacturing jobs, which once had powered its economy, plummeted by 40 percent. Abandoned houses dotted once vibrant neighborhoods as more than a quarter million citizens fled to the suburbs or elsewhere, forcing city officials to slash essential services to compensate for the dwindling tax base. Homelessness skyrocketed, roads fell into disrepair, trash went uncollected, and racial tensions flared amid entrenched segregation and heavy-handed policing.

These tensions were exacerbated by the rise of Frank Rizzo, a former police commissioner who served as Philadelphia's mayor from 1972 to 1980. Through a racially incendiary agenda that, among other things, aimed to restrict public housing, thwart busing to desegregate schools, and crack down on crime, Rizzo appealed to the same white working-class base most likely to embrace Philadelphia as a blue-collar town powered by citizens who supposedly earned what they got through hard work, not handouts. Those most likely to be affected by Rizzo's policies harbored different perceptions. Chet Walker, who played for the 76ers in the 1960s, asserted that Rizzo was "to black people, like some nightmare sheriff who'd followed them from Mississippi or Alabama." They were the targets, the scapegoats, the receiving end of an administration predicated on "law and order." Rizzo wasn't subtle in his messaging. While attempting to change a city charter that would've allowed him to run for three consecutive terms as mayor, Rizzo encouraged his supporters to "vote white." In this context, the "We Owe You One" slogan took on a more charged subtext. It signaled to the 76ers' disproportionately white ticket-buying base that they were owed a title from the disproportionately Black team that hadn't lived up to the city's ideals.

The NBA as a whole was similarly riven by racial strife. At the end of the 1970s, it had an asymmetrical dilemma: roughly 75 percent of players were Black while roughly 75 percent of ticket holders were white. How well a majority-white customer base could relate to a majority-Black labor force became the league's central preoccupation. Certain executives were blunt in their skepticism. In 1979, the year before he bought the Cleveland Cavaliers, businessman Ted Stepien told reporters, "This is not to sound prejudiced, but [if I owned the Cavaliers,] half the squad would be white. I think people are afraid to speak out on the subject. White people have to have white heroes. I, myself, can't equate [*sic*] to black heroes. I'll be truthful, I respect them but I need white people. It's in me. And I think the Cavs have too many blacks."

Enduring prejudices that painted Black athletes as naturally gifted hindered ticket buyers from forging the same emotional bonds that they did with the white benchwarmers for whom general managers often reserved end-of-roster spots. Black players faced dual barriers to becoming fan favorites: their successes were more likely to be attributed to biology than effort, which ignored the innumerable hours that had gone into developing their talents, and their shortcomings led to accusations of laziness or an overall lack of character.

These prejudices, too, were fueled by reports of rampant drug consumption in the NBA. In the absence of league-mandated screening, many players dabbled in illicit substances without fear of repercussions. To shake off the effects before games, several popped green-colored uppers that were known as "Christmas trees." Dawkins claimed that during breaks in the action, certain players bantered about the goods they'd scored. Afterward, they slipped into each other's locker rooms to hand friendly opponents a sample. With security lax, brazen dealers sometimes turned up in clubhouses, peddling their wares. Addiction derailed the careers of several stars. Spencer Haywood, for one, hit rock bottom after drifting off to sleep during a practice in which he'd shown up high on quaaludes, which set in motion his expulsion from the Los Angeles Lakers. While the drug crisis was real—Dawkins estimated, perhaps exaggeratedly, that half the league snorted cocaine and 90 percent smoked marijuana—it often was used as an excuse to smear Black players in general as out of control.

Similarly, physical play that sometimes tipped into brawls fed the impression that the league was failing to police its labor force. On December 9, 1977, in a game that pitted the Houston Rockets against the Los Angeles Lakers, Rudy Tomjanovich, a white forward for the Rockets, sprinted toward a scuffle that had broken out in the backcourt. Detecting someone closing in from behind, Kermit Washington, a Black forward for the Lakers, wheeled around and decked Tomjanovich. The force of a fist colliding against his own acceleration fractured Tomjanovich's skull. As he left the court, the bitter taste of leaking spinal fluid coated his mouth. Doctors had to reconstruct Tomjanovich's facial bones with the meticulousness of a paleontologist piecing together the splintered shards of a fossil. Replays of the incident hardened perceptions of the NBA as a troubled league, disorderly and prone to violence, with standoffish and militant stars who were incompatible with the more genial, nonthreatening persona that advertisers and television networks favored in Black athletes.

If any player could bridge this stark racial divide, Erving seemed best suited to do so. Equal parts revolutionary and conservative, he had the uncommon ability to be all things to all people, to cater to white mainstream tastes without sacrificing his identity as a proud Black man. Black audiences took pride in Dr. J's streetball bravado; white audiences felt at ease with Erving's accommodating presence. "His style of play did not dictate his personality," Sixers guard Al Skinner said. "He was aggressive on the court, dunking over guys like he did, but that wasn't who he was off it. Once he stepped between the lines, he was Dr. J. But when he wasn't, he was Julius Erving."

Unlike his more politically engaged peers, Erving distanced himself from the protests and Black Power activism coursing through the country. When sprinters Tommie Smith and John Carlos raised their gloved fists on the medal podium at the 1968 Summer Olympics, Erving considered it shameful: "I love America. I'm buying the American dream. We should solve our problems through negotiation, arbitration, mediation. Not with a raised fist. What does that solve?" Erving seemed more in tune with Black athletes from an earlier generation, those like Jackie Robinson and Joe Louis who sought crossover acceptance through respectability politics, by projecting dignity and composure on and off the playing field. "'Crossover' became an important term for me, because it wasn't a black thing anymore," Erving said. "All of a sudden, you had white adults telling their kids to grow up and be like Julius Erving."

It was a stance that attracted the attention of large corporations, even Hollywood. Converse executives claimed that Erving's specific shoe, a plain white high-top adorned by a red star and bent red stripe, was the highest-selling basketball shoe in the country, even if Erving himself received no royalties for each pair sold. In 1978, a movie producer named Gary Stromberg, who'd garnered success with his first film, *Car Wash*, approached Erving about playing the lead in his next project, *The Fish That Saved Pittsburgh*, a strange concoction that blended off-the-wall humor, musical interludes, and basketball montages. The resulting film revolved around a flatlining basketball franchise that turned its fortunes around by teaming together players with the same astrological sign. At one point in the movie, Erving wooed his love interest by taking her to a playground court and dunking in his street clothes. In a bit of poetic foreshadowing, the name of Erving's character was Moses.

The movie opened in 1979 to baffled reviews and sparse audiences. That same year, the Sixers were eliminated in the Eastern Conference Semifinals by the San Antonio Spurs, failing for the second straight season to advance to the NBA Finals. "Internally," Erving said, "I was restless, empty in a way. I was void of the happiness trip that should come with things being as they were for me."

His thirtieth birthday on the horizon, Erving was a player and a person in search of a new identity.

In the summer of 1979, a reunion was planned for the Williams family, the last name of Erving's paternal grandmother. A committee was convened to identify distant relatives and to trace the family's history as far back as possible. On July 6, more than three hundred members gathered at Eisenhower Park on Long Island. For Erving, it proved to be a profound spiritual awakening. On a scroll that was unrolled, the family's genealogy was revealed, from enslaved ancestors in the early 1800s to those before him in the present. With this larger understanding of his lineage fresh in mind, Erving took to heart something one of his uncles told him there: "A long time ago, long before you were born, our family was blessed, and you are the result of that."

For months, the words rattled around in his head. "I started thinking about destiny," Erving said. "What is destiny all about? You hear about that all the time. You wonder if there is a master plan, a grand design of things."

The reunion came at the exact moment that he'd been questioning the meaning of Dr. J. Had that persona subsumed Erving the individual? Was a rebalancing in order? Searching for answers, Erving turned to the Bible and various books on Christianity. He soon came to the realization that a stage of his life was ending and another beginning. "I divided my life into three periods," Erving explained. The first concluded at age eleven, when his father died in a car accident. The second carried on until his brother, Marvin, passed away while Erving was a freshman in college. "In the third phase," Erving continued, "I just went on taking things as they came, and I became Dr. J, and that lasted until I was 29. That was when I accepted Christ. Then I realized I was in a fourth period, the one I'm in now. I see how sheltered I've been, how passive. That's the thing I need to change."

Shortly thereafter, in a gesture loaded with symbolism, Erving pared down his trademark Afro. He was cutting off the old in order to conjure up something new. The '70s had been the decade of Dr. J; the '80s promised to be the decade of Julius Erving.

CHAPTER 9

THE PHILADELPHIA REBOOT

Two things stood out when Julius Erving reported to training camp at the start of the 1979–80 season: his hair was shorter, and his knee braces were off.

The dawn of a decade promised a fresh start for Erving. Centered in himself, regenerated from a summer of stretching and strengthening his knees and groin, he made it clear that his days of deferring to others had ended. "He looked so good, so determined," said Sixers assistant coach Chuck Daly. "He took off those knee braces and he ran like a youngster. We could sense a different attitude about Julius too. He was very serious about everything we did in practice. Mentally, he was on top of everything. He was very much the leader, the captain. It was as if he had made up his mind this was going to be the year."

It helped that Erving was now surrounded by teammates who complemented, rather than cut against, his style. Much of the credit rested with Sixers head coach Billy Cunningham. Chalk-white and redheaded, nicknamed the "Kangaroo Kid" for the springs in his legs, Cunningham had competed during his playing days with the combative fervor that characterized the city he'd grown up in. A New Yorker through and through, Cunningham used to scale fences as a kid so that he could continue shooting late into the night on the schoolyards of Brooklyn. "He looks soft and young but he always got a seat on the subway. That's a good sign of aggressiveness," said fellow New Yorker Frank McGuire. Joining the 76ers as a sixth man in 1965, Cunningham fit the mold of a Philadelphia athlete. He emoted, he sparred, he left it all on the floor. His crucial role in sparking the Sixers to their first—and at that time only—championship in 1967 elevated him to iconic status. Cunningham, Sixers general manager Pat Williams declared, was "more popular in Philly than soft pretzels."

Although a gruesome knee injury forced an early retirement in 1975, Cunningham's work in Philadelphia wasn't done. When the Sixers stumbled to a 2–4 start in 1977–78, the season after they'd blown a 2–0 lead in the NBA Finals, the front office's patience with Gene Shue and his hands-off approach to coaching finally ran out. Cunningham was tapped to be Shue's replacement. Thrust suddenly into a position for which he had no experience, Cunningham resorted to sideline histrionics in an effort to will his club to victory: he flailed about when referees whistled fouls against his players; he stomped the floor so hard that he developed shin splints; he hurled clipboards with such frequency that assistant coaches were ready to duck at a moment's notice. After games, the sweat had to be wrung out of his three-piece suits. His intensity was consistent with what George McGinnis remembered of Cunningham as a player during the lone season they'd overlapped. "He'd be busting, chasing loose balls, going for everything, playing like he always had," McGinnis said. "I'd say, 'Billy, the ball is out of bounds, you had no chance. Let it go.' He couldn't accept that, he couldn't play that way."

Cunningham also couldn't coach that way, not with players like McGinnis, who didn't grasp the value of hurtling after lost causes in meaningless scrimmages. When the Washington Bullets bounced the 76ers from the playoffs in May 1978, Cunningham advocated for a housecleaning. It was clear that the Sixers couldn't simply stockpile stars and prance to glory. They'd tried their hand with talent; what they needed now was chemistry. So over the next two offseasons, the front office dismantled its one-on-one road show piece by piece, retooling a roster front-loaded with ego into one that more closely resembled the selfless Portland Trail Blazer squad that had upset the Sixers in the Finals. "We trimmed out a lot of flamboyance," Pat Williams said of the decision to shed McGinnis, Lloyd Free, and Joe Bryant, among others.

The McGinnis trade epitomized the club's new philosophy. In exchange, the Sixers received Bobby Jones, a sunken-chested forward from the Denver Nuggets who seemed the antithesis of what McGinnis represented. McGinnis could beat clubs with the ball; Jones could beat them without it. McGinnis puffed cigarettes during halftime and practices; it was said that Jones couldn't stand the smell of smoke. Even profanity, the lingua franca of professional sports, grated on Jones. "Anyone who cursed around Bobby felt like shit," wrote Charles Barkley, who played two seasons with Jones. McGinnis voiced misgivings about being obscured by the long shadow cast by Dr. J; Jones was happiest in the shade. "I didn't want to be the center of attention," Jones explained before the trade. "That's why I'm glad David Thompson is on the [Nuggets]. He gets the publicity, which is fine. I would just as soon be in the background. I don't care how long I play or even if I play."

Jones was the quintessential role-player, someone who boxed out, set picks, and hugged his man so tightly on defense that, one writer claimed, Jones would know in an instant the flavor of the gum the other player was chewing. A devout Christian who studied Bible verses on road trips while his teammates thumbed through *Playboy*s or sports magazines, Jones was guided by the faith-based principle of self-sacrifice. How many points he scored didn't seem to concern him. "I quickly figured out," Jones later stated, "that if I could get steals and block shots, that would be my goal because those are unselfish stats. Those are stats that help your team gain more possessions." Basketball never became his identity or his all-consuming obsession. He bore down in games, then let it go entirely. "Bobby Jones gives you two hours of his blood, showers, and goes home," Pat Williams said. During the offseason, Jones preferred lazing in a hammock to bouncing a basketball. Which wasn't to imply that he was a pushover or uncompetitive. Jones, columnist Mark Whicker wrote, "always has combined elements of off-court reluctance and on-court fanaticism. He's a guy who says it really isn't that important who wins, then runs himself into exhaustion contradicting himself."

A roster heavy on soloists and light on collaborators might've seemed an uneasy fit for Jones, but he intuited immediately why the Sixers had pursued him. "If you have five guys that need the ball, then it's a bad situation. And that's what Philly faced when they traded for me. They had all these guys who were scorers. And so it was a perfect scenario for me, who didn't need the ball, to go to a team that had plenty of guys who could take care of scoring." Steve Mix, who'd joined the Sixers in 1973, making him the club's longest-tenured veteran, sensed the change at once. "For the first time since my first season here I could see a team begin to take shape," Mix said, adding, "Nobody was stabbing anybody in the back, all of the sudden everybody knew their roles."

The thornier challenge involved selling Sixers fans on the wisdom of swapping the onetime franchise redeemer for someone whose worth was measured more in intangibles than statistics. For Billy Cunningham, it all came down to the team's now-undisputed captain: "A lot of people were saying, 'How are you trading somebody with a twenty-point, ten-rebound track record for somebody who's maybe averaging twelve points and five or six rebounds?' But Bobby allowed us to turn the team basically over to Julius Erving. At that point, I think that Julius had tried to accommodate everyone else and wasn't taking control of the situation. We had to put him in the position where he was comfortable. And from that point on, it was a different type of atmosphere. The team was completely restructured."

Equally key to the Sixers' reboot was a little-known point guard from an out-of-the-way college in the Texas panhandle. Maurice Cheeks had come to the team's attention through Jack McMahon, a basketball lifer and Sixers assistant coach who never seemed so happy as when he hit the road. Several times a year, map in hand, McMahon set off along two-lane country highways on days-long treks to faraway colleges so that he could assess unheralded players whose hardwood feats had generated regional buzz. It was lonely work, built on solitary nights in shabby hotels dining on snacks from lobby vending machines.

After catching wind of a senior at West Texas State University who'd earned All-Missouri Valley Conference honors for three years running, McMahon hightailed it to El Paso and then sped northeast in a rental car for seven hours, thinking, "This kid better be worth it." What McMahon found was what he hoped every scouting adventure would unearth: buried treasure. Here, toiling away in a corner of the country so remote that Maurice Cheeks would complain that he had to travel seventeen miles to the next town just to get good pancakes, was a hardy, turnover-averse point guard.

Selected late in the second round of the 1978 draft, Cheeks journeyed from anonymity to spotlight, elbowing his way into the Sixers' starting lineup his rookie season. Cheeks played the way he carried himself: methodically, unobtrusively, with maximum efficiency and minimal fuss. One writer characterized Cheeks as being "as insistent and consistent as an Atari character." He made whatever he did on court seem like the only thing he could've done. His Sixers teammates discovered that the six-foot-one Cheeks could dunk only when he unexpectedly did so during a game against the Detroit Pistons. Dashing down the lane on a fast break, Cheeks was met at the rim by a taller opponent. Uncertain whether he could loft the ball over the defender's outstretched fingers, Cheeks flushed it through the hoop instead, dunking not as a flourish but as the surest way to finish.

Indifferent to applause or publicity, his mouth set in a permanent grimace, Cheeks thwarted the press's best efforts to profile him. His quirkiest off-court feature was his diet, which tended toward chocolate chip cookies and Hawaiian Punch. A remarkably durable player, Cheeks seemed more likely to visit the team's trainer for jaw cramps from eating a bag of jelly beans than for a sprained ankle. He was so devoted to sweets that his teammates once staged a cookie challenge after practice. Blindfolded, Cheeks nibbled on five different chocolate chip cookies, accurately identifying the brand and price of each one. Even taking part in such a challenge seemed a stretch for the reserved Cheeks, who otherwise tried to blend into the scenery. As a result, it took a while for him to be recognized as a rising star. "Not being a vocal person off the court got him overlooked," said Franklin Edwards, who would spend three years as Cheeks's backup on the Sixers. "He liked it that way."

For Julius Erving, there was a certain irony to the changing makeup of the Sixers. He went from being surrounded by players who didn't pass enough to ones who passed too much. He found himself doing something he couldn't have imagined even a year earlier: encouraging his defensive-minded teammates to shoot more. "I remember during timeouts in the first or second quarter, Billy Cunningham would be talking and Julius would say, 'Hey, Billy, we haven't gotten Maurice or Bobby a shot yet. Let's get them a shot,'" Bobby Jones recalled. "So here's a guy who's leading the league in scoring, but he's thinking, 'Let's get everybody else involved because you feel better when you scored a point or two.'"

Such exchanges left little doubt: this was Erving's team. The power struggles that had roiled his NBA infancy were settled. But that didn't mean Erving reverted to his high-flying ways. Arthritic knees and aging legs had forced him to conserve his energy in any way possible, to play the game as much with his head as his body. His renowned aerial assaults now manifested in bursts rather than as a matter of course. "If you try to rev yourself up every night," Erving said, "you'll burn out your motor." Unperturbed by the ground-level jostling that enflamed other players, Erving remained so coolheaded that one writer described guarding him as akin to "leaning against a block of ice." On off-days, he packed his aching body in ice "like a mackerel." Less spectacularly but more efficiently, Erving boosted his scoring average during the 1979–80 season to nearly twenty-seven points per game, close to his ABA baseline, while sinking a higher percentage of shots than ever before.

After years of disharmony, the Sixers clicked. They reeled off fifty-nine regular-season wins, the most Erving had amassed as a professional. The only worrisome sign was that their home attendance plunged, falling by more than 25 percent from its peak in 1976–77. Part of the reason was that following the unloading of such maddening yet enthralling personalities as McGinnis and Lloyd Free, the Sixers had become, in one writer's words, "about as exciting as high tide on the Jersey Shore." Fans, too, had grown pessimistic that the "We Owe You One" debt would ever be paid in full.

Going deep in the playoffs wouldn't suffice. To win back the city, it was championship or bust.

Bursting into the NBA that season were a pair of basketball savants whose rivalry had begun in the 1979 NCAA Championship Game. Thirty-five million viewers had tuned in to watch Earvin "Magic" Johnson's Michigan State Spartans clash with Larry Bird's Indiana State Sycamores, making it the most watched college basketball contest ever, a record that still stands. By landing on the league's most storied franchises—the Los Angeles Lakers and the Boston Celtics—the charismatic rookies inspired hope of a decades-long West Coast–East Coast rivalry that would buoy a league mired in drug scandals, perceptions of violence, and grind-it-out games. Straight out of central casting, Johnson and Bird were a bonded pair whose opposing characteristics—Black and white, urban and rural, sociable and shy—pulled in fans from all demographic groups. In many ways, their styles of play—expressive and brash, peppered with no-look passes and steeped in trash talk—seemed to owe more to the league that had nurtured Julius Erving and Moses Malone than to the NBA. But neither Johnson nor Bird carried the stigma of those who'd crossed over from the ABA. They offered a blank slate on which professional basketball could inscribe a more mainstream and marketable future.

Three seasons of postmerger messiness had crowned three different NBA champions—the Portland Trail Blazers, the Washington Bullets, and the Seattle Supersonics. Each had seemed a missed opportunity for Erving and the 76ers. The years that could've cemented Erving's legacy instead shook the foundation on which it had been constructed. And now, as Johnson's Lakers and Bird's Celtics rose to the top of the standings, finishing the 1979–80 season as the only clubs to secure sixty or more wins, the two rookies appeared to be on a collision course to meet again in the NBA Finals. Their ascendance placed Erving in an unfamiliar spot. He was, for once, the spoiler, a barrier to seemingly the only matchup that might dissuade CBS executives from scheduling NBA playoff games late at night on tape delay.

Since Larry Bird, like Erving, played in the Eastern Conference, he was the more familiar opponent. Erving, with his aerodynamic physique and elongated limbs, looked the part of a basketball star. No one would've said the same of Bird. As one writer described him, "His hair is as ruly as alfalfa and his complexion as adolescent as measles. From top to bottom, a distance measured to be 6 ft. 9 in., Bird could not be whiter if he were a professional blood donor. His yellow mustache suggests a gulp of buttermilk." Despite Bird being as earthbound as Erving was airborne, what he lacked in athleticism, he made up for in savvy. No matter where the ball bounced, there Bird seemed to be. The year before Bird's arrival, the Celtics had burrowed into the cellar of the Atlantic Division, the first time in thirty years the club had ended a season in last place. The addition of Bird in 1979 hurtled the Celtics from worst to first, swinging from twenty-four games below .500 to forty above, two ahead of the revamped 76ers.

As expected, the two clubs met in the Eastern Conference Finals during the playoffs. Contrary to expectations, the matchup was anticlimactic. Over five games, Erving and Bird battled to a standstill individually, with Erving netting more points and Bird snagging more rebounds. Collectively, however, the Sixers had too much size, experience, and urgency. While the Celtics were still discovering themselves, the latest iteration of the Sixers knew that they had no time to waste. After the teams split the first two games, Philadelphia ran off three straight victories, punching the Sixers' ticket to the NBA Finals.

Erving cast the media out of the locker room afterward so that his teammates could gather in prayer. Reporters returned to a subdued scene: players undressing, showering, and packing, the mood relaxed and muted. "The Sixers of two or three years ago would have had an orgy," Philadelphia sportswriter Ray Didinger quipped. But those days were gone. "I don't think there's anybody who could watch us now and say, 'Yeah, that's the same old Sixers,'" Erving said. "This is a team, in every sense of the word. This series should erase a lot of the negative things that have been said about the Sixers."

Having dispatched one rookie, Erving braced for another.

A year before, when Magic Johnson was debating whether to turn professional after winning the NCAA Championship during his sophomore year, agent Irwin Weiner had invited him and his Michigan State teammate Greg Kelser to New York City to feel out their interest in signing with him. As a sweetener, Weiner made arrangements for the two to travel to Philadelphia to spend the weekend with his star client. "So we went to Julius Erving's house," Kelser remembered. "He greeted us; he was an incredible host. Both Earvin and I were at the Doctor's house. It was like a fantasy or something. We were trying to be calm and cool, but we were inside out." Erving proffered advice on thriving as a pro athlete, on negotiating the demands and drudgeries of an eighty-two-game season. Johnson departed with promises of staying in touch. Now, twelve months later, in the moments before the tipoff of Game One of the 1980 NBA Finals, Erving embraced the twenty-year-old. "Forget everything I told you," he whispered.

Johnson had no intention of waiting his turn. Wherever he'd played—high school, college, and now the pros—his presence had converted average clubs into championship contenders almost overnight. Physically, Johnson was uncategorizable—a Swiss Army knife of a player who could slot into any position, someone with the body of a forward but the mind of a guard. At six foot nine, similar in height to Moses Malone, Johnson towered above nearly every other guard in the league, affording him unparalleled views of the court. Teammates held their hands high when Johnson dribbled the ball, knowing that an unforeseen pass could zip their way when least expected.

Just as important, Johnson had the ability to infect teammates with his own enthusiasm, elevating their games to levels they might not otherwise have reached. "He helped me to become a winner. He brought a winning attitude, a culture, a mindset, all wrapped up in one person," Kelser said of their years together at Michigan State, adding, "He had a knack for bringing elements that were missing from the club that made everyone better." Johnson, too, possessed a magnetism tailor-made for television. He showed up at the Forum, the coliseum-like venue that hosted the Lakers, with what one writer called "an ear-to-ear grin of a kid who has just gotten a new bike for Christmas." When Magic pranced downcourt and whipped a bullet pass to a teammate he couldn't possibly have seen, bringing the Hollywood celebrities in the courtside seats to their feet, it gave the sensation that professional basketball was finally mushrooming into something bigger—a scene, a spectacle, the go-go sport for a decade soon to be synonymous with excess. It was fast and it was breathtaking. It was Showtime.

In Johnson's first game as a rookie, Kareem Abdul-Jabbar had swished a buzzer-beating skyhook for the win. Overcome with emotion, Johnson had wrapped the Lakers center in a bear hug, celebrating as if they'd just clinched a title. In the locker room, Abdul-Jabbar had reminded his new teammate that the trick to surviving the NBA grind was never to get too high or too low after a single game. Their opposing reactions underscored the differences between the two players who would form the backbone of the Lakers' success. One was an animated extrovert bubbling over with exuberance, the other a self-contained introvert closed off to the world below his seven-foot-two frame.

Reserved and studious, Abdul-Jabbar retreated into himself as a coping mechanism for a world he'd never been able to find refuge in. As a child, his preternatural height had drawn gawking stares. In college, the NCAA had outlawed dunking partly to stymie his dominance at UCLA, where he won three straight championships. In the pros, he often was cast as aloof and brooding, locked into cruise control on the court and emotionally unavailable off it. Interviewing Abdul-Jabbar was fraught with challenges. "Kareem would get a big book, a thick book, and sit down there and act like he was reading it," beat writer Steve Springer said, unaware perhaps of Abdul-Jabbar's budding literary aspirations. "If you asked him something, he'd be like 'Excuse me, I'm busy reading here. Can you leave me alone?'"

As someone who'd boycotted the 1968 Summer Olympics to protest injustices against Black Americans and who'd changed his name from Lew Alcindor when he'd converted to Islam early in his career, Abdul-Jabbar was no stranger to backlash or being misunderstood. The racial slights and power imbalances that afflicted Black athletes were never far from his mind, and he often pushed back against them by declining to open himself up in ways expected of a high-profile figure. "All the attention, even the praise," Abdul-Jabbar once wrote, "was like a storm to get out of." His signature move, the skyhook—a silky one-handed shot launched high above his head—fit him to a tee. It was as unreachable to defenders as Abdul-Jabbar often was to the public.

During the 1979–80 season, Abdul-Jabbar collected his sixth MVP award, a feat still unmatched. He'd come a long way from the playground courts of New York City, where he'd grown up as the only child of artistic parents in upper Manhattan, a short distance from Rucker Park. A few years older than Julius Erving, he'd first crossed paths with his fellow playground legend in 1969 at a beach in the Rockaways. The two had sized each other up not by playing one-on-one but by pressing their palms together. Improbably, even though he was seven inches shorter than Abdul-Jabbar, Erving had bigger hands.

Now, eleven years later, Abdul-Jabbar and Erving prepared to square off for the first time on basketball's biggest stage. Los Angeles's top-line strategy in the 1980 NBA Finals was simple: "Don't let the Doctor go wild," Lakers head coach Paul Westhead told his club, adding, "Any time the Doctor scores two baskets in a row, do *anything* to stop the game—call timeout, fake an injury, throw ice on the floor...anything. When he gets it going, he turns on his teammates, the crowd, and the whole game changes." The strategy proved effective in Game One. Whenever Erving dribbled, the Lakers ran additional defenders at him. They held a rhythmless Erving to a quiet twenty points while coasting to a 109–102 victory.

In the second game, Erving used the Lakers' game plan to his advantage. He attacked the lane, forcing defenders to rush toward him, and then kicked the ball out to a teammate for an uncontested jumper. "When I got the ball, I'm the bait," Erving explained. "I'm baiting 'em to come get me. Sometimes three of 'em do. Then, there's got to be somebody open." Erving and four other Sixers scored in double figures as Philadelphia knotted the series at one.

After mostly sticking to the ground in Game Three, another loss for the Sixers, Erving sensed the home crowd's impatience during the following game. Fans pleaded with him to stop being the bait and start being the instigator, to bust out Dr. J no matter how many defenders mobbed him. Late in the fourth quarter, with the 76ers protecting a slim lead, Erving obliged.

It started when Bobby Jones threw the ball to Erving on the right wing, just outside the free-throw line. Aware that his defender, Lakers forward Mark Landsberger, had overplayed the pass, Erving dribbled once along the baseline, charging toward the hoop as if to dunk. The second that Erving left his feet, Abdul-Jabbar collapsed on him, cutting off his straight-on route. "I tried to look for Darryl [Dawkins]," Erving explained. "I figured Darryl might be rolling to the hoop, since Kareem was guarding him. But I couldn't find him. So I held the ball out in traffic while I looked." Frozen at the height of his jump, his right arm extended parallel to the floor, more out of bounds than in, Erving was trapped behind the backboard, out of options. For any other player, gravity would have forced a turnover. But a lifetime of creating something out of nothing had imbued Erving with the confidence to trust his instincts while in the air, even when the situation appeared hopeless. Unpanicked, he continued floating to the other side of the basket while curling his right arm around the outstretched hands of Landsberger and Abdul-Jabbar. Just before landing, he spun the ball backward off the left side of the board with impeccable English.

For those who'd never seen Dr. J in the ABA, it was unlike any move they'd witnessed. But for those like Mike Littwin, who'd covered Erving as a beat writer since his first training camp with the Virginia Squires, it was a throwback to his premerger self. "I know that's a play that everyone could talk about forever," Littwin said, "but it's a play that he made five times a game in the ABA." Erving himself, who'd been dreaming up and then executing precisely those sort of sui generis moves since childhood, didn't see what all the fuss was about. "Just a reverse layup," he said with a shrug, a line so understated that it struck many as absurd. "It was like calling Kilimanjaro a goosebump," sportswriter Gary Smith claimed.

Philadelphia held on for the win but then dropped Game Five in Los Angeles. Despite being on the brink of defeat, down 3–2 in a best-of-seven series, the Sixers flew home in a hopeful mood. Midway through the fifth game, an ankle sprain had hobbled Abdul-Jabbar, who'd finished strong with forty points and fifteen rebounds but then limped away from the Forum on crutches. Rushed to Centinela Hospital, he was informed by doctors that while the X-rays had come back negative, the injury appeared critical enough to limit his availability for the rest of the series. A split-second decision was made: Abdul-Jabbar would stay put in Los Angeles, resting up for a potential do-or-die seventh game. In an instant, the odds swung hard in the Sixers' favor.

Philadelphians, forever suspicious of good fortune, refused to believe it. In the lead-up to Game Six, rumors of Abdul-Jabbar sightings, in taxis and on the street, in hotels and restaurants, shot through every corner of the city. The Sixers fans who thronged the Spectrum on May 16 fully expected the Lakers center to unveil himself during warmups. What they saw instead was stranger: the team's lead guard lining up for the tipoff.

On the flight to Philadelphia, in a symbolic gesture, Johnson had plopped down in Abdul-Jabbar's customary seat in first class. "Have no fear!" he'd announced. "Motherfucking Magic Johnson is here!" Johnson went on to play all five positions in Game Six while racking up forty-two points, fifteen rebounds, and seven assists. In some ways, having a formidable but familiar foe like Abdul-Jabbar emerge from the shadows would have been preferable to Johnson's fast-break assault, which caught the lumbering Sixers flat-footed. "I think we played our poorest game of the series," a stunned Erving mumbled afterward, not yet able to process his team's 123–107 loss.

Conventional wisdom credited the Lakers championship to Abdul-Jabbar's fortitude and Johnson's fire. But the numbers told a different, more mundane story. Lost amid Johnson's heroics was the fact that the Lakers had outrebounded the Sixers 52–36 in the final game, upping their rebounding advantage to a devastating

308–223 over the entire series. With all games but the last being decided by a handful of points, what doomed the Sixers was their ineptitude at recovering missed shots.

After years of falling short, the 76ers had remade themselves on the fly into a Finals-caliber team, less entertaining but more cohesive. Still, they lacked a key element, and it didn't takc a tactical genius to identify what that was. "Rebounding is an area we have to improve in," Erving acknowledged. Without it, they seemed likely to keep suffering the same fate.

CHAPTER 10

COLLISION COURSE

To Carroll Dawson, it all came down to footwork. A former scout for the Dallas Cowboys, Dawson had been lifted from obscurity to round out the Houston Rockets coaching staff for the 1980–81 season. Handpicked to assist Del Harris, who'd taken over as the Rockets head coach after Tom Nissalke had jumped to the Utah Jazz a year earlier, Dawson arrived at camp intimidated and circumspect, more comfortable observing than instructing. One question in particular intrigued him: "How the hell does [Moses Malone] get to everything?" The answer revealed itself during the first scrimmage. "The ball would go up, and everybody turned into a statue watching it," Dawson said. "But Moses's feet would never quit moving, like a boxer's. So he could move to the ball when it didn't come to him. That's why he got so many rebounds."

There was, however, a glaring flaw in Malone's game: he was one of the worst-passing big men Dawson had ever seen. His outlets to initiate fast breaks hung limp in the air, vulnerable to being picked off. So, mustering his courage, Dawson, who went by the nickname "CD," pulled Malone aside and asked him to stick around after practice so they could work on making his wrists firmer when he passed the ball. "He stood there and looked at me for a minute," Dawson remembered. "And I thought, 'Oh my goodness, what have I done?' He said, 'CD, 'round here, they don't pay me to pass.'"

Self-assured and plainspoken, his résumé burnished with an MVP before his twenty-fifth birthday, Malone put management on notice: if he didn't want to do something, he wasn't going to do it. Once, the Rockets front office dropped $25,000 on a twenty-foot plastic rocket with flashing red lights on top and a smoke machine at the bottom that simulated takeoff. The plan was for the players to run through the smoke during pregame introductions. Malone took one look at the rocket and declared, "I ain't doing it." When executives explained that they couldn't afford to let such an expensive prop go to waste, Malone shrugged. "Put Murph in it and shoot it to the moon," he grunted, referring to Calvin Murphy, the Rockets' diminutive point guard.

Malone even objected when the public-address announcer called him the NBA's reigning MVP. "I don't dig superstar status," Malone explained. "The way I see it, there are 244 players in this league, and we're all just players." It was all part of what Rockets forward Major Jones identified as Malone's overriding philosophy: "Moses always said, 'It's us. It ain't about me. It's us.' He wanted [his teammates] to share in the same light he had."

Tired of being bumped and shoved by brawnier opponents, Malone had loaded up on starchy food and hit the weight room in the offseason. He tromped into the '80s with thirty extra pounds on his frame. The T-shirts that comprised a sizable portion of Malone's wardrobe now strained across his beefed-up shoulders and lifted above his waistline. Gerald Govan could hardly believe the change from the coatrack-thin rookie he remembered from their time on the Utah Stars. "I said, 'Man, you put on too much weight!' Because I thought he had. But [Malone] was so quick. He said, 'Oh no, you just wait. They push me too much here.'" Malone still motored about with inexhaustible energy, but he could also plant himself immobile in the lane, fortified against the jostling that big men had to withstand on each possession.

Malone was thriving; his team was not. Rick Barry, who ended his Hall of Fame career in Houston, deemed the Rockets "probably the most talented team I've ever been on." But for various reasons, the talent didn't translate to wins. They were a club out of step with the direction the league was taking. Unlike Erving's Sixers or Johnson's Lakers, whose fast-breaking brio poured in points, Malone's Rockets brought the pace to a standstill, dragging quick-footed clubs into the murky tar pit of their sluggish style. Starting in 1980 with the acquisition of Billy Paultz, a six-foot-eleven plodder colorfully known as the "Whopper," the Rockets clogged the lane with big men. Houston, sportswriter Bob Ryan joked, "has three speeds: slow, slower, and Billy Paultz." A typical offensive set involved walking the ball up, milking the shot clock, then crashing the offensive boards. It was more rugby scrum than track meet, so aesthetically displeasing that critics dubbed it "ugly-ball," though the Rockets themselves preferred, simply, "Rocketball." Del Harris characterized Rocketball as "tough individual defense, no frills, no tricks, no mirrors"—the spitting image of Moses Malone himself.

Since going toe-to-toe with the 76ers in the 1976–77 playoffs, the Rockets had stumbled through a string of pedestrian seasons. Hoping to add outside playmaking to their inside bulk, they signed perennial all-star Rick Barry in 1978. At that time, when a team acquired a free agent, it had to compensate the club that lost that player with someone from their roster. The twist was that the league front offices settled on the compensation, which left clubs in danger of losing a player of greater value than the free agent they hoped to sign. This was what happened to the Rockets, which had to surrender John Lucas, their valuable young point guard.

Barry and Malone tried to make the most of it. At Fonde Recreation Center, the two spent a summer perfecting a pick-and-roll routine. When they unveiled their offseason labor at training camp, however, the coaching staff brushed it off as unrepresentative of the team's style. Though he could still light it up on occasion, Barry had too little left in his thirty-four-year-old legs. Amid a ten-point dip in his per-game scoring average, he turned into a scapegoat for the team's stagnation. After one tough loss, general manager Ray Patterson lashed out at Barry in frustration. "Ray just totally clobbered him with distasteful words, ripped him while Rick was naked in the shower," remembered sportswriter Tommy Bonk.

From 1978 to 1980, the Rockets had twice wound up second in the NBA's Central Division and twice been bounced early from the playoffs. Heading into the 1980–81 season, the club faced dissension on all fronts. Its fans were apathetic, and several players were becoming aggravated with the slowdown offense. "You don't make thoroughbreds walk," Calvin Murphy said decades later. "Of course it stymied us." Because points were at a premium, blowout wins came around as often as snowstorms in Houston. "We never had any margin to work with, we never had a night to laugh," Del Harris told journalist Phil Jasner. "We had to give it everything every night."

The difference between the playoffs and the cellar was Malone. Attesting to the pounding he absorbed inside, Malone, in addition to recovering the most missed shots, led the league in free-throw attempts in 1980–81. Thirty points and fifteen rebounds became regular occurrences, so much so that Harris groused about the media taking notice of Malone only after games in which he fell short of those astronomical numbers. "Any time Moses takes the floor," Kansas City Kings coach Lowell "Cotton" Fitzsimmons stated, "his team can play with anybody. Moses and four guys off the street could compete in the playoffs."

Fitzsimmons's theory was put to the test during a season in which the Rockets, despite Malone's nightly heroics, never once rose above the .500 mark. Only by winning four of their last five games did the Rockets manage to sneak into the playoffs with a 40–42 record. Their reward, everyone was certain, would be a surefire exit in the first round against the league's reigning champions.

After losing to the Lakers in the 1980 NBA Finals, the Sixers upgraded their roster in the offseason through shrewd drafting. Once again, they relied on the tireless wanderings of assistant coach Jack McMahon. This time, the small-circuit scuttlebutt led him to Lafayette, where a six-foot-three shooting guard for the University of Southwestern Louisiana was torching the Gulf State colleges that made up the Southland Conference. What sold McMahon was seeing the fear in defenders' eyes whenever Andrew Toney sized them up. "When I scout," McMahon said, "one of the bottom lines is, 'Would I like to play against this guy?' I asked myself that about Andrew, and said, 'Bleep no.' That kid would have had me back on my heels, muttering 'Please don't let him drive.'"

Long-armed and deceptively strong, so much so that Bobby Jones claimed "you would just fall off him when you tried to guard him," Toney brimmed with the arrogance of a gym rat who'd yet to come across someone who could stop him from scoring. "Andrew had the mentality that if you can't guard him, then you shouldn't be on him. Because he would try to score on you every single time," Sixers backup point guard Franklin Edwards said. Whenever he went on a shooting streak during scrimmages, Toney would turn to the teammate defending him and ask, "You not practicing today?" Once, after he sank several jumpers against Michael Cooper, a Lakers guard widely regarded as the league's best lockdown defender, Toney whispered in Cooper's ear, "Ain't you first-team all-defense?"

Toney's form was unconventional—an arms-extended shot that he released with a spasm, as if he'd suffered a slight tremor at the height of his jump—but he'd honed it to perfection through monomaniacal repetition. When he was recruiting Toney out of high school, Bobby Paschal, the head coach at the University of Southwestern Louisiana, was told that janitors and security guards used to shoo Toney out of local gyms late at night. In college, Paschal remembered rolling up to the team's practice court before sunrise and spotting Toney already there, alone with a basketball and a boom box. Once, a reporter asked Earl Cureton, a bench player for the 76ers, how he'd stop Toney. "Close the gym," Cureton said.

"No," Sixers center Caldwell Jones shot back, "he'd still make 15 or 20 through the keyhole."

Toney's belief that his shooting range extended from one baseline to the other tried the patience of the Sixers head coach. Excitable under ordinary circumstances, Billy Cunningham grew downright apoplectic when his impulsive rookie broke plays with hair-trigger jumpers. His sideline cries would reverberate across arenas: "Aaaaandreeeeew!" Cunningham started Toney, benched him, left him in for an entire game, then sat him the next. Eventually, Cunningham phoned Paschal for advice on coaching someone so unpredictable. Paschal urged a lenient, hands-off approach. "At some point in every game," Paschal told Cunningham, "there's a good chance that Andrew is gonna get hot, gonna get in that zone, and he's gonna start scoring and be impossible to stop. When that happens, he can almost shoot the other team out of the game. By him going in and out, you might be missing that time when he gets hot and scores ten points in a row."

For a less assured player, the yo-yoing minutes would have wreaked havoc on his confidence. But Toney was unbothered. He lacked what athletes referred to as a conscience, that nagging voice in the back of their minds that made them hesitate after consecutive misses. Toney instead abided by a simple philosophy: "I know I can't make 'em all, but I'll never shy away from taking them." He could win or lose a game for the Sixers, and the following morning, no one would be able to tell the difference. Julius Erving dubbed Toney the "X factor," a chaos agent who could devastate defenses single-handedly when the game was on the line. "When Andrew gets that rhythm," Erving said, "it's all over. You can turn out the lights, it won't make a difference. He'll still put it in the hole."

Nothing captured the early-'80s essence of Julius Erving better than the retail venue that he launched in 1980 through The Erving Group, his newly formed corporation dedicated to helping him pursue financial opportunities beyond basketball. It was a Fifth Avenue–style boutique in Philadelphia's historic Society Hill neighborhood that specialized in shoes, a natural fit for a professional athlete. Sneakers, however, would have no place on the store's shelves; instead, its designer leather dress shoes and heels targeted the sort of upwardly mobile clientele who aspired to the urbane, mature lifestyle that Erving was now projecting.

The normally risk-averse Erving sank thousands of dollars into the venture. To hedge his bets, his business advisers had urged him to name it Dr. J's Shoe Salon, but Erving declined. "I want to move away from Dr. J," he explained, "because I want the shoe store to stand on its own merits." A newspaper advertisement announcing the salon's grand opening featured a photo of a well-coiffed Erving and Turquoise decked out in tailored formal wear next to a tagline that read "What do Salvatore Ferragamo, Garolini, Bally, Bruno Magli, Halston, Johnston & Murphy, Palizzio, Givenchy, Ralph

Lauren... and Julius and Turquoise Erving have in common? The Doctor's Shoe Salon!"

For Erving, it was all part of a diversified business portfolio. Over the next few years, he would invest in a Coca-Cola bottling plant and a business that distributed high school class rings, sit on the board of a company that produced television commercials, and star in his own ads for products ranging from Converse to ChapStick. Finally committing to Philadelphia, Erving purchased a 2.8-acre, hedge-lined estate in Villanova, along the storied Main Line associated with the city's upper crust. On off-days, he sometimes attended to customers at his store, a budding tycoon holding court in a setting befitting of the crossover ideal that Erving treasured. "I have that feeling," Erving told a reporter, "that belief that comes from the mail I get from parents and kids. From people coming up to me from all types of backgrounds, saying, 'I really like what you stand for, what you say, how you handle yourself, and I'd like my son to grow up to be like you.' And that's a white father talking about his son. That Chapstick commercial was designed to give them entry into the Black market."

Shoppers, however, didn't share his vision. The shoe salon was a bottle of Dom Perignon in a shot-and-a-beer town. It was, Erving learned, harder to attract customers with class and taste than with dunks and athleticism. Within eighteen months, the salon shuttered its doors.

It was a lesson that the 76ers were learning at the same time. The squabbling team from Erving's initial NBA season had shattered franchise attendance records, filling the Spectrum with more than fifteen thousand fans per game. The breakup of that roster set the Sixers on surer footing but drained the color and controversary that had sparked fan interest. Especially after Erving shaved off his Afro and fashioned a more corporate look, endless ink was spilled on the riddle of professional basketball in Philadelphia.

How could a championship-caliber team that sported the league's most breathtaking star fill less than half the Spectrum's seats on any given night?

Sportswriter Bill Livingston posited that the Sixers had become more a national attraction than a cherished local team, one that "stirs fans across the breadth of the land with the exploits of Dr. J, but which is unheeded and unloved in its own city." Even during their streak of twenty-two wins in twenty-three contests near the start of the 1980–81 season, the Sixers often struggled to top five figures in attendance at home. They didn't sell out the Spectrum until early February, more than fifty games into that season, then went on to sell it out just twice more. On the road, in contrast, they played before packed houses nearly two dozen times. Privately, some players admitted that they preferred away to home games. "Because they hear noise," explained Jack McMahon. "Hey, they're performers. It's probably tough for a comedian to be his funniest when the house is half empty."

The dip in attendance baffled the club. "It was a team that you would think would represent the city," Billy Cunningham said decades later. "It played hard. You never had to worry about the effort. I never could understand it." Some believed that two other championship-level teams in Philadelphia were sucking away the attention: the World Series champion Phillies and the Super Bowl–bound Eagles. Others, like Lou Scheinfeld, a former vice president of the Philadelphia Flyers who had been hired as CEO of the 76ers in 1980 with a mandate to increase attendance, laid much of the blame at the feet of the team's patrician owner, Fitz Dixon. "He was a bad symbol," Scheinfeld said. "He was preppy, he was elitist and distant, the total opposite of [Flyers owner] Ed Snyder, who was passionate and colorful and everybody loved him." During games, Dixon sometimes sat in the front row alongside his bodyguard, who prohibited anyone, vendors and photographers included, from walking in front of his boss. For fun, Dixon used to wager a quarter with his bodyguard on a scoreboard diversion known as the dot game, in which two pixelated circles raced each other across the screen. The sight of Dixon among the people but not part of them rubbed fans the wrong way. Scheinfeld recalled telling Dixon, "You have got to get off the floor, come up to the box. You can't be like Nero sitting down there with guards around you."

Given the changing demographics of both the league and the city—after decades of white flight, African Americans made up 37 percent of Philadelphia's residents in 1980—it seemed that the Sixers could've cultivated new customer bases. But Scheinfeld pointed out that the franchise not only had no Black employees among its front-office and coaching ranks but also did little outreach to African American communities. It was to the Sixers' detriment, since playground basketball proliferated in those communities like nowhere else outside New York City. Philadelphia's streetball ambassador was Sonny Hill, who, like Holcombe Rucker in Harlem, helped numerous adolescents land scholarships at major collegiate programs. Many iconic players, most notably Earl "the Pearl" Monroe, whose twirling moves spun as much oral mythology as Erving's dunks, cut their teeth in the Baker League, the city's premier playground basketball showcase, which was centered on two outdoor courts in North Philadelphia, one at the intersection of Twenty-Fifth and Diamond Streets and the other at Twelfth and Oxford Streets. Years earlier, in 1973, Caldwell Jones, a second-round draft pick for the Sixers out of Albany State, had been cut during the team's rookie camp. Instead of returning home, Jones had stuck around to play in the Baker League, where he'd caught the eye of Wilt Chamberlain, who had been in town to attend a wedding. His playing career over, Chamberlain had been named head coach of the San Diego Conquistadors, a bumbling ABA squad. Impressed by what he saw, Chamberlain convinced the Conquistadors to consider Jones, who subsequently stuck in professional basketball for seventeen years, attesting to the power that the Baker League had in building and rehabilitating reputations.

Rather than wooing these basketball-hungry communities, the Sixers expended tremendous energy on retaining their core base of ticket holders, many of whom had since fled to the suburbs. Reports of robberies, dice rolling in the restrooms, and marijuana smoke wafting through the Spectrum's upper reaches, no matter how overblown or racially coded, made white ticket holders in particular reluctant to venture to South Philadelphia on game nights. One writer went so far as to state that some fans "feared for their lives" when coming to the Spectrum. In response, Sixers executives beefed up security around the arena and in parking lots. They also improved the lighting in restrooms, cracked down on smoking in the stands, and did whatever they could to signal concern for fan safety.

Even then, executives fretted over whether the issue was, at its core, structural: would white fans ever turn out in sufficient numbers to watch a Sixers starting lineup that consisted of five Black athletes? When pressed on the question, the players grew visibly uncomfortable. "I would like to say that race is not involved," Erving said, choosing his words carefully, "but I'm afraid that would be naive."

Hanging above it all was the debt that the team continued to accrue. "Our fans still feel we let them down and have not delivered what we're capable of delivering," Erving said. "They have broken hearts."

It'd been a dozen years since an NBA team had won back-to-back titles, not since the Boston Celtics had reeled off two straight in 1968 and 1969. Too often, injuries, fatigue, and ego derailed the best-laid plans to repeat. The Los Angeles Lakers learned this lesson the hard way in 1980–81. Their troubles started when Magic Johnson missed half the season with torn cartilage in his left knee. Norm Nixon, a gifted young point guard perpetually overshadowed by the roster's brighter stars, picked up the slack while his injured teammate recuperated but then chafed at stepping back into a more subordinate role when Johnson returned. The tension between the two simmered as winter turned to spring.

And then there was the bumpy education of the team's accidental head coach. Arriving in Los Angeles at the same time as Johnson, Jack McKinney had been the strategic mastermind behind the transition-oriented offense that came to be known as Showtime. But he never got the chance to reap the rewards. Fourteen games into his tenure, McKinney suffered a near-fatal head wound upon crashing his bicycle. His recovery was slow and his memory spotty. Months after the injury, McKinney bumped into Lakers owner Jerry Buss at the Forum. When Buss greeted him, McKinney kept walking, appearing not to recognize his boss. Replacing him on an interim basis was Paul Westhead, a former Shakespearean scholar and head coach for the La Salle University men's basketball team who was mere weeks into his first NBA job as the Lakers assistant coach. Untested and deferential, Westhead kept in place the system that McKinney had implemented, riding it all the way to the Finals. To sportswriter Scott Ostler, Westhead compared himself to a jockey. "He said, 'I gave [the players] a hand ride as opposed to going to the whip,'" Ostler recalled. "He just basically didn't try to overcoach them."

That changed in 1980–81. A championship under his belt and the "interim" removed from his title, Westhead began to tilt the offense more toward the team's linchpin. The fifth-oldest player in the NBA at thirty-three, Kareem Abdul-Jabbar thrived in half-court arrangements in which he could loft skyhooks from the post. Slowing down the tempo to accommodate their aging center rankled the Lakers' impatient young gunners. Steve Springer, a beat writer for the *Los Angeles Times*, claimed that certain players passed around matchbooks emblazoned with the slogan "Trade Kareem." Toting them in their pockets, they'd flash the matchbooks to one another both as an inside joke and as an actual grievance about being unable to run as often as they preferred.

Normally, a first-round encounter with a sub-.500 team would serve as a postseason warmup, but the Lakers, divided and vulnerable, had reasons to fear the Houston Rockets. For one, the series was best of three, which meant that a single loss would bring Los Angeles to the verge of elimination. For another, Houston matched up unusually well with them. The Rockets' superior offensive rebounding and leaden pace stifled what was left of the Lakers' fast-break tendencies. More important, no one gave the six-time MVP fits quite like Moses Malone. "Kareem is probably the greatest finesse player ever," Del Harris said. "He was like a ballet dancer. His coordination and everything about him was smooth and polished. He was a polished diamond. Moses was a rough cut." Abdul-Jabbar, Scott Ostler claimed, "just wanted to play basketball. He thought, 'You shoot a basket. You don't try to knock guys down and stuff like that.' And Moses's game was pure pit bull. Kareem not only couldn't guard him but didn't like to guard him. He just didn't want any part of Moses. Anytime the Lakers went against him, they were like 'Oh shit, what are we gonna do with this guy?'"

It was a question that the Lakers were asking themselves after the first game. Abdul-Jabbar proved helpless in stopping Malone, who amassed thirty-eight points and twenty-three rebounds, eleven of them off the offensive glass, which matched the Lakers' entire team effort. "When I'm scoring and rebounding like that, we win a lot of games," Malone said matter-of-factly.

In the wake of the Lakers' 111–107 loss, an article ran in the *Los Angeles Times* in which Norm Nixon voiced his dissatisfaction with playing second fiddle to Magic Johnson. "You know when you write something that's going to be a shitstorm," said Mike Littwin, the article's author. "But I wrote this without any idea that it would be a shitstorm. It was basically a sympathetic look toward the situation Norm was in, and it was about Nixon not understanding that he's not just competing with another player. He's competing with a *legendary* player." Rather than sloughing off Nixon's gripes, Johnson fired back through Littwin days later. "They think I hog the endorsements. I turn half of them down. I don't go out looking for publicity," Johnson stated in exasperation, adding, "If [Nixon] wants the ball more, he can have it. I don't need the ball. I just want to win."

Even though the Lakers managed to eke out a victory in the second game, they staggered into the series-deciding contest no longer able to paper over the friction just beneath the surface. Five minutes before tipoff, Lakers assistant coach Pat Riley, walking into the locker room, saw a team in no condition to compete. In one corner Johnson was insisting, "I didn't really say any of those things in the paper," while in the other several teammates were yelling, "If it wasn't true, they wouldn't have printed it!"

Houston carried on with its strategy of forcing Los Angeles to swap Showtime for Rocketball. "The Lakers wanted to get out and run," Rockets forward Major Jones stated. "But as long as we had Moses on the floor, it was gonna be hard. They had to put two guys on him to stop him from getting every rebound." Slow-walking the ball up the court, the Rockets drained the shot clock, fought tooth and nail for offensive rebounds, then kicked the ball back out to drain twenty-four more seconds. It was sludgy, brutish, and ugly as sin—just as Del Harris had drawn it up. The Rockets shot a ghastly 35 percent from the field in Game Three, but their edge in offensive rebounding and turnovers enabled them to attempt fifteen more shots than the Lakers.

In the waning seconds, with the Rockets ahead by a single point, Westhead called for Johnson to lob an entry pass to Abdul-Jabbar in the low post. Instead, in an illustration of the ongoing power struggle between the young guard and the old center, Johnson took matters into his own hands. "Magic got into the lane, and he was about six feet away from the basket when he laid it up," Littwin remembered. "The ball went about five feet—never hit the rim." The airball sealed the Rockets' shocking 89–86 upset on a night when Johnson missed twelve of his fourteen shots. Until then, Johnson's life had unfolded like a Hollywood script—from one championship to another along every rung of the basketball ladder. But now the twenty-one-year-old was heading into an early offseason with newfound doubts about whether he could mend the rifts that had, at least for the moment, upended the Lakers' potential dynasty.

In the Rockets locker room, Malone, who'd piled up twenty-three points and fifteen rebounds while playing the full forty-eight minutes, dismissed Showtime in one succinct sentence: "We don't care nothing about no fancy lineups or cute names."

After Johnson's last-ditch shot fell short, 76ers general manager Pat Williams danced across his living room in Philadelphia, screaming with joy. "I never thought," Williams said, "I would so blatantly be cheering for Houston."

The Lakers' abrupt elimination affirmed a vague yet unshakable sense that this would be the Sixers' year. It was a narrative that had taken hold when, after dropping two of their first three games, the 76ers had ripped through thirty-two of their next thirty-four contests. The day after Christmas, their record had stood at a gaudy 33–4, the second-fastest start in NBA history, behind only the Sixers of 1966–67, a club that then romped to the championship. With the Lakers no longer looming, the path to the title had cleared considerably for whichever team survived the stacked Eastern Conference.

It was a narrative that had taken hold equally because the 1980–81 season seemed like the climax of the second act of Julius Erving's professional career. Five years after winning three straight ABA MVPs, Erving became the first noncenter to win the MVP in the NBA since Oscar Robertson had done so in 1963–64 and the second ex-ABA player behind Moses Malone to garner the top individual prize. The award wasn't given to him because of a dramatic team turnaround or drastically improved statistics—the Sixers won sixty-two games that season, three more than in the previous one, and Erving's scoring average actually went down two points from the previous year, from 26.9 per game to 24.6. Instead, his steadiness had won over his NBA skeptics. "What he did night in and night out, consistently giving fans what they wanted, was what made Erving special," teammate Al Skinner claimed. "There were some players who could do what Erving did maybe once a week. But he was able to make that style of play consistent. He could put on a show every single night." But the show, like Erving himself, was now mellower, as elegant as it was well-rounded.

The playoffs started promisingly for the Sixers with a sweep of the Indiana Pacers. Their path next wound through Milwaukee. Quietly, with few outside Wisconsin taking notice, the Bucks had racked up sixty wins, third best in the NBA, only two behind the Sixers. Although not as nationally resonant as the league's biggest names, the Bucks' intimidating, no-nonsense trio of Bob Lanier,

Marques Johnson, and Sidney Moncrief was more than capable of bullying smoother clubs into submission.

For six games, the Sixers and Bucks seesawed, with neither team managing to swing the momentum to its side. After Philadelphia had forged a 3–2 advantage, Milwaukee buried the Sixers on the boards in Game Six, outrebounding them 55–29. Back in Philadelphia for the deciding game of the Eastern Conference Semifinals, Erving looked around at the vacant red seats that, one writer noted, gave "the Spectrum the texture of a bowl of cold tomato soup." Turning to teammate Ollie Johnson, Erving said, "It looks like we've got to do it for ourselves."

The resulting contest resembled trench warfare, a draining battle between two clubs contesting every inch of the court. "It was a helluva game," Bucks center Bob Lanier said. "In fact, it was hell." Erving later called it the most physical series he'd ever been part of. After the Sixers limped away with a narrow 99–98 victory, Erving slouched on a clubhouse stool, ice packs fastened to his knees and hips. When someone informed him that a mere 6,704 fans had turned out, the smallest playoff crowd for the Sixers in seventeen years, he shook his head. "We get more people than that on our charter flights," Erving muttered.

The Bucks in the rearview, Erving was besieged with questions about the series ahead. "It was," one reporter wrote, "like cornering a Battle of the Bulge veteran on V-E Day and asking if he'd like to catch the next plane to Okinawa." It was also consistent with what everyone in the locker room knew: the NBA playoffs didn't kick off in earnest until Philadelphia faced Boston.

CHAPTER 11

THE BOSTON MYSTIQUE

On April 21, 1981, the Philadelphia 76ers undressed in a damp, dingy locker room they were all too familiar with. Six times in 1980–81, the 76ers had squared off against the Boston Celtics, winning three at home and dropping three away, including the final game of the regular season. It was a consequential loss. After sprinting out to a 54–13 record, the Sixers had sputtered to an 8–7 finish. The Celtics, who'd been nipping at the Sixers' heels since the start, had caught them at the end. The two teams had wound up with identical 62–20 records. Because the Celtics had won more games against the other teams in the Atlantic Division, home-court advantage in the playoffs was their reward. It was a situation that the Sixers had hoped to avoid at all costs. They understood from experience that visiting teams to the ramshackle gym incongruously known as a "Garden" had to contend not just with the Celtics but also with the Boston mystique.

Mystique, let alone tradition, was in short supply in a league as young as the NBA. Only the Celtics possessed it. Ever since Arnold "Red" Auerbach, the Celtics' pugnacious head coach, had advocated trading for a defensive-minded rookie named Bill Russell in 1956, the Celtics had clinched more than 50 percent of all NBA titles—thirteen in twenty-four years. The smoke wafting off the cigar that Auerbach lit after each Celtics victory, often before the game's final buzzer sounded, was an apt symbol of Boston's supremacy—a gesture of arrogance befitting the basketball mastermind who relished tweaking his enemies almost as much as winning championships.

When questioned in 1981 about whether he'd suffered from ulcers during his head-coaching tenure, the balding, gnomelike Auerbach waved his hand. "I didn't get ulcers," he asserted. "I gave them." The secret to his sustained success boiled down to an insistence that sheer talent could take a club only so far. Auerbach instead sold players on sacrificing a percentage of their individual statistics for the betterment of the collective team and on uncomplainingly slotting into predetermined roles that would lubricate the overall system. At the same time, Auerbach attempted to squeeze every last advantage out of his home court by subjecting opposing players to a host of mind games and indignities. On cold nights in Boston, Celtics attendants switched off the heat and opened the windows in the visitors locker room; on hot days, they sealed the windows shut. "One hundred twenty degrees one time in. Twenty degrees the next," Billy Cunningham remembered. Cold water streamed from the showers; the towels arrived sopping wet. By the time visiting clubs emerged into the drafty barn perched two floors above a rumbling train station, they were already rattled. Even the court at Boston Garden, pieced together by blocks of parquet, vexed players unfamiliar with its fabled dead spots, which turned dribbling into a guessing game.

From these precepts, the Boston mystique was born. It meshed pride, pettiness, and unselfishness in equal measure. It was also inextricably tangled up with the team's chief rival.

"What makes the Celtics the Celtics?" a reporter once asked Boston benchwarmer M. L. Carr. "Philadelphia," Carr responded.

Defining one franchise by evoking another might have seemed strange, but professional basketball in Boston couldn't be assessed without mention of Philadelphia, and vice versa. The decades-long rivalry between the two East Coast cities helped bring the NBA out of the long shadow cast by the college game. It also shaped both the character of the two clubs and the psyche of their fan bases, imbuing the Celtics with their storied mystique and the Sixers with their hard-bitten fatalism.

Initially, Philadelphia seemed to be the better-positioned city. Basketball and Philadelphia had gone hand in hand from the start, thanks largely to a short, rotund immigrant from Ukraine. Surviving in a freshly birthed sport took nerve and street smarts. Eddie Gottlieb possessed both in abundance. In 1917, at age nineteen, Gottlieb threw together a squad of mostly Jewish players and barnstormed his club, dubbed the Philadelphia Sphas, up and down the East Coast, weathering basketball's tumultuous growing pains by competing wherever he could make a buck—in dance halls, YMCAs, high school gymnasiums, and armories.

Three decades of hustling put Gottlieb at the forefront of a rapidly professionalizing game. When the Basketball Association of America was founded in 1946, the team that Gottlieb managed, the Philadelphia Warriors, clinched the league's inaugural championship. Through every bump and milestone in those early seasons—the merger that created the NBA, the folding of numerous franchises, the signing of Black players in 1950—the one constant was Gottlieb, whom Temple University head coach Harry Litwack described as "about as important to the game of basketball as the basketball." He shaped the rules, drafted the schedules, and, after purchasing the Warriors in 1951, captured another title five years later.

Basketball had hit the big time in Philadelphia. In 1955, a quintet of local colleges—the University of Pennsylvania, LaSalle,

Saint Joseph's, Temple, and Villanova—formed what was known as the Big 5. Doubleheaders between them at UPenn's Palestra, the so-called Cathedral of College Basketball, routinely packed in fifteen thousand on wintry weekends. Across the city, rec leagues and playground courts sprouted, fostering a generation of basketball-first athletes. One of them, a lanky seven-footer from Overbrook High School in West Philadelphia, rose like Goliath above all others.

Drafted by the Philadelphia Warriors as a territorial pick, which enabled NBA franchises to nab popular local players to juice attendance, Wilt Chamberlain shook up the league on impact. Until then, no player had ever averaged thirty points per game. Chamberlain blew through that mark during his rookie season of 1959–60, draining buckets at a thirty-seven-point clip while grabbing twenty-seven rebounds. It was a great leap forward, the launch of an uncontainable talent destined to rewrite NBA record books and bring glory to his hometown. Only one obstacle stood in Chamberlain's way: Boston.

There would have been no rivalry between Boston and Philadelphia were it not for Chamberlain and his Celtics counterpart, Bill Russell. These two gifted giants were divided as much in ideology as in temperament. Chamberlain came across as equal parts brooding and flamboyant, prone to excess whether in wooing women or piling up points. Russell was serious-minded and socially conscious—white reporters painted him as militant for his outspokenness on racial inequities—a selfless competitor who was always thinking beyond himself. Their near-annual springtime clashes in the playoffs, which began during Chamberlain's rookie year, doubled as referenda on many of basketball's enduring binaries: star versus ensemble, numbers versus intangibles, dominance versus role-playing. More often than not, Chamberlain—and, by extension, Philadelphia—wound up on the losing end.

It was true in 1960 and again in 1962. Afterward, the Warriors got whisked away to the West Coast, landing in the Bay Area. Philadelphia officials convinced the Syracuse Nationals to migrate south in 1963, rechristening the club the "76ers" to commemorate the city's revolutionary heritage. Improbably, the Sixers vaulted into the NBA's top tier in only their second season by trading for none other than Wilt Chamberlain. Whatever flicker of hope accompanied Chamberlain's return was doused when a familiar pattern took hold: over the next two seasons, the Sixers advanced to the Eastern Division Finals; in both series, they were routed by the Celtics.

By the time he turned thirty, Chamberlain, despite having shattered every conceivable scoring record, found himself ringless. Russell, meanwhile, was one ring short of being able to adorn each finger. Fans' perception of Chamberlain shifted from awe to disappointment. "There was a reaction to [Chamberlain] because he was so big," Dick Jerardi of the *Philadelphia Daily News* said. "It was sort of, 'Why didn't he win all the time?'"

Finally, in 1966–67, Philadelphia snapped the Celtics' streak of eight straight championships. The Sixers went on to defeat the Golden State Warriors, the same franchise that had fled Philadelphia five years earlier, in the NBA Finals. Heavily favored the following season, the Sixers jumped to a 3–1 lead in their inevitable postseason clash with their chief rival. But then the Celtics swept the final three games, derailing any dream of a Philadelphia dynasty. In the offseason, Chamberlain demanded a trade. Stripped of their center, the Sixers fell on hard times. In 1972–73, the team bottomed out at 9–73, a stain of futility that remains the worst win-loss record in an eighty-two-game NBA season.

Boston exited the Russell-Chamberlain era with ten championships and unshakable confidence. Philadelphia came out with one title and an inferiority complex as tall as the William Penn statue atop City Hall. The rivalry lay dormant over the following decade, awakened briefly in 1977 for a seven-game series that Philadelphia eked out. A new matchup, Julius Erving versus Larry Bird, reignited the spark. "Perhaps the biggest thing I learned [my rookie season]," Bird wrote in his autobiography, "was how important beating Philadelphia was to everyone in Boston."

Erving had won round one in 1980. Bird now looked to even the score.

If the 76ers held any advantage in 1981, it was that the Celtics' banner-draped shrine meant nothing to Andrew Toney. "I'm not into that, man," the rookie snapped whenever the Boston mystique was brought up. "I'm into reality." As if he were suiting up at the local YMCA, Toney dismantled the Celtics at Boston Garden in Game One, his clinching free throws at the end capping a twenty-six-point performance.

Toney's coolness was matched by Larry Bird's. Following the Celtics' 105–104 loss, reporters pestered Bird about what was on his mind. "Getting my yard mowed," Bird replied. His grass presumably cut, Bird bounced back the next day with thirty-four points. In the final seconds of the Celtics' 118–99 blowout, the crowd feted him with a standing ovation, which made Bird want to crouch under the bench. "I hate to show any emotion," he explained, "because we haven't won the series yet."

Game Three featured something Philadelphia had lacked all season: a rowdy home crowd. Police mounted on horseback were dispatched to control the scrum of fans jockeying for tickets. Even the upper reaches of the Spectrum filled up, giving the Sixers their first sellout in that year's playoffs. Beforehand, head coach Billy Cunningham made a fateful decision. In the first two games, Bird had run Caldwell Jones ragged, pulling the Sixers' most effective rebounder away from the boards. To defuse Boston's most potent weapon, Cunningham switched the assignment to his most athletic player.

Reminiscent of the Philadelphia-Boston matchups of the past, where Wilt Chamberlain and Bill Russell had shadowed each other from end to end, Julius Erving now tailed Bird through screens and thrust an oversized hand in his face for forty long minutes. With Bird hampered, scratching out a tough twenty-two points, the Sixers sprinted to an early lead that they never surrendered. The same pattern played out in the fourth game. Erving hounded Bird into a one-for-eight first-half shooting performance as the Sixers surged ahead by seventeen. But then, little by little, they frittered the lead away. In the final seconds, with Boston behind by only a bucket, Celtics point guard Nate "Tiny" Archibald, initiating a fast break, spotted Bird stalking along the baseline. As soon as the ball left Archibald's hands, Bobby Jones, with the speed and instincts of a football cornerback, streaked down the court to intercept the pass. "Relief," Sixers center Darryl Dawkins muttered about the play that preserved the two-point win. "Plop plop, fizz fizz."

Flying back to Boston, the Sixers held a commanding 3–1 edge in the best-of-seven series. History had taught them, however, that putting Boston to bed was something that Philadelphia could never take for granted. Already, they'd come within a Bobby Jones's fingernail of blowing the previous game. "That fourth win will be murder," Sixers trainer Al Domenico predicted.

Making the trip to Massachusetts was Sixers general manager Pat Williams. He watched from the stands as Philadelphia carried a six-point lead and the ball into the final ninety seconds of Game Five. All around him, Celtics fans slunk to the exits, some of whom shook Williams's hand and wished him luck. What followed flipped the congratulations to condolences so suddenly that Williams had no time to process it. A blocked Andrew Toney layup, a botched inbounds pass, a missed Bobby Jones scoop shot, and eight consecutive Celtics points derailed the Sixers' fast track to the Finals. "I remember that night just walking away and saying, 'Oh boy, that was our golden opportunity,'" Williams said about the Sixers' 111–109 loss. Michael Madden of *The Boston Globe* wrote that Boston showed itself to be "a team of character," Philadelphia to be a team "in need of the Heimlich maneuver."

Ending the series in Philadelphia was imperative. No one wanted to risk returning to Boston for a winner-take-all contest. In Game Six, the Spectrum crowd, raring for a fight, bombarded the Celtics during warmups with ice, beer, and expletives. Larry Bird claimed never to have seen worse sportsmanship. "They get 10,000 one night, 18,000 the next...I guess they don't know how to act," he said, taking a shot at Philadelphia's fair-weather tendencies. The slurs strayed so far beyond the boundary of ordinary fan abuse that midway through the third quarter, Celtics forward Cedric Maxwell charged five rows deep into the seats, which struck the Sixers as unwise. "A man runs into the stands here," Darryl Dawkins stated, "he doesn't know what those people have in their pockets. He could have his throat cut and wouldn't know it until his head fell off." Maxwell claimed that a fan in the stands stuck him with a pointy object, later believed to be a pencil. "It was just the emotions of the game, sort of an out-of-body experience," Maxwell said decades later. "But it galvanized us."

In the first half, the Sixers had thundered to a double-digit lead; the Celtics battled back through their newfound strength: physicality. During the previous offseason, Celtics president Red Auerbach, the shrewdest wheeler-dealer in the NBA, pulled off one of his biggest heists, sweet-talking the Golden State Warriors into sending him underachieving center Robert Parish and a first-round draft pick, which he used to select Kevin McHale, a gangly forward from northern Minnesota. A frontline once deficient in height was now stocked with length and heft. Unlike in the previous year's playoffs, when Philadelphia had brushed Boston aside with minimal drama, the Celtics turned this one into a bar fight, never more so than in the sixth game. In the final quarter, columnist Peter Vecsey noted, "Each stampede to the basketball was an act of courage. Each rebound was a test of manhood. Each shot was a violent effort." There were skirmishes in the stands and on the court, a pileup of bodies and limbs, playing directly to the Celtics' advantage.

With tempers running high, Billy Cunningham employed an unorthodox strategy. Rather than lashing out, he channeled his emotions inward—toward the one untouchable player on the roster. "Doc was struggling a little bit and I needed him so badly. The team needed him to step it up. And the only way I knew how was to jump on him, which I'd never done before, get him upset with me and then have him respond on the court," Cunningham recalled, adding, "That was something I felt at the moment. I needed to get him mad at me so that he would take it out on the Celtics." Tuckered out from guarding Bird, a player nearly seven years his junior, Erving seemingly had too little left to muster his usual offensive energy, shooting an abysmal five-for-seventeen. Ahead by as many as fifteen points in the third quarter, the Sixers coughed up the lead with minutes to go, losing 100–98.

The tension between Cunningham and Erving erupted in the clubhouse afterward. Behind closed doors, they barked at each other loudly enough for the press to hear. Erving emerged uncharacteristically tight-lipped, shooing reporters away. Writer Joe Klein was struck by how exhausted Erving looked at that moment, hunched alone by his locker, toweling the sweat out of hair now flecked with gray. "I'm our best offensive player and I had to face-guard Bird, which was the most demanding defensive assignment," he later said. "*You* try chasing that guy around the floor sometime."

A grounded thirty-one-year-old straining to anchor both sides of the court, Erving didn't need tough love from Cunningham. He needed help.

Tailgating in the streets surrounding Boston Garden commenced hours before the tipoff of Game Seven. It was May 3. The warm, cloudless Sunday weather heralded the delayed start of spring across New England. Inside, organ music piped through the arena's speakers. Unlike their flashier counterparts on the West Coast, the Celtics made few concessions to modernity—no cheerleaders, no mascots, no Top 40 hits. Everything was old in Boston Garden, down to the team's radio announcer, Johnny Most, whose cigarette-corroded voice crackled across the airwaves like a dispatch from a distant era. Even the everlasting stench of spilled beer and cigar smoke lent the venue an aura of timelessness.

In a season of sellouts, the Celtics never had to worry about civic apathy. Fans streamed in by the thousands, some decked out in green suits, some festooned in bells, some with "Let's Go, Celts" painted in lipstick across their midriffs. Mirroring each other all year long, the Sixers and the Celtics had split their six games in the regular season, then split their six in the playoffs. Seemingly no two clubs had ever been more evenly matched. Whatever edge Boston held that afternoon was tied to the teams' shared history, to the mystique that for decades had haunted Philadelphia's players the second their sneakers touched the parquet floor.

The game proceeded no differently from the others. The Celtics came out cold; the Sixers bursted to an early lead. The Celtics crashed the boards; the Sixers began to buckle. In desperation, as if sensing that a Lakers-free Finals might never come his way again, Erving shrugged off the hesitancy and indecision that had plagued the Sixers in the second half of the last few games. He nailed a midrange jumper, swooped past the Celtics' big men for a finger roll, threw down a forceful fast-break slam, sank another outside shot, and spun in a reverse layup. Soon, a four-point Sixers' deficit swelled to a seven-point lead.

Then it all fell apart.

"One point?" Erving asked in the locker room afterward.

"One free throw in five minutes and twenty-three seconds," a reporter affirmed.

"One point?" Erving repeated, less a question than an expression of disbelief, as if some mathematical error had been made. The Sixers couldn't have collapsed so completely.

After Erving's spurt of buckets, the tenor of the game shifted once again. It started, as longtime *Boston Globe* columnist Bob Ryan remembered, when the referees "put their whistles in their pockets. The Celtics played, let's just say, rather aggressive defense and got away with it." Now, when gliding toward the hole, Erving got body-checked so viciously that it felt like he'd been tossed through a windshield. It was, Larry Bird declared, an "all-out war. I've never been through anything so brutal."

Whether because of nerves or noncalls, the Sixers froze up. Shots stopped falling; the ball drifted into the wrong hands. At one point, Erving lobbed a pass that Bird picked off. Shortly after, Bobby Jones threw the ball again to Bird. "It looked like every time the Sixers got the ball at the end they wanted to give it away," Bird said with a laugh. With a minute left, Darryl Dawkins caught a pass in the post while, according to Ryan, "half of

Eastern Massachusetts swarmed all over him." True to what columnist Peter Vecsey called the "no autopsy, no foul" ethos of the final quarter, the referees stood silent as Dawkins heaved the ball toward the basket. Seizing the rebound, Bird chugged downcourt, pulled up twelve feet from the hoop, and banked the ball softly off the glass to put the Celtics ahead by two, 91–89.

Down to their last chance, Erving again surrendered the ball to the Celtics, but point guard Maurice Cheeks eventually recovered it and managed to do the impossible: draw a foul. Near the free-throw line, Celtics forward M. L. Carr, brushing by Cheeks, whispered, "Don't choke." Needing both foul shots to pull even, Cheeks sank just one.

Over the game's final few minutes, the Sixers clanged six shots, coughed the ball up five times, and bricked a game-tying free throw. They'd held leads late in the fourth quarter of three consecutive games in which they could've eliminated the Celtics. In any of those contests, if the Sixers had simply hit one more shot or turned the ball over one less time, the series would've swung the other way. They lost Game Five by two points, Game Six by two, and Game Seven by one. During a season in which Boston and Philadelphia had run neck and neck from October to May, a lone free throw separated them in the end. It wasn't so much that Boston emerged victorious. It was that the Sixers failed to exorcise the ghosts of playoffs past. They'd become, as Harvey Araton surmised in the *New York Post,* "victims of the gremlins in their minds."

Hours later, when the Sixers' bus pulled away from Boston Garden, Celtics fans, delirious with joy and liquor, climbed its sides and crawled onto its roof, rocking the vehicle back and forth as if to tip it over. One sprawled across the windshield and began banging on the glass with his bare fists. "I thought they were gonna have to drop a helicopter in there to get us out," said Sixers benchwarmer Ollie Johnson. Unable to shake the revelers, the driver yelled, "OK, we're going!" and floored it. "I was sure somebody was going to get hit," Cunningham said.

In back-to-back seasons, Erving had been beaten first by Magic Johnson and then by Larry Bird. Something was missing: a killer instinct when the game was on the line, an enforcer who could punch back, someone to relieve the burden of the league's aging MVP.

Everywhere the Houston Rockets turned in the runup to the NBA Finals, they saw signs of disrespect: vendors hawking T-shirts prematurely celebrating Boston's fourteenth title, posters proclaiming the Celtics "NBA Champions, 1981," newspaper columnists musing that the Rockets should forfeit the Finals to spare themselves the embarrassment. It was a joke among Celtics fans that their club would run away with the best-of-seven series in three games. On the Rockets' bus heading to Game One, center Billy Paultz called out, "All right, is Rodney Dangerfield here? He belongs on this team. That man could sympathize with us now."

On some level, the lack of respect for the Rockets was understandable. After Houston had eliminated the Los Angeles Lakers in the playoffs' first round, the basketball-minded public had shifted its full attention to the Eastern Conference. At the same time that the Sixers inched past the Bucks and fell short against the Celtics, the Rockets stunned the heavily favored San Antonio Spurs in seven games, then dispatched the Kansas City Kings in the first and last Conference Finals matchup between two clubs that boasted sub-.500 regular-season records. The coverage was sparse—quizzical profiles of a grumbly superstar and his merry band of underdogs who were grinding down the competition out West.

As soon as they'd reached the Finals, however, the press started treating the Rockets as a joke that had gone too far. Facing the Rockets after the Sixers was, *Boston Globe* writer Michael Madden quipped, "a bit like Lawrence Welk following a warmup set by the Stones."

Since 1979, the Rockets had dropped thirteen straight games to the Celtics. Coming into the opening contest, Houstonites tried to brush off their recent futility in Boston. "We never had a jinx against the Celtics," Moses Malone asserted. "We just never won any games against them." And few expected them to start doing so now. If there were any doubts about the outcome of the Finals, they revolved around whether the Celtics might suffer an emotional letdown against an opponent so unworthy of gracing the Garden parquet. "Trying to get up for Houston," Bob Verdi wrote in the *Chicago Tribune*, "is like trying to get excited over cornflakes for breakfast."

The Rockets, per usual, refused to roll over. Periodically throughout the playoffs, Malone had set the tone by swaggering into shootarounds with red boxing gloves knotted around his neck, a boxer's mouthpiece dangling from his lips. "Ain't nothing going to change because I'm in the final," Malone asserted. "I'm going to be doing the same things I've been doing."

In the opening game, the Rockets punched the unsuspecting Celtics in the mouth. Expecting to witness a coronation, the Garden crowd sat in bewilderment as Houston took a six-point lead into halftime. It wasn't that the Rockets were playing beyond their capabilities. If anything, they were laboring through an off-night. The reason was simple: Malone couldn't buy a bucket. Almost everything he threw at the basket missed the mark. Knowing he needed more from his franchise player, Rockets head coach Del Harris goaded Malone during timeouts. "I always talked around

Mo because Mo had tremendous pride, and that was something that carried him," Harris explained. "But this time, I said, 'Mo, you gotta wake up and get on the boards.' And he said, 'Fuck you, Coach' and a bunch of other stuff, and I said, 'Mo, we'll talk about our sex lives after the game, but right now, I need you on the boards.'" While Malone did grab fifteen rebounds, he let a crucial one slip through his fingers at the end of the game, which could have stemmed the Celtics' second-half comeback. What's worse, he sank only four of his seventeen shots. Even an average shooting performance would've put the Rockets over the top. Instead, they lost their grip in the final quarter as the Celtics edged past them, 98–95.

The Rockets had no choice: they would have to play uglier—*much* uglier. No running downcourt, no jumpers until the shot clock ticked nearly to zero, no unpunished forays into the paint. In the first game, the Rockets had attempted ninety-nine shots, too many for Del Harris's liking. In Game Two, they attempted only eighty-five. They hit 40 percent of them. They were outrebounded and dished out fewer assists than the Celtics. They repelled viewers and put the Garden to sleep. Yet somehow, behind Malone's thirty-one points and fifteen rebounds, they departed from Boston with an unsightly 92–90 win.

Before Game Three, the theme song from *Rocky* blared through the Summit's speakers. Texans waved mass-produced cardboard signs that declared YES WE CAN in yellow block letters. But the Celtics, setting the pace early, buried the Rockets by twenty-three points. In Game Four, Houston dragged Boston back into the mud. "You'd hate to be behind these guys when they come to a tollbooth," one columnist sneered about the Rockets. "They probably shut their engines off." Again, they heaved bricks toward the hoop, shooting a ghastly 36 percent from the field. Again, behind the offensive rebounding of Malone and Robert Reid, who recovered nineteen of the Rockets' sixty-six misses, they staggered away with an ugly five-point victory.

On the way back to Boston, the Rockets stopped in Chicago for a layover. Browsing through the newspapers, they saw scathing columns about the Celtics needing to end this "pointless" series before the Rockets sullied the sport further. Something snapped in Malone. Before the fifth game, he did something wholly atypical. He gave the press a peek into his innermost thoughts. "They ain't that good," Malone said of the Celtics. "I could take four guys from off the street in Petersburg and beat them."

Decades later, there is still wide disagreement about why Malone chose to speak out at that particular moment. Rockets guard Calvin Murphy claimed that his statement was a joke. "He said it to be funny," Murphy said. "Mo didn't understand about stuff that motivates other people. You don't grab Superman's cape, and Mo didn't understand that." Steve Patterson, the son of Rockets general manager Ray Patterson, called Malone's comments a "polite F-U" to the basketball establishment. "The man had great pride in his craft," Patterson stated. "[The disrespect] was insulting to him as a great practitioner of his craft." Perhaps the most thoughtful interpretation came in the moment from Robert Reid, the Rockets small forward, whose suffocating defense was frustrating Larry Bird. "We are all so sick of being ridiculed every time we pick up a newspaper and every time we turn on the TV. The people in the East have been unbelievable. We have been called a farce and a disgrace and all kinds of trash. We've been treated like outcasts and given the same kind of respect you would give a man who broke into your house," Reid explained, adding, "For four games we kept our mouths shut, thinking that if we won a game or two, that trash would stop. But it didn't.... I think this is [Malone's] reaction to all of that stuff that has been said about us."

Bird, for one, cited Malone's comments as the turning point in a hard-fought series deadlocked at two games apiece. "There was no way they were going to beat us after we read that," Bird declared. "The coach made sure we had carbon copies of what he said before Game 5." All night long, Boston benchwarmers yelled at Malone, "Moses, you better get those four guys from Petersburg because the four guys you got now ain't working out so well." The Celtics ended up trouncing the Rockets by twenty-nine points in Game Five. Even then, Malone refused to back down. "The Celtics are still chumps," he snarled afterward, adding, "I spoke from my heart and I still believe it: Boston is not that good. Philadelphia should have beaten them. I've got a lot of pride. I was raised in the ghetto and I grew up believing you should say what you believe."

Angry and rejuvenated, motivated, according to Celtics point guard Nate Archibald, to make Malone "eat some of those damn words," Boston romped to the title. It was a disheartening finish to an otherwise competitive NBA Finals. Malone had dragged his club to within two wins of a championship, but even someone as tireless as Houston's leader wore down from months of exertion. Malone hit only 48 of the 119 shots he attempted in the Finals, well below his 52 percent shooting average in the regular season.

In the locker room after the Rockets' 102–91 loss in Game Six, Malone appeared drained but unbowed. When asked if he still believed that he could whip the Celtics with four nobodies from his hometown, Malone replied, "Oh yeah, we'd take 'em. We got good players down there [in Petersburg], the best. We'd take 'em."

Days later, from the fourth-floor balcony of Boston's City Hall, Larry Bird glanced out at the fifty thousand residents who'd taken time from their lunch hour to celebrate the latest in a seemingly endless string of Celtics titles. Some of the handmade signs being held aloft congratulated the players; others took aim in vulgar language at the newest villain in Celtics lore. One in particular caught Bird's eye.

"After all the hollering and screaming," Bird boomed into the microphone, "I look out on the crowd and I see one thing that typifies our season: Moses does eat shit."

CHAPTER 12

OF REBOUNDS AND PLANETS

Fitz Dixon had had enough.

Never a basketball fan to begin with, the Sixers owner hadn't even bothered to show up to Philadelphia's seventh game in Boston. "The 76ers were like a toy to him," assistant equipment manager Ron Rabena stated, and by then, it had become too scuffed and costly to elicit much joy. Besides, Dixon had other sporting options to choose from, some more in line with his blue-blooded background. His show-jumping horse, Jet Run, was competing at the Valley Forge Grand Prix, and Dixon was there in Wayne, New Jersey, to watch him leap to a first-place finish. Afterward, basketball reporters reached out for comment on the Sixers' collapse. Dixon made himself unavailable.

For five years, Dixon's and Julius Erving's fates had been yoked together. Over that span, the Sixers had won 273 games in the regular season and 42 in the playoffs, the most in the NBA. It was a record of success that other owner-superstar combos would've killed for. But the absence of championships and box-office abundance had colored the period in more somber shades. The Boston Celtics had just won a title that had been the Sixers' to seize, and it seemed possible heading into the 1981–82 season that fan apathy might spiral even further into abandonment. "That doesn't mean we're unloved because we're loved wherever we go around the league," Erving asserted defensively. "When I traveled in the offseason—in Israel, Italy, Aruba—all people wanted to talk about were the Sixers. In Philly we're taken for granted, and no matter what we do, the only thing that will satisfy our fans is a championship. I can accept that, but I get disappointed when I hear us referred to as losers. That's one thing we definitely are not."

Dixon could deal with losing; what he couldn't stomach was the money pit that the franchise had become. It was estimated that in his half decade as owner, Dixon had incurred $10 million in losses—a pool of red ink too deep even for someone whose inherited wealth could last several lifetimes. "It's impractical for me to continue much further," Dixon stated after fewer than seven thousand spectators had sprinkled through the Spectrum to watch the Sixers fight for their playoff lives against the Milwaukee Bucks in April 1981.

As soon as Dixon's musings about unloading the franchise hit the newsstands, Laurence Shaiman, a Philadelphia-based attorney, began working the phones. Harold Katz, Shaiman's client, wanted to own the Sixers. And what Katz wanted, he usually got.

When Harold Katz turned twenty, he took a job as a door-to-door salesman peddling Fuller brushes. This might've seemed an ordinary career starter for the son of a neighborhood grocer in North Philadelphia, but Katz entered it with a sizable disadvantage: he stuttered. Since childhood, he'd tripped over certain syllables, so much so that his classmates cruelly nicknamed him Porky Pig. Rather than shying away from professions whose success depended on verbal dexterity, Katz charged headlong into them, convinced that he could overcome a lifelong impediment through sheer force of will. "Stuttering made me a stronger person," he asserted. "I'm convinced of that. You think putting together a big business deal, hundreds of millions of dollars, is scary? Try selling some bad-tempered housewife some Fuller brushes when it takes you five minutes to get your own name out of your mouth."

As a young man, Katz excelled at selling fruit and brushes and insurance, but he was always aiming higher. What he envisioned was a level of wealth that would entitle him to tell the rest of the world, all those snickering classmates and doubtful elders, to go screw themselves. Casting about for up-and-coming trends, Katz stumbled onto the blossoming realm of dieting. Since the mid-'60s, the dominant player in weight loss had been Weight Watchers, which offered support groups, cookbooks, and frozen meals to those struggling to shed pounds. In 1972, Katz muscled onto their turf with Nutrisystem, a meal-delivery provider and champion of the liquid protein diet. Within a decade, Katz had opened seven hundred brick-and-mortar franchises and, more importantly, amassed his screw-you money, enough to adorn his outfits with diamonds, his stretch limousine with red velour, and his office with chrome. His adulthood ambitions fulfilled, Katz now looked back to his boyhood passion: basketball.

A year younger than Wilt Chamberlain, Katz had grown up during an era when Philadelphia basketball was coming into its own. Though he was a shooter at heart, Katz had recognized that runty, unathletic teenagers seldom clawed their way onto high school varsity squads by jacking up jumpers. He'd caught the coach's eye instead by passing, suppressing his scorer's instincts in order to set up his more physically gifted peers. His playing career had peaked during a game against Overbrook High School, when he'd goaded Chamberlain into goaltending a handful of his shots.

Katz's basketball fanaticism never waned. Even in 1973, when the Philadelphia 76ers failed to crack double digits in wins, Katz could be found at the Spectrum, settling into his usual game-time perch: Section U, Row 13. Upon gaining his fortune, Katz constructed a basketball court at his mansion and splurged on satellite television, which allowed him to fall asleep while watching college basketball games taking place on the West Coast.

Vain and garish, his hair blow-dried and his fingers ringed in gold, Katz appeared the very picture of new money, a stark contrast to the refined owner who surrounded himself with bodyguards. Dixon had been born to the estate, Katz to the streets. While negotiating the ownership rights for the 76ers, the two never met in person. Upon the announcement of the sale in July 1981, Dixon was as unreachable as ever, chartering his yacht, the *Grindstone*, up and down the rocky coast of Maine. Katz, meanwhile, thrust himself into the teeth of a media horde. "Many people have called me crazy," he declared when asked about purchasing a franchise that was bleeding cash. "You have to be a little bananas. But I feel I can increase attendance."

Dixon's disregard for what had made Philadelphia basketball distinctive shone through during his first face-to-face meeting with Katz, a chance encounter on the street in September 1981. According to Katz, Dixon tendered one bit of advice: "Fire everybody." Not only did Katz disregard the suggestion, he rehired a fixture of Sixers games whom Dixon had unceremoniously let go the year before. With his close-cropped gray hair and slender frame, Dave Zinkoff didn't look the part of an eccentric trendsetter, but no one did more to establish the public-address announcer as a meaningful character in the game. Since the 1950s, his rhymes and alliterative turns of phrase ("Dipper dunk!," "Dr. J puts it away!") had been an indelible part of the aural atmosphere at the Spectrum. Professional basketball in Philadelphia without Zinkoff seemed so unthinkable that upon his dismissal, classical musician Isaac Stern wrote a letter to Dixon that began "In case you don't know me, I am a world-class violinist. I consider Zink a world-class announcer. You might want to reconsider."

Zinkoff, one Boston writer scoffed, treated every Sixers field goal "as if it were the invention of electric light," which was the exact tone that Katz hoped to set in his inaugural season as owner. Katz realized that if fans had stopped turning out for a team whose roster included the most exciting player in the game, then doubling down on basketball alone wouldn't suffice. Every game would need something extra, a dash of entertainment to draw disillusioned Philadelphians back to the Spectrum. So Katz tasked general manager Pat Williams with mapping out promotional plans for all forty-one home games. Williams booked halftime shows featuring bears who wrestled humans and unicyclists who rode on tightropes so high that they could be reached only via forklift. He gave away baseball bats and posters and minibasketballs. "Pat came up with the idea of a God-and-country night for the churches, and then Harold came up with a salute-to-Israel night for the synagogues," marketing director Jack Swope remembered. "So there was a competition between Pat and Harold about who would turn out more: the Christians or the Jews." When the Houston Rockets came to town, the Sixers staged Calvin Murphy night, where adult men shorter than five foot nine, Murphy's height, could buy one ticket and get another free.

A loyal season-ticket holder, Katz had waited and waited and waited for the title owed to him from five years earlier. Failure to deliver it in the upcoming 1981–82 season threatened to upend the ongoing Erving era. "The whole charisma of the team changed when Harold bought the team," sportswriter Mark Whicker claimed. "I think people felt like he represented them. He was impatient. Sixers fans were impatient." Katz made it clear that if another spring passed without a championship parade marching down Broad Street, then a roster overhaul was in order.

For now, Katz focused on adding what his club needed most: rebounding.

On November 18, 1981, three weeks into the new season, the Houston Rockets returned to New England. Outside Boston Garden, as a sellout crowd filed in, vendors peddled green T-shirts emblazoned with three now-familiar words: "Moses Eats Shit." Before tipoff, fans in the balcony unfurled a banner with the same slogan, decorated with a cartoon of a defecating dog. Throughout the game, chants of "Moses eats shit" drowned out the squeaking of sneakers.

Impervious to the taunts, Malone ripped down eleven rebounds and racked up thirty-seven points, twenty more than Larry Bird. It was a performance superior to any of his games from the previous year's Finals, yet the Rockets barely inched past the Celtics, 106–104. Seven players from Boston scored in double figures; only three from Houston did. Relying on Malone's garish statistics to overcome the Rockets' persistent lack of depth burdened him with unrealistic expectations—either he put up herculean numbers or his team lost.

Afterward, the press found Malone unexpectedly chatty in spite of the rude reception. "I think these people here love me," Malone said, a sly grin creeping across his face. "They talk about Jesus—why can't they talk nice about Moses?"

"What'd you think about the shirts?" one reporter asked.

"I think some smart man made some money off some ignorant people," Malone replied.

For two hours he'd been mocked and demeaned, jeered and cursed. Malone, *Boston Globe* columnist Leigh Montville wrote with an undercurrent of disgust, "had been treated as if he were some great beast that had been brought by the conquering Roman legions. He had been a captured grizzly to be taunted, the paying customers running to yell things at him." Malone had weathered the abuse stoically. His witty retorts in the locker room gave him the last word, swinging sympathy to his side. He emerged that afternoon with his dignity intact. From then on, whenever he returned to Boston, any talk of Malone feasting on excrement was minimal.

The Philadelphia 76ers roster that Harold Katz had inherited carried a handful of players—Julius Erving, Andrew Toney, Maurice Cheeks, Bobby Jones—who were performing near their peak, scraping every iota of talent from their wiry frames. And one who was not. Six foot eleven and strong enough to tear a rim off a backboard at will, Darryl Dawkins was, at age twenty-four, a man of infinite possibilities. But the results, so far, had been limited. As a salesman, Katz seemed to have the golden touch. But selling Dawkins on unlocking his vast potential through hard work and dedication would tax even Katz's considerable persuasive powers. Easier, one writer claimed, "to try and sell oil to the Arabs, pork to the Israelis."

Dawkins's contract would expire at the end of the 1981–82 season; Katz made it clear that if Dawkins expected the new owner to cut him a sizable check, his statistics would need to hew closer to those that his fellow prep-to-pro star was putting up in Houston. Ever since they'd been selected straight out of high school in consecutive drafts, Malone and Dawkins, as different from each other as oil and water, had cut contrasting figures. Through blinkered devotion to his craft, Malone had made up for his lack of collegiate seasoning by the time he'd reached legal drinking age. Dawkins, in contrast, had seen the word "potential" curdle into an insult when applied to him. "His size told me he should get at minimum ten rebounds a game, and he wasn't close to it," Katz later said of Dawkins. Despite averaging half as many points and rebounds as Malone, Dawkins shot to national prominence by being as hungry for publicity as Malone was for the ball. "I'm an entertainer," Dawkins explained, adding, "I do whatever I think is going to make me known, to make me marketable so that I can do commercials, appearances, whatever."

In the late 1970s, *Philadelphia Journal*, a fledgling tabloid, tried to beef up circulation by enlisting stars from Philadelphia's four professional sports teams to write weekly columns. When Julius Erving declined, the choice on the Sixers was obvious. Every week Dawkins would sit in the corner of the team's practice court with his ghostwriter, Fran Blinebury. Stem-winding tales of his alternate life on the planet Lovetron in the fictitious solar system Dawkins claimed to hail from flowed from his lips as fluently as if he were recounting what he ate for breakfast. "He just let his imagination run wild," Blinebury said. "He came in one day and told me he doesn't live on Lovetron anymore. He's on a neighboring planet called Chocolate Paradise and he reigned as Chocolate Thunder and his queen was Juicy Lucy, and he'd go on and on and on." The subsequent columns read like a cross between surrealist poetry and dime-store novels about intergalactic adventures.

Dawkins's fame broke nationally when he began breaking backboards on the court. The first came in Kansas City on November 13, 1979. It happened with alarming suddenness—one second, Dawkins was leaping for a two-handed jam; the next, shards of glass were raining down on Bill Robinzine, the Kings forward camped under the hoop. Already, Dawkins had taken to coining outrageous nicknames for his rim-rattling dunks—the "In-Your-Face Disgrace" and the "Turbo Sexophonic Delight," among others—so reporters crawled over one another to scoop what Dawkins would christen this slam. Catching Dawkins's eye in the locker room, Blinebury shook his head. Dawkins got the message. "Well, I've got a name for the dunk," he announced, "and you can read all about it in my column in the *Philadelphia Journal*." Later, Dawkins slipped a piece of paper to Blinebury. On it was written: "The Chocolate-Thunder-Flying, Robinzine-Crying, Teeth-Shaking, Glass-Breaking, Rump-Roasting, Bun-Toasting, Wham-Bam, Glass-Breaker-I-Am-Jam." Weeks later, he ripped another backboard to shreds. Dismayed at having to sweep glass off the court multiple times a season, the NBA was forced to adopt a spring-loaded, bounce-back rim that not even Dawkins could destroy.

Dawkins became a bona fide superstar who'd never so much as sniffed an All-Star Game, a handsomely paid big man who'd never finished among the top-ten league leaders in rebounds. Perhaps unsurprisingly, it was the colorful and gregarious Dawkins, not the brusque and walled-off Malone, who landed a coveted advertising deal with Wheaties. Even for an owner who was latching onto any gimmick that could bring fans to the Spectrum, Katz let it be known that he expected production, not eccentricity, out of Dawkins. "The number one subject we have constantly talked about is all that stuff about being on Lovetron. All of that double-talk... Those phrases, the 'in-your-face-disgrace' dunks, aren't what people care about anymore. I want to see him perform on the floor," Katz asserted, adding, "He's paid to perform, not give out Lovetron quotes."

All that season, Katz focused his attention on Dawkins. After games, depending on the performance, Katz would either wrap Dawkins in a bear hug at his locker or launch into condescending lectures about the importance of grabbing rebounds with both hands. Whenever Dawkins brought up his expiring contract, Katz didn't budge: "Darryl, until you get ten [rebounds] a game, the money you talk about isn't going to happen." Katz claimed that Dawkins responded, "I don't even have ten jumps in me a game."

It was a line that head coach Billy Cunningham had heard before. After one playoff game against the Atlanta Hawks in which Dawkins had scored thirty points and pulled down eleven rebounds, Cunningham grabbed him and yelled, "That's what we need!" To Cunningham's dismay, Dawkins point-blank told him, "Don't expect that from me every night." When Lionel Hollins, a key member of the Portland Trail Blazers club that had upset Philadelphia in the 1977 NBA Finals, got traded to the Sixers, Dawkins pulled him aside. "Why are you going so hard? It's just practice," Dawkins said. "You can't win a championship in practice."

Hollins shot back, "That's why we beat you guys."

Dawkins dominated one night, disappeared the next, his only consistency being his inconsistency. Julius Erving stated that Dawkins was "one of the leading players in the league where you put a question mark after his name." Once, during practice, Cunningham whistled the action dead when he spotted Dawkins going through the motions. Crowding into his face, Cunningham berated him for his lack of effort. Chastened, Dawkins promised to work harder. Then, as Cunningham walked away, Dawkins stuck out his leg and tripped him.

Taken aback, Cunningham could do nothing but laugh. Dawkins was who he was. No amount of threats or encouragement could change that.

A year after lugging his club to the Finals, Moses Malone seethed at the Rockets' hesitancy to proffer a new contract. A free agent the next summer, Malone had urged his agent, Lee Fentress, to hammer out an extension that would root him for life in the unassuming city that suited him. It had almost happened in November 1980, when Fentress and Rockets owner George Maloof Sr. had huddled together to negotiate. Days later, Maloof had suffered a heart attack. In the hospital, barely able to muster a breath, Maloof had turned to his children and asked, "How many did Moses get last night?" Maloof's son Gavin claimed that they were his father's last words.

Maloof Sr.'s untimely death altered Malone's fate. "If he'd stayed alive," Rockets forward Major Jones claimed, "it would've worked out, and Malone would've remained in Houston." Inheriting the Rockets were two of Maloof's sons, twentysomething businessmen too inexperienced and financially insecure to commit seven figures to the team's star, even if losing him could sink the franchise. "If we start next year without Moses," Rockets general manager Ray Patterson stated in February 1982, "we might as well forget it. We're dead." But this supposed urgency didn't reignite negotiations. The Rockets, Malone sensed, weren't being straight with him. "I have never, ever gone around and claimed that I am the best player or the greatest player in the league," Malone said. "But I have always thought that I am certainly one of the hardest workers. And over the last five or six years, I've always thought that I've worked as hard as possible to help make the Rockets better and I don't understand why they wouldn't try to reach an agreement with me on a new contract long before this one ran out."

Malone unleashed his frustrations on two tried-and-true fronts: by punishing opponents on the court and by stiffing reporters off it. No player in 1981–82 mattered more to his team than Malone. He attempted a quarter of all Rockets field goals, exceeding thirty points per game for the first time as a professional. The ball swung down low to him so often that Malone ended up committing the third-most turnovers in the league. Once again, he lapped his competition in rebounding. His 558 total offensive rebounds were nearly 40 percent more than those of his nearest peer. In a game against the Seattle Supersonics on February 11, 1982, Malone corralled thirty-two rebounds, twenty-one on the offensive glass alone, a single-game record that still stands. Decades later, the memory of trying to box out Malone remained burned in Sonics forward Greg Kelser's brain. "Moses had no flair," Kelser explained. "He was like that jackhammer that kept pounding and pounding and pounding. As you wore down, he just kept going." Worried about his superstar's workload—Malone averaged forty-two minutes per game, two more than any other NBA player that season—head coach Del Harris once offered to rest Malone for a game. The very idea rankled Malone. "Rest? I can rest at night!" he exclaimed. As Major Jones said about Malone, "You would have to handcuff him and put him in jail to get him to sit out."

Neither career-defining feats nor wins against top-tier clubs could loosen Malone's tongue. "I got nothin' to say tonight," Malone snapped after his thirty-one-point, twenty-rebound performance had downed the Philadelphia 76ers in late January. It was a vow of silence that, with few exceptions, persisted through the winter and into the spring. "In 1982, the deal was that Moses decided that he wasn't talking to the media," said Fran Blinebury, who'd left the *Philadelphia Journal* for the *Houston Chronicle* in the early '80s. "I was never told a reason for it. It was just an accepted thing that Moses wasn't talking." Malone had never played better—and never looked more miserable doing so.

It was a sour season overall. Fed up with a sluggish offense that stifled any semblance of a fast break, players whispered among themselves in airport terminals and hotel lobbies about staging a mutiny against head coach Del Harris, though it never came to pass. Calvin Murphy still hadn't gotten over being benched for the entirety of Game Four in the previous year's Finals. "I was through after that one game mentally. Del took my game. He did to me what an opponent couldn't do: he took my mental state of basketball away," Murphy claimed, adding, "That's why the next year, I just went through the motions—got my money and ran." The Cinderella club of 1981, the Rockets didn't even make it out of the first round of the playoffs in 1982.

That the Rockets front office hemmed and hawed while Malone's contract wound down registered as a breach of trust. Deep down, Malone abided by old-fashioned values: loyalty, industriousness, pride. He played his heart out for the Rockets; in turn, he expected them to reward him accordingly. "I never wanted to be a free agent," Malone asserted. "I've hoped all along that we could get something worked out, but they didn't have that much respect for the things I have done."

Not even a joyous occasion like receiving his second MVP award in four years could curb Malone's anger. Upon presentation of the trophy, Malone grumbled, "I'll bet this is the first time an MVP was on unemployment."

On April 11, 1982, a week before the playoffs were to begin, Harold Katz stomped into the locker room at the Spectrum in a rage. The Sixers had just blown a game to the Celtics in which they'd led by thirteen points at halftime. In the second half and into overtime, the Celtics had outrebounded the Sixers 34–17. On the offensive boards, the Celtics had built an eye-popping 29–10 advantage, resulting in twenty-seven more total shots. "How do you win a championship the way we rebound?" Katz screamed in between a torrent of four-letter words.

Players had grown used to Katz prowling around after games, tossing off unvarnished opinions, but never with such fury. "Our guys are too nice," Katz groused. "Check it out. Our team leads the league in picking up guys off the floor."

Katz's experiment with Darryl Dawkins had failed. Even before a fractured fibula in his right leg had sidelined Dawkins in January, his rebounding numbers had hovered stubbornly below double figures. For months, general manager Pat Williams searched the far corners of the basketball world—everywhere from Europe to the developmental leagues—for anyone who could round up missed shots. At one point, Katz even put out feelers to forty-five-year-old Wilt Chamberlain, who'd last seen NBA action in 1973. "I know it's off the wall—way, way off the wall," Katz said, "but the situation we're in, I don't want to leave any stone unturned." So desperate was Katz that he reportedly offered Chamberlain a half-million dollars for a half-season's work. When Chamberlain expressed reservations about travel, Katz promised to exempt him from road games. Chamberlain passed; Williams's search came up empty. What Katz had aimed to fix when he purchased the club remained broken as the playoffs loomed.

The Sixers wound up dead last in the league in offensive rebounding for the season, fourth weakest in total boards. Opponents outrebounded the Sixers in fifty-one of their eighty-two games. Everywhere else—points, assists, steals, blocks—the Sixers put up numbers more consistent with a championship contender. Merely above-average rebounding would've eased their apprehension about the upcoming postseason. "Either we get [our rebounding] straightened away this week or we'll have a very early summer," Billy Cunningham said with a sigh.

Even so, the Sixers managed to finish with the NBA's second-best record, five games shy of the team whose postseason path always seemed to wind through Philadelphia. "I try to play every game as if the Celtics don't exist, but it won't go away," Erving said. "Not many of us will admit it, but the Celtics are always somewhere in the back of our minds." From the second their series had ended the previous May, both teams had known: a rematch between Boston and Philadelphia was inevitable.

CHAPTER 13

THE END

By the time the 1982 playoffs got underway, exhaustion had settled in across Philadelphia—for the fans, who'd packed the Spectrum to capacity only four times that season; for the new owner, who made no bones about blowing up the roster should the 76ers again collect a consolation prize; and, most importantly, for Julius Erving, who told Mike Littwin of the *Los Angeles Times*, "This is the first year when sometimes I'm driving to a game and I wish I was still in bed." One way or another, the Dr. J era was nearing the end.

Perennially coming up short had taken a toll on Erving and his teammates. It had turned them inward, fostered an embattled us-versus-the-world mentality. "We're proud, but we're not cocky," Erving explained. "It's a difference from last year to this, but not a drastic one. We're just not a group that goes bananas. Maybe that's because we've also known disappointment. In our privacy, we show more of ourselves, but under scrutiny, in front of the media, we tend to show less." Still the most accessible basketball star, Erving had become adept at masking his annoyance at the increasingly audible whispers that painted him as a choker, a transcendent ABA showman whose aerial style hadn't translated to NBA titles. A dreaded question threatened to hover over his retirement and beyond. "If I have to go through the rest of my life being asked about my quest for a championship," Erving groused, "I'd at least like to have a ring to show for it."

After cruising through the opening rounds, brushing aside the Atlanta Hawks and the Milwaukee Bucks, the 76ers showed up in Boston on May 9 for their fourth postseason faceoff against the Celtics in six years and their ninth in the last eighteen. In each of the recent matchups, the opening game had been decided by three points or fewer. Not so this time. The Celtics rode a seventeen-point lead into halftime, then proceeded to crush the Sixers by forty. It was the most lopsided playoffs defeat in franchise history, a drubbing so memorable that Boston writers immortalized it in Celtics lore as the Mother's Day Massacre.

True to their reputation of being "as unpredictable as a paper cup in a wind storm," the Sixers swept the next three games. Perversely, holding a 3–1 advantage in a best-of-seven series inspired hope not in Philadelphia but across New England. Before the opening tipoff of Game Five at Boston Garden, a loudmouthed Celtics fan hollered at Philadelphia's head coach, "Three to one, Billy! Now we've got you right where we want you!" Cunningham smiled, having heard worse. But the pressure to win had slimmed him down ten pounds since the start of the playoffs. One well-meaning friend had mailed Cunningham a good-luck card with two Rolaids taped inside.

Cunningham, it turned out, could've used the entire roll. That Wednesday evening, so deeply did the Celtics bury their opponents that with three minutes left and the Sixers trailing by thirty-four points, the Boston Garden crowd, certain that the series would go the distance, burst into an impromptu chant of "See you Sunday!" Hours later, when the Sixers returned to the Sheraton in downtown Boston, a group of construction workers hollered at them from across the street, "See you on Sunday! See you back in Boston!"

Arrogantly for someone whose club was still facing elimination, Celtics forward Kevin McHale said, "The coffin lid is still open, and now we've got one leg out."

Hours before Game Six on Friday, May 21, Julius Erving stretched out on a trainer's table at the Spectrum as Al Domenico swathed his ankles in tape.

"So here we go again," the Sixers trainer said to Erving.

"Yeah. But each one is different in its own way," Erving replied.

Or maybe not. From the start, Game Six evoked an unmistakable sensation of déjà vu. The Sixers' glassy eyes said it all. "You could look at their faces and see they were shell-shocked," said Celtics forward Cedric Maxwell. "Some of them didn't even want the ball." Up fifteen early, the Sixers tallied a paltry twenty-seven points after halftime, the lowest-scoring half in the playoffs since the advent of the shot clock in 1954. It was ugly and dispiriting, a slow-motion nightmare unfolding over twenty-four excruciating minutes. Erving heaved up a pair of airballs; Andrew Toney hit only one of eleven attempts, his shots missing the mark so widely that Sixers reserve Steve Mix, rummaging through his gym bag afterward, joked that he was searching for Toney's jumper. Outmuscled by Boston's rugged frontline, the Sixers ended up with nineteen fewer rebounds than the Celtics.

When the buzzer sounded on Philadelphia's 88–75 loss, the fans at the Spectrum boiled over with anger, unleashing all the fury and frustration they'd bottled up from six years of near-misses and blown leads. The players scurried off the court, seeking shelter from the barrage of insults and jeers that pulsed through the arena. It was the rageful, mournful sound of a city forsaking its team.

In the days leading to the seventh and deciding game, Philadelphians lathered themselves up into a mutinous frenzy. If the Sixers were to choke away a 3–1 advantage for the second straight year, one writer claimed, "they might as well move the team to Memphis or somewhere. They never could go back to Philadelphia." Another suggested that the results of the game could swing the franchise's fortunes by millions of dollars, since a defeat would trigger a mass cancellation of season tickets. Dave Sims of the *Daily News* painted an even bleaker scenario: "Philadelphia will disown [the Sixers] for good. Julius Erving will be busted from doctor to ambulance attendant. The Spectrum will become a furniture warehouse. A new blue law will be passed that will prevent big men from dribbling basketballs in front of large crowds." When a local journalist was asked why he intended to travel to Boston Garden to witness the inexorable heartbreak, he shrugged. "For the same reason that you agree to be a pallbearer, I guess."

At practice the following day, Billy Cunningham huddled the players together. Steamed at the hometown press for prematurely writing the team's obituary, he said, "You know what I wanna do? I wanna walk in tomorrow [after the game] and tell the media to go fly a kite—but with different words." Casting out the coaching staff, Erving convened a players-only meeting. The theme was the same: to recover their pride, the Sixers had only themselves to rely on. "Nobody thinks we have a chance," Sixers reserve Clint Richardson said. "Man, the coaches left. The fans gave up. Nobody in Boston thinks we can win. Nobody in Philly thinks we can win. It's just us." They set off for Massachusetts united in anger and grievance.

May 23 broke gloomy and overcast in eastern Massachusetts. Roaming the aisles of Boston Garden were fans draped in white sheets with "The Ghosts of Celtics Past" scribbled across the backs. "That's when I got scared," Erving said. "I thought it was the Klan." The chant of "See you Sunday!" that had rung out four days earlier now was replaced with an ominous "This is Sunday!"

Midway through warmups, the Sixers hastened back to the locker room. There, amid desert-level heat from a cranked-up thermostat, Erving roused the roster by again reminding them that everyone in the building expected them to fail. To counterbalance the soaring rhetoric from the team's spiritual leader, Darryl Dawkins performed his role as club jester. With clever jabs and gentle roasts, he loosened up his tight teammates. "The way I figured," Dawkins explained, "if somebody tells a joke, you've got to laugh. Even if you're at a funeral, you have to laugh at a good joke." On the blackboard, among banal directives like "Don't Rush Shots" and "Screen and Execute," was a phrase that summed up the Sixers' mindset: "Kick Their Ass."

Early in the game, Bobby Jones, wrestling for a rebound, tumbled alongside Kevin McHale into the seats beyond the baseline. "We both were almost sitting down in the laps of the people right there," Jones recalled. "The ref stood there and just looked at us. No call. That was the way it was going to be." It was part of Philadelphia's game plan: bully Boston into the stands if necessary—whatever it took to match the Celtics' physicality. When calls went against them, the Sixers smirked or exchanged high fives, interpreting each questionable foul and unfavorable whistle as further evidence that the world, referees included, had lined up against them.

Physicality was far from the only key to beating Boston on its home court. Philadelphia also needed Andrew Toney to recover his rhythm. Hours after the previous game, Maurice Cheeks had stopped by Toney's house to deliver a direct message: relax, forget about the past, come out firing. An off-night never rattled Toney.

A clutch performer, he'd averaged 16.5 points per game for the season, but against Boston, that number soared to 25.2. The bigger the stage, the more Toney rose to the occasion. "There's not many players that the NBA doesn't have an answer for," Celtics center Robert Parish said. "Andrew Toney was one of them. You've never seen anything like Andrew Toney. Nobody had an answer for him. I called him a B-I-T-C-H. He was a *bitch* of a cover." Cedric Maxwell claimed that Celtics guards used to pore over game tape, studying Toney's footwork for any clues on how to stop him. "Then they'd get to the game," Maxwell said, "and none of that shit worked."

In Game Seven, Toney demonstrated how much the center of gravity was shifting for Philadelphia. The Sixers remained, in spirit and in character, Erving's club. He arranged team meetings, he set the locker-room tone, he acted as player spokesperson. Yet in crunch time, the ball bypassed his fingers more and more. Once able to improvise at will, Erving, his knees sheathed in gray wrappings, had had to make concessions about what was still possible physically. "Before," Erving said, "I would just do something without ever planning it. Then afterward I would analyze it. Now, sometimes I find myself thinking about a particular move *before* I execute it. I think about it first and then I do it." Increasingly it was Toney who broke plays when his instincts dictated, who demanded the ball as the clock expired. That afternoon, the two directed the offense jointly, combining for sixty-three points: thirty-four for Toney, twenty-nine for Erving. So clutch was Toney that a nickname was passed on: the Boston Strangler.

Even as the Sixers opened up a twelve-point lead after three quarters, the crowd's faith in nail-biting finishes breaking Boston's way never waned. This time, however, they waited in vain for Philadelphia's nerves to fray. "We were overconfident," Cedric Maxwell admitted. "We were certain the same thing as last year was going to happen. But the Sixers didn't get the memo." When it became apparent that the Sixers weren't going to choke, Celtics fans swallowed their pride and paid tribute to their long-suffering rivals, chanting in the game's final minute, "Beat L.A.! Beat L.A.!"

Following his team's 120–106 win, Billy Cunningham, true to his word, came out swinging in the postgame press conference. "I'm going to be real quick," he said. "I only have two things to say. Number one, I want to thank the Celtics' fans for the way they responded at the end, because it was a real show of class. Number two, I'm ecstatic for the twelve [Sixers players] and the coaches, and that's it. Everyone else buried us. Period. Goodbye. That's it for me, babe. I've had enough of you guys."

Bobby Jones, the most upstanding player in the league, was waiting for Cunningham at the clubhouse door. "Did you do it?" Jones asked. Cunningham laughed. "Of all the people in the world you think of," he said decades later, "[Jones] was so proud of exactly what I said."

Meditative and cool, Erving took the long view. Still, bits of anger seeped through. "It's been like a six-year chase," he said. "I think all too often it's gotten taken out of normal perspective and put in abnormal perspective. For every person who can be content with the success we've had, there's another ten who can't feel it and can't feel good about all we've done until the last hurdle is cleared.

"So it has become," Erving concluded, "sort of a haunting situation."

After the emotional high of what Julius Erving deemed the most important game of his career, there was nowhere to go but down. "In 1982, we got so caught up in beating Boston," Sixers backup center Earl Cureton said. "And when we finally did, I think that we took a breath. It almost felt like we'd won the championship, but then we still had to play another series against the Lakers. It was a letdown."

These were not the same Los Angeles Lakers that had fumbled a best-of-three series to the Houston Rockets. Their season had gotten off to a shaky start when head coach Paul Westhead had once again insisted on slowing the offensive pace in favor of halfcourt sets centered on Kareem Abdul-Jabbar. Caged in and fed up, Magic Johnson soon demanded a trade. Within three weeks, Westhead was replaced by a former Lakers benchwarmer named Pat Riley. Slick-haired and high-strung, smeared in gel and cologne, Riley shifted the Lakers offense into high gear, swapping unhurried post-ups for a fast break that whooshed downcourt like a tidal wave. "There were times when the ball never touched the floor," sportswriter Steve Springer recalled. "They passed it from one end to the other, and they ran and ran and ran. They just went."

Hardly breaking a sweat, the Lakers skated through the anemic Western Conference. They swept the Phoenix Suns and the San Antonio Spurs, then indulged in nearly two weeks of rest while waiting for their Eastern Conference counterparts to wrap up their prolonged slugfest. The Sixers staggered into the NBA Finals physically and emotionally spent, having played almost twice as many playoff games as the Lakers. No team had ever come out of the postseason undefeated. The way the Lakers were rolling, their sights were set on making history.

Before the opening game on May 27, Sixers fans, as penance for abandoning the club against Boston, decorated the Spectrum with signs that read "Oh Ye of Little Faith" and "Past 5 Years Best Record, You Owe Us Nothing." At tipoff, both teams burst from the starting blocks. "Cattle stampedes," Bill Lyon wrote in *The Philadelphia Inquirer*, "have been conducted at a more leisurely pace." By the third quarter, the 76ers had sprinted to a fifteen-point advantage. The Lakers snuffed it out by tearing through a 40–9 run. The Philadelphia crowd had remained on its best behavior all evening, bursting into applause on routine jumpers, but as the Sixers' comfortable lead vanished, fans could no longer suppress their natural tendencies. Once more, boos drowned out the cheers.

Not even a Sixers win in Game Two, behind twenty-four points and fourteen rebounds from Erving, could lend drama to the series. Over the next two contests in Southern California, the Lakers demolished the Sixers with such ease that Los Angeles fans, disappointed that they weren't witnessing Magic squaring off against Bird, started chanting, "We want Boston!" Again feeling disrespected and dismissed, the Sixers channeled their anger into a 135–102 blowout in Game Five—the worst defeat the Lakers had suffered in three years.

Game Six found both teams at their finest. The Sixers tumbled behind by nine at halftime but then roared to life when Erving strung together eight straight points at the start of the third quarter. Feisty yet overmatched, Philadelphia clawed to within three with four minutes left but couldn't get any closer. A season of angst and tumult wrapped up with a 114–104 loss. For the series, the Lakers grabbed thirty-four more rebounds than the Sixers, fourteen more in the final contest alone. "Rebounding, or the lack thereof," George Shirk wrote in *The Philadelphia Inquirer*, "has become such a perennial problem in Philadelphia that when a Sixers fan thinks of glass, he or she cringes by force of habit."

In the sixth game, Erving had thrown in thirty points, snatched eight rebounds, stolen five passes, and hounded the Lakers on defense. "There was Erving," columnist Bill Lyon wrote afterward, "the eternal Don Quixote in sneakers, all these years dunking over windmills and still without an NBA championship ring. The league's most noted astronaut, a driven man, somehow coaxed yet one more level of altitude out of his ouchy knees."

It was among his greatest performances, a valiant stab at beating back the forces of time and generational turnover. So there was some solace in knowing that if this was the last gasp of Erving-led squads vying for NBA titles, he was walking away from the Finals with his head held high.

Moments after the final buzzer, Erving was sitting zombielike in the visitors locker room. The exuberant sound of the Lakers' celebration seeped through the concrete wall that separated the Forum's two clubhouses. As the captain of the losing club, Erving knew what he had to do. Straight-faced, his sweat-drenched red uniform clinging to his slender frame, Erving set out toward the glowing exit sign. "It takes ten or fifteen seconds to get from one [clubhouse] to the other," one writer noted, "but when Julius Erving began the painful trek Tuesday night, he might as well have been walking from here to eternity."

On the other side of the wall, amid television cameras and network lights, uncorked bottles and champagne streams, everything appeared bright and rosy, as sunny as the Southern California weather. There, Erving performed the rituals expected of every superstar whose title aspirations had run aground: the rote handshakes, the strained smiles for tomorrow's front pages, the vigorous nods each time an opposing player murmured into his ear that a couple of lucky breaks here or there could've swung the series his way. Pat Riley recognized the anguish Erving must have felt. "When you lose in the Finals," Riley later said, "it takes a tremendous toll. You lose a little bit of your basketball life."

Erving fulfilled his obligations dispassionately. But then, upon returning to the Sixers' clubhouse, emotions that he'd kept buried through more than a decade of rigorous self-control bubbled up all at once.

Few realized that the detached calm Erving exhibited on and off the court—the coolness that was central to the Dr. J persona—had been born partly of personal tragedy. In the days leading up to the Finals, Erving had told reporters, "After my brother died, I cried for a year and then stopped crying." Through the highs and lows of a professional basketball career that had spanned states and leagues, Erving had never once shed a tear. As he'd said numerous times over the seasons, "I don't know what it would take to make me cry again."

Now he had his answer. Shuffling from locker to locker, attempting to console his teammates, Erving wept. So surprised were Sixers officials that they sealed off the room. Erving's sobs soon spread to everyone around him, from the executives to the coaching staff. When asked what had gone on behind those closed doors, Harold Katz said, "I kept thinking of Doc. The emotion..." He took a beat to collect himself. "To see grown men work their butts off and lose... There were tears in that locker room. I cried too, and I'm not ashamed to admit it."

After his emotions crested, Erving dried his eyes, then went out to face the media. "It hurt," Erving told them. "I feel much more disappointment this year than the other two times. I don't know why. But it's there." At several points during the press conference, Erving tried to bend the narrative in a more positive direction, but his heart didn't seem to be in it. "Maybe there will be a day," he said, "when all the victories are ours."

It was a hopeful line, but some writers noted that Erving spoke it wistfully, unconvincingly, as if trying to conjure a future that had already been lost. His tears betrayed a different truth: it was the last run. Undoubtedly, Erving's legs could withstand the grind for a few more seasons, but barring a revamp that would plug up the roster's holes, ones that would enable the Sixers to slay Bird and then Magic one after another, the Dr. J era was already fading away. More likely than not, Erving would exit professional basketball as the most consequential star never to win an NBA championship.

On and off the court, Julius "Dr. J" Erving was the picture of 1970s chic. (credit: © Associated Press)

Moses Malone won back-to-back Virginia state championships at Petersburg High School, turning him into the country's most sought-after prospect. (credit: © Associated Press)

Julius Erving's aerial artistry in the American Basketball Association legitimized playground moves in professional settings. (credit: © Walter Iooss Jr. / NBAE via Getty Images)

The first prep-to-pro basketall player, Moses Malone made an immediate mark through his signature skill: rebounding. (credit: © Bettmann via Getty Images)

Julius Erving soars from the free-throw line during the slam-dunk contest at the last ABA All-Star Game. (credit: © Carl Iwasaki / *Sports Illustrated* via Getty Images)

Julius Erving sits alongside Philadelphia 76ers owner Fitz Dixon at the press conference to announce his signing with the Sixers on October 21, 1976. (credit: © Bettmann via Getty Images)

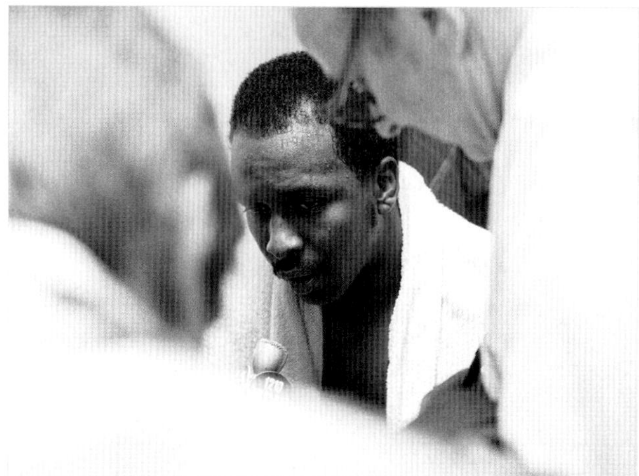

Moses Malone engaged in his least favorite activity: talking to the press. (credit: © James Drake via Getty Images)

The matchup between Julius Erving's Philadelphia 76ers and Bill Walton's Portland Trail Blazers in the 1977 NBA Finals was framed as a series that pitted two distinct styles and leagues against each other. (credit: © Associated Press)

Darryl Dawkins could shatter a backboard but struggled to snag rebounds off it. (credit: © Bettmann via Getty Images)

Sixers head coach Billy Cunningham strains to reach Andrew Toney, the team's brilliant, maddening shooting guard. (credit: © Focus on Sport via Getty Images)

No two teams were more evenly matched—or more bitterly opposed—in the early 1980s than the Philadelphia 76ers and the Boston Celtics. (credit: © Tony Tomsic / *Sports Illustrated* via Getty Images)

Even though the Houston Rockets finished the 1980–81 season below .500, Moses Malone powered the club to the NBA Finals. (credit: © Paul Kennedy / *Sports Illustrated* via Getty Images)

Harold Katz purchased the Philadelphia 76ers in July 1981. (credit: © Manny Millan / *Sports Illustrated* via Getty Images)

Moses Malone melded with Philadelphia sports fans from the start. (credit: © Manny Millan / *Sports Illustrated* via Getty Images)

Six years after the "We Owe You One" campaign, Julius Erving finally delivered a championship to Philadelphia in 1983. (credit: © Manny Millan / *Sports Illustrated* via Getty Images)

Billy Cunningham wipes the sweat off Moses Malone's brow as Julius Erving looks on after the Philadelphia 76ers swept the Los Angeles Lakers in the 1983 NBA Finals. (credit: © Associated Press)

PART III

MERGER

CHAPTER 14

THE UNANTICIPATED SUITOR

"I'm twenty-seven, my body is getting older, and I'm becoming a tired old man."

It was mid-June 1982, and Moses Malone was ruminating on his future. He was struck by a realization similar to the one that had brought Julius Erving to tears just a week earlier: a chapter in his basketball life was nearing its end.

Houston offered Malone comfort, relative anonymity, and ample spaces to practice his craft, but it demanded too much of him in exchange for too little. The production expected from Malone simply so that the Rockets could reach the playoffs was, he recognized, unsustainable. "I don't want to have to play for a team where I will have to carry most of the offense," he mused in a rare moment of public introspection. "I don't want to have to be the leading scorer every night. It would be real nice to get into a situation where I could play 35 to 38 minutes every night and have a good, solid backup center to come in and let me get a rest for 10 or 12 minutes."

Never before had an NBA player entered free agency on the heels of winning an MVP. The two previous recipients, Kareem Abdul-Jabbar and Julius Erving, both took home annual salaries that topped out at $1 million, the highest in the league. What Malone might command staggered the imagination. "Start the bidding at $3 million per season," *New York Times* sportswriter

Harvey Araton speculated. "Offer a house, a car, a garage, a television station, a trip to Saudi Arabia, all its oils. Raquel Welch. Beg. Weep." A bidding war between clubs in the nation's biggest media markets—the Los Angeles Lakers, the New York Knicks, and the New Jersey Nets—seemed certain to break out, which could bump Malone's multiyear contract into uncharted eight-figure territory.

Weeks after their brusque ejection from the playoffs, the Rockets had been sold to a local businessman named Charlie Thomas, who owned two dozen car dealerships across Houston. After having sunk more than $10 million into the purchase, Thomas was cautious about committing the same amount to a single player. There was a coldness to his approach, a distance that he maintained between himself and the star of his newly purchased franchise. "I never met him," Malone said of Thomas. "If he walked past me right now, I wouldn't know who he was. He never came to negotiations, always sent someone to represent him." The overall tenor of the talks did little to assuage Malone's ongoing concerns about the organization.

The opening bid that the Rockets put forth, around $1.7 million per year, was record-breaking but below what Malone's agent was seeking. Even though Malone declined it, the offer sent waves of panic through front offices across the league. Dismayed that the Rockets had established too high a floor right off the bat, several owners placed private calls to general manager Ray Patterson to urge restraint. They fretted that paying Malone close to $2 million would throw the NBA's salary structure off-kilter, leading to ever-escalating contracts that could topple several sputtering franchises. Already, the average NBA player took home $218,000 in annual pay, the highest in team sports despite the league's unsteady financial footing. Magic Johnson and Larry Bird had helped lift the fortunes of their respective clubs, but for almost every other franchise, yearly losses around $700,000 left owners questioning when enough was enough.

In 1982, the Philadelphia 76ers wound up roughly $1.5 million in the red, which forced Harold Katz to hike ticket prices by 45 percent for the following season. Never one to hold his tongue, Katz deemed Houston's introductory offer to Malone "absolutely crazy." Professional sports "is no different than running a grocery store. You have to have fiscal responsibility," Katz stated, adding, "So I think you're going to see less ridiculous salaries. Malone isn't going to get that $2 million everybody thought."

The collective bargaining agreement struck between the owners and the National Basketball Players Association in 1980 was due to expire during the upcoming season. Owners were girding for clashes over changes that they planned to push for, most notably the implementation of a salary cap that would establish a maximum payroll for each club. And they knew that forking over millions of dollars to a single player, even one as consistent and deserving as Malone, would undermine not only their bargaining position but also their overriding message about the urgency of curbing spiraling salaries.

Months passed; no other offers materialized. Big-market clubs kept their checkbooks sealed. As training camp loomed, Malone found himself bereft of options. A return to Houston at a price below what his pride could stomach seemed unavoidable.

But then, at the eleventh hour, an unanticipated suitor emerged.

Late in August 1982, Harold Katz phoned Billy Cunningham and posed a series of questions: "Would Moses help our team? Would he fit in?" Taken aback, Cunningham vouched for Malone's talent but doubted that Katz would follow through. This was, after all, the same big-talking owner who'd been a strident critic of the Rockets' negotiation tactics.

Panic changed his position. The Sixers roster, despite Katz's vow to shake it up, remained fundamentally unaltered by summer's end. His efforts to peddle Darryl Dawkins had come up empty. Fearful that the Sixers would lose one of their big men to free agency while getting little in return, Katz put his misgivings aside and signed Dawkins to a contract extension. But that didn't change Katz's desire to offload him. "General managers didn't want him. If you called a general manager and asked, 'How would you like a backup center who averages twelve points and ten rebounds?' they'd all say yes right away," Sixers forward Steve Mix said, exaggerating Dawkins's actual rebounding statistics. "But then you'd say, 'It's Darryl Dawkins,' and they'd say, 'No, no, not interested.'" It wasn't until late August that Philadelphia was able to pawn Dawkins off on the New Jersey Nets for a first-round draft pick.

In some ways, it was the end of an experiment. It'd been seven years since Dawkins and Bill Willoughby had followed Malone into the league out of high school; since then, both players had struggled to unlock their potential. A consensus emerged that Malone, who had once seemed the grand marshal of a parade of adolescents marching straight into the NBA, was singular, the lone prep-to-pro player to become a superstar. As a result, NBA franchises shied away from drafting high schoolers over the next two decades.

Whatever relief the Sixers might've felt in getting rid of Dawkins soon mutated to dread. It was late in the offseason, and the Sixers were down a player. In desperation, Katz began working the phones. He placed a personal call to San Diego Clippers owner Donald Sterling to request permission to speak with Bill Walton, whose agonizing foot injuries had limited him to fourteen games over the past four seasons. Katz also attempted to pry the rights to the second and third picks from that year's draft—Terry Cummings and Dominique Wilkins—from the clubs that were struggling to sign them. Nothing worked. Undersized already, the Sixers were careening into training camp with less height than before.

The week before Labor Day, Katz was vacationing at Lake Tahoe, unable to enjoy the scenery. Midway through, he phoned the team offices and, aware that general manager Pat Williams had set off to China with Julius Erving on a goodwill tour, asked to speak with assistant general manager John Nash. Katz's request was straightforward: find out whether Malone's return to the Rockets was a done deal.

The next morning, Lee Fentress informed Nash that while his client was still on the market, time was running short. During the first two weeks of September, several Nike-sponsored NBA players were taking off on a two-week trip to Europe, where they would play a slate of exhibition games against international competition. In the early 1980s, Malone wore Nike's new Air Force 1, its first sneaker to feature internal air cushioning. Hampered with the unenviable task of building a marketing campaign around a publicity-averse player, Nike coaxed Malone into donning a biblically inspired tan robe and clutching a staff resembling the company's signature swoosh. The resulting poster showed Malone, seashells and basketballs strewn about his feet, glaring unsmilingly at the camera while a hardwood gym parted like water around him. A single word was printed in stone letters at the bottom: MOSES.

Still a free agent, Malone had agreed to join Nike's traveling European road show. He was to depart Houston on Wednesday, September 1, making a brief stopover in New York City. If the Sixers were to make an offer before training camp started, that was where they would have to do so. The Sixers front office had a day to figure out its pitch to Malone and slap together what undoubtedly would add up to the most lucrative contract in team sports.

Like Katz, Billy Cunningham was on vacation, relaxing at Pinehurst Resort, a historic golf course in North Carolina. Unable to reach Cunningham directly, Nash called the pro shop there and begged someone to scour the course until they'd located the Sixers head coach. An hour or so later, Cunningham was measuring up his shot on the tenth tee when a worker bowling toward him in a golf cart interrupted his swing. After getting the message, Cunningham dropped his clubs, rushed back to his hotel room to pack, sped to the Raleigh-Durham airport, and caught a flight to Newark.

At 7 in the evening on September 1, Katz, Nash, Fentress, a bevy of lawyers, and Malone and his wife, Alfreda, huddled together at the Grand Hyatt hotel on Forty-Second Street in Manhattan. "We're all there except Billy," Nash remembered. "We're trying to cut the tension a little, but with each passing minute it's like 'Where the hell's Billy?'" Cunningham had requested to speak with Malone first to gauge his willingness to make sacrifices to fit in with the team, so negotiations couldn't commence until he'd shown up. An hour elapsed. Finally, the head coach burst in, agitated and blustery. "Do you know how much they want for a cab ride from Newark airport?" Cunningham ranted. Outraged at the $40 that taxi drivers were charging to Manhattan, Cunningham instead had boarded a slow-moving bus. The irrationality of his decision hit Cunningham hours later. "Wait a second," he thought, "I just took a freaking bus, and Moses is getting two million bucks?"

One-on-one, Cunningham grilled the foremost practitioner of Rocketball on whether he could adapt to the Philadelphia system. Running was central to the Sixers offense, Cunningham made clear, so if Malone couldn't keep pace, he'd struggle. "Hey, I'm no dummy," Malone replied, brushing aside the worry. "I like the easy buckets. The more fast breaks, the more easy buckets. All I want to do is win." The more pressing concern was one that Cunningham had experience with. His first season as head coach, he'd tried to manage two superstars, Julius Erving and George McGinnis, who'd continually stepped on each other's toes. Determined not to replay that drama, Cunningham asked point-blank whether Malone could defer to another MVP-caliber player. "This is Doc's team," Malone reportedly told Cunningham, in reference to Erving. "I'm just here to help Doc. Wanna get Doc a ring. This is his team, not Mo's."

Satisfied, Cunningham gave the thumbs-up to his boss. Negotiations began in earnest. Just as he'd done almost a decade before in Petersburg while listening to offers from competing college recruiters, Malone sat mostly in silence, poker-faced, his occasional low grumble throwing everyone off-balance. When he did chime in, Malone talked not of money but of winning, which only emboldened Katz to lavish millions on a player who spoke his language. Malone's lone stipulation about his salary was "No 'ferred"—a rational request from a former ABA star who would've known numerous players with sizable contracts built on deferred money who were still waiting for their back-end payments to materialize.

The discussions lurched past midnight. Lawyers scribbled out the parameters of an offer sheet longhand. Shortly after 2 in the morning, they'd reached an agreement: six years, $13.2 million, with a million-dollar signing bonus and a raft of incentive clauses that would augment Malone's base salary. The total was more than what Katz had shelled out for the entire Sixers organization a year earlier.

At 3:30 AM, the phone rang at assistant coach Jack McMahon's house. On the other end was Billy Cunningham. Dispensing with all pleasantries, Cunningham rattled off a list of current NBA stars. "If you could have any of those players," he asked, "which one would you pick?"

Groggy and irritated, McMahon didn't hesitate in responding, "Moses Malone."

"You got him," Cunningham said.

McMahon sat bolt upright in bed. "What?"

Malone, Cunningham informed him, had just signed an offer sheet with the Sixers. "Now go back to sleep," he said.

Wide awake, McMahon wandered down to his kitchen. There, he sat in a daze, drinking grapefruit juice while trying to wrap his mind around a starting lineup that melded the league's last two MVPs. McMahon knew as well as anyone else that overnight, the balance of power in the NBA had shifted.

At 7:30 the next morning, Moses Malone called his childhood friend David Mitchell, who was the morning-radio DJ at WSSV, a rhythm-and-blues station in Petersburg. "I just signed with the Philadelphia 76ers," he said. Malone had promised Mitchell the exclusive scoop when his free agency wrapped up, and now, moments before catching his flight to Europe, Malone wanted to make sure that Mitchell broadcast the signing before word leaked to larger media outlets.

The announcement, one Houston sportswriter claimed, "landed with all the impact of a safe being dropped from the 50th floor. There hasn't been such a stunner since a crazy sailor lit out from Europe in the late 1400s and returned home with a wild tale that the Earth wasn't really flat." To Charlie Thomas, the Houston Rockets owner—who, under the NBA's free-agency rules, would have fifteen days to match the 76ers' offer—the whole ordeal smacked of absurdity. "Christ, Ray," he reportedly told his general manager, Ray Patterson, "this is twelve million bucks for one guy. I just paid twelve million bucks for the whole goddamn franchise."

League executives, shocked and dismayed, accused Katz of skewing salaries so far in the players' direction that clubs struggling to mitigate their financial losses would find it impossible ever to turn a profit. Don Nelson, the head coach of the Milwaukee Bucks, questioned how small-market franchises could expect to compete with one that paid two players more than the entire payroll of his team's roster. Malone's proposed contract, an editorial in *The Sporting News* argued, would "push the NBA a bit closer to insolvency."

Katz batted away their criticisms. His desire to deliver a championship to Philadelphia during whatever remained of Julius Erving's prime trumped his loyalty to his fellow owners and their fiscal concerns. "I know there are people who will say a deal like this isn't in the best interests of the NBA," Katz said. "But it is certainly in the best interests of the 76ers."

Fleeing the publicity storm, Malone hopped the Concorde to Europe, where he met up with a squad that included Sixers forward Bobby Jones, a fellow Nike signee. It was a whirlwind tour. During one stretch, they played an exhibition contest in Amsterdam, then drove to Germany. The cramped bus ride left them sore-legged before their next game the following afternoon. As Jones and Malone positioned themselves at center court for tipoff, one of the German players uttered an unmistakable racial slur in his native tongue. "I looked at Moses, and he just lit up," Jones recalled. "I mean, his eyes were just fierce when he heard that. And he had, I don't know, thirty-five points and probably twenty-five rebounds. He just turned those guys inside out."

Stateside, the Rockets were coming to terms with losing the player who'd given their franchise credibility. Philadelphia's offer had been structured in a calculated way. For one, it eschewed deferred payments altogether, requiring the Rockets to cough up an enormous wad of cash up front. In addition, the Sixers crafted a number of incentive clauses based on attendance, performance, and playoff appearances that, should the Rockets choose to match them, would inflict ongoing financial pain on an organization historically beset by ownership churn.

Instead of fighting to keep the reigning MVP, the Rockets turned their attention to wresting a prize from the Sixers as compensation. Years earlier, in 1977, the 76ers had swapped a seldom-used shooting guard named Terry Furlow to the Cleveland Cavaliers for two future first-round draft picks. Since then, the Cavaliers had fallen on hard times, stumbling through the 1981–82 season with a league-worst 15–67 record. Barring a miraculous turnaround, the Cavaliers seemed likely to flounder the upcoming year as well, giving the holder of the upcoming pick a good shot at selecting high in the following draft. Graduating in 1983 was a seven-foot-four senior from the University of Virginia whose length, elasticity, and soft shooting touch had set basketball scouts' imaginations on fire. Losing Malone would sting, but if the Rockets could better position themselves to gain Ralph Sampson—such a game changer that Sampson's likeness graced the cover of *Sports Illustrated* five times while he was still in college—then they believed that they could come out ahead in the long run.

On September 14, 1982, the day before the Rockets' deadline for matching the Sixers' offer, Katz flew out to Houston to meet with Thomas at his spacious home in the ritzy River Oaks District. Over dinner, Katz badgered and sweet-talked Thomas, but the Rockets owner held firm, insisting that the 76ers would have to surrender the first-round draft pick and defensive specialist Caldwell Jones. "If we didn't get what we wanted," Thomas later stated, "we were going to match their offer and sign Moses." Katz jetted back to Philadelphia, stewed for an afternoon, then agreed to Houston's terms.

In praising the deal, Thomas reframed the Malone era as a whole. No longer was it a time of overachievement fueled by the superhuman efforts of a player who'd given the franchise its first taste of national relevance. Instead, Thomas cast it as a period of frustration, when a limited, lead-footed star had struggled to elevate his club into the league's upper ranks. "With Malone, we were going to be a good team, but never a great one," Thomas claimed. "We were going to win 46 or 47 games and be locked into that position. That's not what we want for our fans. We want a team which will grow and prosper and eventually win 59 or 60 games. The Cleveland pick is what really made the deal."

The rift between Malone and the Rockets had become unbreachable. For months afterward, Malone's rage at his former franchise continued to simmer. "Somebody [on the Rockets] should have called Moses," he grumbled. "Somebody should have said, 'You gave us six good years.' But nobody showed [me respect]."

On September 15, 1982, Tim Malloy, the Sixers' assistant group sales director, picked up Malone at the Philadelphia airport and then drove him to the 76ers' offices at Veterans Stadium. Following a quick medical examination and the formal signing of the contract, Katz handed his newest player a bonus check for $1 million. Holding it above his head, Malone beamed. "Have you ever seen anything this beautiful?"

In a crowded storage room beneath the stadium, the team held a hastily assembled press conference. Underdressed per usual, Malone faced the media clad in jeans and a plain brown shirt. Relieved to be casting free agency aside, he answered questions loosely, his laconic responses barbed with dry wit and down-to-earth declarations. When asked about playing alongside Julius Erving, Malone shrugged. "Doc'll still be the show," he said, "but maybe now it'll be a better show." Another reporter solicited his thoughts on the recently traded Darryl Dawkins. "He's got a lot of talent," Malone asserted. "We're both in the same class. I just work harder than Darryl." Inevitably, the talk turned to his unprecedented salary, and Malone, slipping into third person, didn't flinch. "They wouldn't have paid Moses the money if they didn't think Moses was worth it."

Afterward, Malone and Malloy ventured back into the parking lot. It was early evening, the sun just starting to set, and Veterans Stadium was preparing to host a hotly contested Major League Baseball game between the Philadelphia Phillies and the St. Louis Cardinals, two clubs battling for control of the National League East. Hundreds of baseball fans streaming toward the stadium spotted the oversized basketball player stuffing himself into Malloy's compact Toyota Corolla hatchback. Surrounding the vehicle, they pounded on the hood, attempted to wriggle their fingers through the windows, and chanted, "Moses! Moses! Moses!"

For someone who'd sworn time and again that he valued his anonymity in southeast Texas, Malone appeared to revel in the recognition. Lugging a losing club all the way to the NBA Finals hadn't earned him the contract extension he'd sought from the Rockets front office, nor had two MVP awards in four seasons quieted the whispers that Malone was one-dimensional, that he couldn't run, that he'd forced the Rockets to play ugly, that his dominance didn't translate to wins. "Good for you, Charlie Thomas," a column in the *Houston Post* declared. "You realized that it was asinine to pay one employee $2 million a year just so the team could win 45 games and qualify for the playoffs." But there, amid baseball fans who greeted the incoming basketball star with naked adoration, Malone grinned in spite of himself. It was the first time in a long while that he had felt wanted.

Rolling inch by inch through the crowd, Malloy maneuvered out of the parking lot and into the city. As the stadium receded from view, Malone was still shaking his head over how different his life was destined to be in Philadelphia. As Malone revealed to Malloy on the way back to the airport, "I could walk down the streets of Houston at noon, and nobody'd turn his head for me."

CHAPTER 15

PERFECTLY MISMATCHED

When the Philadelphia 76ers gathered at Franklin & Marshall College in Lancaster, Pennsylvania, for training camp before the 1982–83 season, they saw at once that Harold Katz's pledge to overhaul the roster hadn't been bluster. Six members of the previous year's squad, including both centers, had departed. To some, it seemed as if the front office had plowed every last cent into the league's reigning MVP, then swapped pricey veterans for cheap newcomers. "Four rookies and *five* new faces," Julius Erving murmured. "This is not a situation we want to face every year." Even Pat Williams, the general manager who'd orchestrated the transactions, wondered if they'd sliced the roster too close to the bone. "Four rookies are the most rookies ever to play on this club in history. We just have to throw them out there, and this baby will be born."

Moses Malone's arrival calmed everyone's nerves. Following a summer of swimming, skipping rope, and holding court at Fonde Recreation Center against the likes of Hakeem Olajuwon (then known as Akeem)—a seven-foot sophomore from the University of Houston who would credit Malone with toughening him up—he showed up in midseason form and got right down to work. As he told the press, "Moses will take a day, shake all the players' hands, get to know them, then go play ball." It was exactly what Billy

Cunningham needed from him. "The players were not ecstatic, losing friends—Caldwell Jones and Darryl Dawkins—and being so close in the Finals," Cunningham recalled. "But all it took was one practice really, and then they realized why we had made the moves we made."

Katz, clad from head to toe in a blue warmup suit, watched the drills from the bleachers. At one point, spotting the owner who'd brought him east, Malone jogged to the sidelines. Casually, as if relaying a bit of gossip, Malone told him, "We are going to win seventy games." Smiling, Katz took a drag on his cigarette. He was a gambler by nature, someone who relished jetting to Las Vegas for weekend splurges among the high rollers. And the way that Malone's intensity rubbed off instantly on his new teammates reassured Katz that his extravagant offseason bet had been well-placed.

To ward off the power struggles that had downed the George McGinnis–Julius Erving pairing, harmony would need to be established between Malone and the team's undisputed leader. "The thing that helped us the most was when Moses did an interview [at the initial press conference]," backup point guard Franklin Edwards said. "He talked about it being Julius's team and he was happy to be part of it. Everybody loved that. He killed all the talk of ego and whose team it was." Malone carried through with his promise from the opening practice. "Moses didn't have that attitude of 'I'm the man,' as he could have," remembered Russ Schoene, the Sixers' second-round draft pick. "Right away, Moses deferred to Doc. He let Doc lead. He just came in and did what he does, which is all the dirty work."

Even so, Erving felt a sense of loss. His longtime roommate on the road, Steve Mix, was gone, as was everyone else over thirty except Bobby Jones. At one point, Erving turned to Maurice Cheeks and mused, "Where have all our comrades gone?" One player was particularly missed. On a club rife with ego, Caldwell

Jones, a wiry center, had uncomplainingly shouldered the thankless yet essential tasks that won games. Since joining the Sixers in 1976, Jones had scored twenty or more points just four times in the regular season, despite the fact that he'd averaged a shade below that number in his second year in the ABA. "Caldwell was a sacrificial player," Erving said, adding, "He knew what he had to do: just be consistent night in and night out." After games, Jones would crack open a beer and unwind, far from the media scrums that formed around his more famous teammates. Though he seldom generated headlines, players across the league understood his value.

That included Malone. He'd played alongside Jones during his half-season stint on the Spirits of St. Louis years earlier. The two had bonded to such an extent that Major Jones, the Houston Rockets forward and Caldwell's brother, said that Malone became part of their family. When Malone called Major Jones to inform him that he was leaving Houston for Philadelphia, he quipped, "If I can't play with one Jones, I'll go play with the other." Upon finding out that Caldwell Jones was to be shipped to Houston as compensation, Malone almost backed out of the deal. "One of the reasons I came here is to play with Caldwell," he told Pat Williams. "And if he's not gonna be here, then I'm not sure I'm gonna do this." It took a call from Katz to talk Malone down from the ledge.

Erving mourned the loss of Caldwell Jones for deeper reasons. "What I had wanted was to have Caldwell with us when we accomplished our goal," he said days before the season opened. "With CJ, Moses, Bobby [Jones], and me, we'd have had four guys from the old ABA, fulfilling a fantasy, making a dream come true for the red-white-and-blue ball we used to use. I saw us as four old warriors." Malone, too, had turned reflective about the defunct league that had given him his start. "I used to watch the NBA when I was in the ABA," he said. "I never thought the NBA was that exciting. They used to walk the ball down all the time. In the ABA, we used to run the ball down all the time, dunk and showboat. We used to give people their money's worth. In the NBA, they used to bring the ball down, run patterned plays. Then, once the two leagues merged, seemed like everybody in the NBA had to dunk."

This was the start of Erving's and Malone's seventh season in the NBA. The number of active players who'd paid their dues in the ABA had dwindled. Time was running out for them to realize their dream of redemption for a league that had given so much to the NBA—its iconic players, its three-point shot, its playground ethos—yet received so little recognition in return.

For New Yorkers with a nose for drama, the regular-season debut of the most handsomely compensated athlete to dribble a basketball was unmissable. Knicks fans swelled Madison Square Garden to standing-room-only capacity on Opening Day against the Sixers. Malone refused to get swept up in the moment. Pressed for comments before tipoff, he snapped, "No interviews."

His response set the tone for the evening. There were no fireworks, no jaw-dropping moves, no theater to speak of. The fans who'd scrambled for tickets filed out hours later feeling mildly disappointed, as much in the Knicks' fifteen-point loss as in Malone's workmanlike performance. True, Malone had tallied twenty-one points and seventeen rebounds, but those numbers seemed to have piled up almost by default, as surely as water flowing downstream. Even Malone himself was underwhelmed. "I'm only a human being," he told reporters. "I can't get all the boards. The ball didn't bounce right all the time." Malone's apologetic words raised eyebrows in the media. "Seventeen rebounds would have prompted Darryl Dawkins to rename an entire solar system," 76ers beat writer Mark Whicker joked. But Malone saw little reason to celebrate.

"Seventeen boards is all right," he said. "But when I get my mind right and I get used to our players' shots and learn the other teams, I will start rebounding better."

Julius Erving had predicted that Philadelphia's remade roster wouldn't cohere until Christmas. Instead, the Sixers burst from the gates with four straight double-digit wins. In Boston, the Celtics, too, breezed through the season's opening week. The first clash between them came early, on November 6. Even newbies to basketball's oldest rivalry felt the tension. "On the court, Boston and Philadelphia hate the hell out of each other," Sixers rookie Marc Iavaroni sensed.

Years of accumulating his own baggage in Boston ensured that Malone would be a quick study in adopting the proper Philadelphian attitude. In his first game as part of the rivalry, he muscled in twenty-eight points and pulled down nineteen rebounds while playing fifty-six of the fifty-eight possible minutes. Down five at the start of the fourth quarter, the Sixers rallied for a bruising four-point victory in double overtime. It was an early sign that Philadelphia's reputation for choking in close games was under revision.

A win against Larry Bird's Celtics under their belt, the Sixers sought to test their mettle against Magic Johnson's Lakers. They steamed into Southern California on December 5 with the remedy to Showtime in tow: someone capable of shutting down Kareem Abdul-Jabbar in the post while simultaneously curbing Johnson's freedom to bust loose on fast breaks.

That night, Malone grabbed fourteen rebounds—seven offensive, seven defensive—while bullying Kareem Abdul-Jabbar away from the basket. Battered and tormented, Abdul-Jabbar wound up accruing more turnovers (four) than rebounds (two). By controlling the boards, even if by tipping balls out of opponents' hands, Malone stymied the Lakers' ability to streak to the other end for easy baskets. He also kept the Sixers afloat when their offense stalled in the halfcourt. On consecutive plays down the stretch, Andrew Toney bricked a deep jumper and Julius Erving botched a finger roll. In past seasons, these misses would've tightened the Sixers up. This time, warding off any glimmer of a Lakers comeback, Malone converted both into putback buckets. The Sixers held on for a 114–104 victory, swelling their record to 16–3.

Lakers head coach Pat Riley sensed that this was more than a loss. The advantages that his club had held over the Sixers in two of the past three Finals had been wiped out by one free-agent signing. Malone, Riley declared, was "the missing link that [the Sixers] have been looking for," a one-man solution to the team's choking dilemma.

Later that night, long past midnight, Billy Cunningham was loitering in the lobby of the Sixers' hotel. Sleep was the furthest thing from his mind. Cunningham appeared, in one reporter's eyes, "stunned. Shellshocked. Overwhelmed." For once, it wasn't because his players had blown a winnable game. It was because they hadn't.

Turning to a nearby reporter, Cunningham asked how well his team had shot against the Lakers.

"Fifty percent" came the reply. He was also informed that the Sixers had hit 44 percent of their shots against the Phoenix Suns three days earlier and 49 percent against the San Diego Clippers the day after—all comfortable road wins.

Reclining in his chair, Cunningham wagged his head in disbelief. "You know," he said, "last year, to beat the Lakers or the Suns, or to win in San Diego, even, we'd have had to shoot up around 60 percent."

Through twenty games, the Sixers found themselves miles ahead of where they'd been at the same point the season before. They'd bumped their scoring average up from 107 to 117 points and their rebounds from 42 to 50 per game. Their offensive rebounding alone had increased by a whopping 60 percent. That particular evening, the Sixers had attempted 102 field goals against the Lakers, the fifth time that month they'd crossed the triple-digit mark in shots launched over forty-eight minutes. The previous year, they'd hit that number once.

Dumbfounded, Cunningham murmured to no one in particular, "It's amazing what we can do with Moses."

It was amazing, too, what they could continue to do with Dr. J.

One month later, on January 5, 1983, in their second regular-season encounter, Philadelphia battled Los Angeles to a draw through four quarters. Late in the game, with the Sixers ahead by a bucket, Maurice Cheeks deflected a lazy pass from Lakers rookie James Worthy. The ball squirted loose to Erving, who batted it beyond the quick hands of defensive specialist Michael Cooper. Gaining control at halfcourt, Erving dribbled twice, cradled the ball in his right hand, rocked it from side to side like a discus thrower limbering up for a toss, and then left his feet at the exact second that Cooper caught up to him. Orbiting the ball around his body, Erving threw down a dunk so forceful that Cooper ducked in self-defense. The sellout crowd at the Spectrum spilled into the aisles and onto the court. Seven seasons into his Sixers tenure, Erving still was unveiling moves they'd never seen.

That evening, they resembled the Sixers of old, aerial acrobatics and all. While Malone cobbled together his standard twenty-one points and fifteen rebounds, foul trouble and a season-high nine turnovers blunted his effectiveness. Instead, the Sixers leaned on a familiar duo, Erving and Andrew Toney, who combined for fifty-five points, including Toney's game-winning jumper as the clock ticked down in overtime.

Two victories over their Finals adversary through two opposing styles of play—that was the versatility and effectiveness of the Erving-Malone pairing. In past seasons, when Erving's speed game had sputtered, the Sixers had faltered. Now, with Malone under the basket, they could match opponents blow for blow in the halfcourt as well. It was this blend of finesse and force, flow and grind, streetball and Rocketball, that not only unlocked new levels for the Sixers but also evened out the burdens that each superstar shouldered. No longer required to rescue the Rockets game after game, Malone had more time to get acquainted with the bench during blowouts. "I'm a so much better player now with Philadelphia than I was with Houston because I'm not playing all those minutes," Malone asserted. Erving felt the same way: "There are times for stepping back and letting someone else do it. I always felt I had to step in there and make it happen. Now, sometimes, the best thing is to get out of the way."

Together, as if on opposite ends of a seesaw, Erving and Malone balanced each other out. "I might be more of a perfectionist," Erving said of the differences between the two. "Moses keeps batting at the ball until he gets it in. I'm looking for that one perfect play." The transcendence that Erving chased could lead to flashes of visual splendor but also left his team vulnerable to physical clubs that bullied them inside. Malone, in contrast, had little interest in transcendence or perfection or beauty. "I ain't out there to look pretty," he explained. And it was this attitude that reoriented a roster once renowned for elegance and speed, inverting the aesthetics of what Sixers basketball had been since Dr. J arrived. "We used to be a pretty team that looked good winning games,"

Erving reflected. "Now we win games without looking that good. If we put together a perfect game we probably still wouldn't look good, because we have an imperfect approach to playing. Bodies are flying all over the place out there."

As dissimilar as Erving and Malone were on the court, their differences were even more pronounced off it. In the locker room, Erving cut a regal figure. He was someone whose likeness the younger members of the roster likely had had pinned to the walls of their college dormitories. When backup center Earl Cureton found out that the Sixers had drafted him, "I was in heaven—the chance to play with the person I idolized," he said. "My entire generation idolized Doc." It was that exact attitude that, to some degree, ended up separating Erving from his teammates. "The other players on the team always felt like they had to control themselves when Doc was around," claimed Charles Barkley, who would join the Sixers in 1984. "Around Julius," he continued, "you felt you had to. No practical jokes. No craziness. No loud arguments or fooling around. Nothing. Not around Doc."

For rookies in particular, meeting Erving was akin to being in the presence of a higher power. Seemingly aware of these dynamics, Erving went out of his way to connect with newcomers. In his first training camp with the Sixers, Franklin Edwards received a surprise invitation to Erving's house. The private dinner had a dual purpose. For Edwards, it "made Julius more into a person than an object." For Erving, it gave him the opportunity to humanize himself in front of a first-round draft pick who would need to get past his sense of awe for them to work together. As Edwards stated decades later, "I thought [the dinner] was more for him than for me."

Along similar lines, Russ Schoene received an unexpected summons to the empty seat next to Erving on one of his first flights with the Sixers during the preseason in 1982. Seeking common ground with an unheralded draft pick who'd attended a mid-major college, Erving opened the conversation by saying, "You remind me a lot of myself at this stage." It was too much for Schoene to process. The rookie's mind went blank for the remainder of the trip. Despite Erving's best intentions, Schoene's sense of awe remained intact. Overall, Schoene characterized Erving as the roster's older brother. "He looked after the young guys. He wasn't aloof, but he didn't have that 'come on and chat me up any time you want' persona."

Schoene's introduction to Malone was markedly different. Instead of a formal request for a private get-together, Malone roped Schoene and the team's other rookies and bench players into sticking around after practice. Malone, Schoene stated, "would be out there picking teams and talking trash to rookies and having fun. He had a smile on his face. He was laughing. Didn't matter who he was playing against. He was out to win those pickup games." After a while the rookies grew tired, but Malone kept going, cajoling coaches into low-stakes rounds of HORSE. "Here he's making $25,000 a game and I'm making that per year," said John Kilbourne, the Sixers conditioning coach. "I would always lose. We gambled about who would buy lunch, and I can't even count how many times I bought lunch for him, the millionaire player."

In the sanctuary of the clubhouse, Malone was one of the guys. Marc Iavaroni had fond memories of Malone and Toney, the two least effusive Sixers in public, ribbing each other back and forth in increasingly bombastic language. After games, Malone sometimes accompanied teammates to local nightspots, staying out late. Former teammate Steve Green recalled a night out with Malone in Louisville, Kentucky. "Moses was known as a man of few words, but I'm gonna tell you, when he was around the ladies at the disco that night, he was Shakespeare." Franklin Edwards, who would refer to Malone as his best friend in basketball, tried and failed to keep up with his more decorated teammate. "His body was built differently," Edwards said. "We'd be out until one in the morning, and he'd want to keep going. He'd get five hours of sleep and could play the next day."

Erving too maintained a fast pace that others would've buckled under. "So many other things are happening in my life, personally, professionally, in my family life," he said that season. "There aren't enough hours to get it all done." Unable to participate in Malone's postpractice pickup games, Erving quickly changed from gym clothes to executive attire. At his sparsely furnished office in a sleek high-rise in downtown Philadelphia, he sifted through whatever paperwork had piled up at the newly renamed Dr. J Enterprises. There were deals to cut, speeches to deliver, public-service announcements to film. At times, the line between CEO and player blurred. Once, Fred Maglione, the Sixers sales and marketing director, was having trouble wooing a potential client. Word spread to Erving, who subsequently instructed Maglione to invite his client to dinner at Erving's house the following Friday, an off-night for the club. Having learned that their guests were Jewish, Erving's wife, Turquoise, whipped up a spread of brisket and kugel, a bottle of kosher wine on hand to wash it all down. The client soon signed on with the Sixers.

Malone also could be generous with his time and money, albeit more on an individual level. Numerous players spoke fondly of Malone's bigheartedness behind the scenes. Ron Boone claimed that when his wife passed away, Malone was among the first to call and offer condolences. Harvey Catchings said that when Malone was offered a lump sum to attend a basketball camp, he'd convince the organizers to invite retired players who Malone knew were hard up for cash and then distribute a portion of his fee to them. Bobby

Jones remembered calling Malone to gauge his interest in joining a Bible study group and getting only a grunt in return. Later, when one of their teammates started cursing in the locker room, Malone marched over and, aware of Jones's sensitivities, warned him not to use the Lord's name in vain again. Calvin Murphy, the Rockets point guard who doubled in the offseason as a renowned baton twirler, once set out to raise $3,000 so that his twirling group could compete in a national competition. At a fundraising dinner in Houston, Malone showed up unannounced, shoved a wad of cash into Murphy's hands, then disappeared before Murphy could announce his presence. Even members of the Sixers front office vouched for his affability. Fred Maglione recalled Malone swinging by his office to chat. "I was always petrified," Maglione said, "because I said one day, he's gonna come in and tell me that his mother died and I'm just going to giggle and laugh and say, 'That's nice.' I couldn't understand a word he said."

Every NBA player was contractually obligated to make at least four public-service appearances over the course of the season. Erving made more than two dozen in 1982–83. Malone made zero. League-wide stipulations couldn't force Malone to do something he had no interest in. Not even Erving could corral him. At several points, Erving extended a courteous dinner invitation that no other newcomer would have dared turn down. Each time, Malone declined. There was no rift or animosity between them. They simply were two men whose temperaments and priorities were even more divergent than their playing styles.

Malone was relentlessly present on the court, enigmatically wayward off it. Sixers teammate Mark McNamara claimed that Malone drove a car the way he played basketball, hurtling over curbs, snowdrifts, and speed bumps. He was someone who trained his eyes squarely on his job, speeding through all other obstacles that littered his path.

As the Sixers evolved, so did the city's politics. The 1982–83 season took place against the backdrop of a mayoral race whose Democratic primary pitted W. Wilson Goode, a tenant farmer's son–turned–public administrator aspiring to become the first Black Philadelphian to run the city, against Frank Rizzo, the former mayor now running for a third term. The primary was to take place on May 18, 1983, the same week that the NBA Finals were to begin. The timing seemed only fitting since, on some level, the divisions between the two candidates' bases found a faint echo in the divisions between the Sixers' two stars.

W. Wilson Goode subscribed to the same crossover ideology that Julius Erving had exemplified since blowing into Philadelphia. The mid-'70s had been an era, in Erving's words, of "tremendous racial separation," one where "the Fishtowners stayed in Fishtown, Germantowners in Germantown, South Philadelphians in South Philly. You could see the city composed of different pockets of self-interest, and no one was looking out for the whole. I saw this, and my goal was to move about with freedom and respect in all different communities." The same goal would animate Goode's campaign, which aimed to cobble together a diverse coalition by cribbing from Erving's playbook. In public, Wilson donned dark three-piece suits. In stump speeches, he sidestepped divisive rhetoric while waxing eloquent about his administrative accomplishments. Onstage, he declined to appear alongside Black activists whom some might construe as polarizing. It was all part of crafting an image that might register as nonthreatening to the white ethnic enclaves that had been receptive to Rizzo's persona but had grown weary of his divisiveness. Through outreach, acquiescence, and assiduous self-control, Goode managed to peel off 30 percent of the primary's white voters while holding on to an astonishing 97 percent of the Black vote.

While Goode and Erving achieved overwhelming crossover success, it came at a cost. The thin line they had to tread to maintain broad appeal often had the inadvertent effect of flattening them into one-dimensional paragons of humility, patience, and propriety. When Rizzo stoked racial resentments, white audiences by and large chalked it up to him being unafraid of telling it like it is. To his supporters, his crudeness and incendiary rhetoric often came across as "authentic," the unvarnished vernacular of a blue-collar ex-cop who refused to be bound by formal political speech. This sort of verbal freedom was unthinkable to Goode, who remained forever vigilant of language that might be interpreted as inflammatory. Erving, too, perfected the art of speaking often but revealing little, so much so that a reporter once interrupted one of his typical postgame soliloquies with the line "Hold that cliché, Doc. I'll be right back." Both men seemed to be visualizing their words in print the second they were spoken. As a result, there was a discernible distance between them and their audience, a barrier between the person and the model-minority veneer. "You didn't have people saying they loved Wilson Goode," one political consultant said during the Democratic primary. "But nobody hated him either."

It was a conundrum that Erving could relate to. Neither MVP awards nor Finals appearances did much to boost the Sixers' anemic home attendance. To some extent, the very qualities that engendered endless admiration for Erving—his grace, his creativity, his courtliness, his artistry—hindered him from burrowing wholly into the city's hot-blooded heart. The reasons seemed to have more to do with Philadelphia fandom than with Erving himself. "In Philly," Mike Schmidt, the transcendent third baseman for the Philadelphia Phillies, explained, "they want a brawler, they want a guy who doesn't wipe the dirt off, who looks like he's having a tough time getting it done." More than sheer excellence,

Philadelphia rewarded effort. It coveted athletes who, if everything went south, could dust themselves off and seek employment on an assembly line the next week. These were up-by-the-bootstraps scrappers like Pete Rose on the Phillies, Bobby Clarke on the Flyers, and, most notably, Rocky Balboa at the movies.

Released in 1976, a year after Rizzo's landslide mayoral reelection, *Rocky* was a cinematic fairy tale set in Kensington, one of the working-class Philadelphia neighborhoods that had fueled Rizzo's rise. It centered on Rocky Balboa, a down-on-his-luck Italian American boxer who was offered a surprise shot at the heavyweight championship. His opponent, Apollo Creed, was Balboa's reverse image: flamboyant, entitled, and, crucially, Black. While Balboa socked frozen cow carcasses in a meatpacking plant, Creed tended to his financial interests. The optics weren't subtle: here was a white ethnic striver rooted in blue-collar values—the spitting image of how Rizzo's core base conceived of themselves—squaring off against a Black showboat so dismissive of his opponent that he hadn't even bothered to train. On the night of their bout, Creed strutted into the ring festooned in garishly patriotic garb. In a moment rife with symbolism, Balboa floored Creed with one punch shortly after the opening bell. Even though Balboa ended up losing on points after withstanding the full fifteen rounds, *Rocky* at its heart, according to historian Timothy J. Lombardo, "offered redemption to white ethnics who felt like they'd been on the losing end of the civil rights revolution."

Rocky underlined a sports truism of the era and beyond: whenever "blue collar" got bandied about in a sports context, odds were that the athletes in question were white. The term served as a racial code that reinforced the trope that Black athletes were naturally gifted, whereas white athletes earned their success through hard work and sound fundamentals. As much as anyone, it was Moses Malone who turned this belief inside out.

Proud and resilient, unwilling to cede even one missed shot, Malone was the epitome of the hardscrabble civic identity that Philadelphians idolized. His attitude was telegraphed through the boxer's mouthpiece that he slotted across his front teeth before games. "If I could wear a football helmet, I might do that, too," he quipped. His peers recognized his unique appeal for a city whose fandom was infamously moody and demanding. As Sonics center Jack Sikma remarked, "You can do a 360[-degree dunk] and so forth, and that's instant gratification, but over the years you'll see the Philly fans more enamored of Moses for how hard he plays than for how pretty he is."

Unlike Erving, who skated through the action so fluidly that he hardly seemed to break a sweat, half of Malone's body weight appeared to trickle off him every time he suited up. He sweated more each game than Erving appeared to in a season. Once, while nursing a minor injury, Malone requested that a stationary bike be placed on the sidelines during practice. For hours he pedaled, the sweat dripping off him so profusely that coaches had to spread towels across the floor to keep players from slipping. Pat Williams claimed that the Sixers hired an extra employee whose sole responsibility was toweling Malone's moisture off the court during games.

For Malone, sweat was a measuring stick of sorts. Alone at home, he sometimes popped game tapes into his VCR so that he could gauge his effort based on the perspiration draining from his pores. "I wanna see *tension* in my eyes, I wanna see me sweating and getting angry out there—and if I don't see that, it gets me mad," Malone told *Playboy* magazine. "If I look at a tape and see myself relaxing, or laughing and smiling during a game, I say, 'Heck, I ain't doing my work.'" Work was so central to Malone's conception of himself that he disdained the verb commonly used to describe what a basketball player did. "You can't just *play* this game," Malone sneered.

Few mistook Malone for an artist. He bore more of a resemblance to the various laborers—garbagemen, construction workers, plumbers—whose unsung drudgery kept their communities from collapsing. Sportswriters competed among themselves for who could stretch the comparison the furthest. "His factory is the basketball court, the foul line his mill," one wrote. "That's where you'll find him, grunting and sweating, hustling about his job. No clock watching, no thumb twiddling while the boss is away, no sloughing off the dirty work on someone else. Nosir, you sign Moses Malone on a job and you get a day's work at a day's pay."

It didn't take long for Philly fans to embrace Malone. Workers flashed their hard hats and uniforms to him on the street; well-to-do residents splurged on season tickets; casual fans gobbled up the nosebleed seats that had gone unfilled in past seasons. By the end of Malone's first month, the Sixers had matched their box-office haul from the entirety of the previous year. The turnaround was remarkable: a team that until recently couldn't give away tickets found itself among the league leaders in attendance.

Not even Malone's fat paychecks could dent his image. Yes, he was raking in millions, but Philly fans saw those dollars as hard-earned. Even Larry Bird, perhaps the league leader in "lunch-pail" paeans, told sportswriter Bob Ryan upon hearing of Malone's record-smashing contract, "That's the guy. If anybody deserves millions of dollars, it's Moses Malone." Malone himself spoke of his astronomical salary in terms that Rizzo's blue-collar base could appreciate. "You can be rich; you can be poor. Things happen bad, they happen good," Malone said. "I never put myself too high. I was a poor black kid in the ghetto but my mama raised me right. I just work hard. I just do my work."

It wasn't that Malone's emergence eased racial tensions or changed minds in Philadelphia. On the contrary, when Sixers owner Harold Katz donated $50,000 to Rizzo's campaign, Jim

Davis, a columnist for *The Philadelphia Tribune*, the city's century-old African American newspaper, called on Black basketball boosters to boycott the club. "Sixers fans who shout for joy as the team advances in its quest for the NBA championship will probably shed tears of rejection when they realize that their dollars were used to help finance the campaign of Frank Rizzo," Davis wrote, adding, "The spectacular dunks of Dr. J take on a different meaning when they are used to generate funds for a man who will dunk on you, your kids and grandchildren when it comes to a fair shot at a city job or a position in the police or fire department."

The boycott didn't hold. There was too much anticipation, too much hope that this season would end differently, too much curiosity about whether two perfectly mismatched superstars could nonetheless form a fellowship.

CHAPTER 16

THE PHILADELPHIA MACHINE

It was 5 in the morning on January 19, 1983, and the Philadelphia 76ers were trudging through a snow-dusted hotel parking lot. Seven hours earlier, they'd scratched out a narrow victory against the league's sorriest club. It had taken twenty-plus points each from Julius Erving, Moses Malone, and Andrew Toney to subdue the frisky Cleveland Cavaliers. The relentless midseason churn left little time to savor wins or lament losses. The players' flight home would depart by sunrise; tipoff at the Spectrum for their next game would follow twelve hours later.

To save money, Harold Katz had ditched buses on road trips during the 1982–83 season, instead renting four cars at every new city. The four rookies were tapped as drivers for the remaining eight players. It fell on Marc Iavaroni to chauffeur Erving around, a task he found as nerve-racking as the games themselves. Cleveland presented a particular challenge because Richfield Coliseum, the home court for the Cavaliers, lay twenty-five miles southeast of the airport. Skidding on icy highways, the sun not yet on the horizon, Iavaroni had nightmares of jeopardizing Erving's availability for subsequent games or worse. And then there were the more mundane concerns that underscored the reality of professional basketball in the dead of winter: ascending into blizzard-like conditions on cramped commercial flights, nodding off with sore limbs wrapped in ice, suiting up for the fourth contest in six nights shortly afterward.

The game that evening was equally forgettable as the exhausted Sixers mustered up sufficient energy to surge ahead of the hapless Chicago Bulls by seventeen in the first quarter before coasting to a twenty-point win. Forty-eight hours later, they squashed the Seattle Supersonics behind thirty-four points from Malone and twenty-seven from Erving. Sonics guard David Thompson, Erving's slam-dunk equal in the ABA whose drug addiction had grounded him in the NBA, was blindsided by the shock-and-awe onslaught that had buried his club under a twenty-one-point halftime deficit. "I knew they were good," Thompson mumbled, "but I didn't realize they played that *hard*."

It was the Sixers' fourteenth consecutive win, a franchise record. The streak had started exactly a month earlier with a seventeen-point blowout against the Boston Celtics and then gained momentum through the holiday season. There was a matter-of-factness to it, a lack of drama. Each game, Erving scored his customary twenty points, Malone grabbed his customary fifteen rebounds, the odds-and-ends stew of rookies and role-players backed them up. They got the job done, then moved on. "It's all very business-like, less emotional than it used to be. Nobody gets mad about not getting the ball," Bobby Jones said. "This team has just decided it doesn't like to lose."

For more than a decade in Philadelphia, the center position, the axis around which most championship clubs from the era turned, had been manned by a revolving cast of players. "The center by committee rotation didn't bring great results," Erving reflected. "We didn't have the one guy in the middle who was established and who was going to play forty minutes. By having several centers rotating, you couldn't blame one guy; you had to blame them all. The Moses move ended that." Rather than counting on Caldwell

Jones for defense and Darryl Dawkins for offense, the Sixers bundled them together in one package. On his own, Malone surpassed the combined point and rebound totals that Jones and Dawkins had amassed the previous season.

For the first time since Wilt Chamberlain had departed for the West Coast, the Sixers possessed a single big man who could go toe-to-toe with every seven-footer who lumbered into Philly. Malone, sportswriter Mark Whicker stated, "didn't do dumb things. He didn't go over the back. He didn't commit a lot of dumb fouls. He didn't take bad shots. He was just consistent every game." More talkative than he'd been in Houston, Malone repeated variations on the same theme after every game: "All I want to do is win. I love to win. Nothing is more fun than winning. All of them you can." That wasn't to say that Malone was a purely selfless player. Out of earshot, the Sixers sometimes referred to him as "the Black Hole." "You know, once the ball goes in, it's never coming back out, the gravitational thing," said Bobby Jones. "We knew either to get back on defense or to go to the boards because he was gonna put it up."

Malone's metronomic reliability steadied a team prone to losing its bearings under duress. "Having him here was an important thing for us psychologically, just as important as what he brings us on the floor," Maurice Cheeks said of Malone. "Every time we walk on the floor now, we think we're going to win." The fatalism of Sixers fans little by little gave way to hopefulness. Of the fifty-eight games during the 1982–83 season in which they held the lead heading into the fourth quarter, the 76ers emerged on top in all but two of them. Five times the Sixers deadlocked with opponents after forty-eight minutes; in each instance, they escaped with an overtime win. "If you don't get us early," Billy Cunningham asserted, "you're in trouble because we'll get you in the second half"—a statement that would've registered as comical just a year earlier.

Now, when Andrew Toney hoisted hair-trigger jumpers from long range, Cunningham didn't wail his name loudly enough to vibrate the balcony. Free to fire at will, Toney fulfilled his destiny of being a twenty-point-per-game scorer. Maurice Cheeks, too, reveled in the freedom that Malone's presence afforded him. Since Cheeks's professional debut four years earlier, Cunningham had begged his point guard to shoot more. This season, Cheeks finally took his coach's advice, attempting nearly seventy-five more shots than the previous season despite playing fewer minutes. Asserting himself on offense, however, came at a cost for the introverted Cheeks, who squirmed amid the accompanying media scrutiny. "Being in the spotlight doesn't matter, especially with the kind of guys we have on this team now," he said. "With Andrew, Doc, and Moses, there's not much room *left* for the spotlight. They can have it."

Four-fifths of the Sixers' starting lineup—Erving, Malone, Cheeks, and Toney—landed roster spots in the All-Star Game, with Cunningham serving as coach of the Eastern Conference. The exception was a rookie who, months earlier, had been living in a van while auditioning for a training camp invite. It had been four years since Marc Iavaroni had graduated from the University of Virginia, and his professional résumé consisted of stints in the Italian Basketball League. His luck turned when the Sixers, in dire need of big bodies following the departures of Dawkins and Jones, not only tendered the twenty-six-year-old forward a contract but also thrust him into the frontcourt alongside Erving and Malone. "I was starting every scrimmage," Iavaroni said about his first training camp with the Sixers, "and I told [assistant coach] Jack McMahon, 'Hey, I appreciate starting, but I want to get used to coming off the bench.' And he said, 'Shut up and do your job, rook.'"

Moving to the bench was Bobby Jones. Cunningham intuited that Jones, a defensive specialist, would be better suited as an anchor of the second unit, someone who could stabilize the lineup when the big guns needed a blow. True to his selfless nature, Jones made the best of the situation, winning the inaugural Sixth Man of the Year Award while continuing his eight-year streak of being named to the first team of the All-Defensive squad.

Amid this bounty of riches, Malone revived an idea last attempted in the All-Star Game during the ABA's messy final season: "Why not just take the 76ers and let us play the rest of the league?"

For the first time that decade, Sixers games were a scene. Pregame ceremonies amped up boisterous crowds with two diametrically opposing sounds. Grover Washington Jr., a Grammy Award–winning jazz saxophonist who lived in Philadelphia, was a Spectrum regular, kicking off festivities on numerous occasions with a silky, soulful rendition of the national anthem. "I never play it the same way twice," Washington explained. "It depends on how I feel. I'll look into Doc's face each time and the phrasing will depend on what I see." Washington shared with Erving a propensity for letting his instincts guide his artistry. Their bond ran so deep that Washington composed a song for Erving entitled "Let It Flow (For Dr. J)."

If Washington's saxophone was smooth and funky, Dave Zinkoff's voice was coarse and unmelodious. His announcement of the starting lineups alternated between elongated vowels and staccato bleats. At its conclusion, amid deafening applause from an audience that hung on the public-address announcer's every stretched-out syllable, Zinkoff yelled, "Number six, captain of the Philadelphia 76ers, Julius the Doctor Errrrrrrviiiiing!" Opposing players used to scoot closer to the scorers' table to bask in Zinkoff's idiosyncratic delivery.

A sellout in Philadelphia provided more than noise. The crowd could rattle opponents just as much as a Dr. J jam could. Forward Cedric Maxwell said that when the Celtics bus pulled into the Spectrum, Sixers fans would be lined up, their middle fingers extended, from adults down to children. During warmups, fans were prone to pelting opposing players with whatever they'd purchased from the concession stands. One writer noted that each trip to Philadelphia tacked on additional dry-cleaning costs. "I don't know what it is about the City of Brotherly Love that makes the people more abusive than any other city in the league," center Wayne Embry said. No other fan base was as foulmouthed or detailed in their trash talk. "The fans in the Spectrum would make it personal," stated Celtics center Robert Parish, who went by the nickname "Chief." "When I got audited by the IRS, the fans would scream, 'Chief, pay your fucking taxes!'"

After years of performing to half-full houses, the Sixers had finally recovered their homecourt. Nearly 200,000 more spectators piled into the Spectrum than in 1979–80, when Philadelphia had rebooted its roster. It was enough to give Erving a second wind. With Malone rampaging to another MVP season and with the fans out in force, Erving had the luxury of picking and choosing his spots, of enjoying himself even. Following a blowout win against the Utah Jazz in late January, Erving marveled at the pleasure that came with having Malone by his side. "Tonight I felt that I could watch the game. I was there, on the floor, but I wasn't really involved in it a lot of the time. I was running up and down, not getting winded, feeling good, watching the other people play. I had a good time."

Fresh-legged and rejuvenated, Erving turned back the clock at the All-Star Game. Only four NBA games were broadcast nationwide during the regular season, so this was a rare opportunity for casual fans to see the full Dr. J experience. Spurring the East to victory, Erving dropped twenty-five points, ten on sky-walking dunks.

The differences between the Sixers superstars were never starker than in the locker room after the All-Star Game. Having garnered MVP honors, Erving fielded questions for nearly ninety minutes, not budging until the last reporter had shut his notebook. Malone stomped about in his street clothes, grumbling at anyone who approached him. "Where's the checks?" he asked no one in particular. He'd put in his day's work and now expected to be paid in a timely manner. When his check arrived, Malone made sure that it was written for the full $2,000 winners' share, then disappeared without taking a single question.

The midseason break didn't dull the Sixers' momentum. After their fourteen-game win streak was snapped on January 23, they started another six-game tear and then followed that one with ten consecutive wins. All in all, from mid-December to early March, the Sixers came out ahead in thirty of thirty-two games, ballooning their record to 50–7, the fastest start in NBA history. Seventy wins, Malone's prophecy during training camp, no longer seemed far-fetched.

Their chief rival couldn't keep pace. Trying to catch Philadelphia, Boston Celtics head coach Bill Fitch remarked, was "like chasing Raquel Welch for 365 days and not even getting to shake her hand." Confidence suffused the Sixers locker room. "It's gotten to where we know we're going to win," Bobby Jones stated. "It's just a question of how many points."

It had all the makings of a fairy-tale season. Until it didn't.

The Sixers on their own were helpless to alleviate one threat that had the potential of leaving the season unresolved. The collective bargaining agreement between the NBA and the National Basketball Players Association was set to expire on April 2, 1983, two weeks before the playoffs were to commence. If a new deal wasn't struck before then, a players' strike would ensue. "It would be the crowning irony," columnist Bill Lyon wrote in *The Philadelphia Inquirer*, "if, in the year when the Sixers were finally about to realize what they believe is their manifest destiny, the players would hit the bricks and erase the playoffs."

The stickiest issue involved the owners' insistence on a salary cap to rein in contracts like the one Moses Malone had signed months earlier. Malone's salary, exorbitant as it was, hadn't sunk the Sixers' finances. Just the opposite—for the first time in years, the Sixers were poised to turn a profit. Not only had attendance skyrocketed, but the viewership for Sixers games on local television had spiked by 85 percent from the previous season. A union-entrenched city like Philadelphia would've seemed likely to side with players over management, but this was no ordinary season. Clint Richardson, a versatile shooting guard who served as the Sixers' player representative, received stacks of sharply worded letters from local workers urging him to come to terms with the league before the playoffs started. During games, while Richardson sat on the bench, fans barraged him with profanity-laced invective.

The other major threat was injuries. Over the season's first five months, the roster had remained remarkably healthy. Little credit could be claimed by the team's longtime trainer, Al Domenico. A streetwise man from the North Philadelphian rowhouses, Domenico had survived two decades as the Sixers trainer with little medical background beyond night courses from Temple University. He was more likely to spout off about the benefits of smoking than to delve into the particulars of human anatomy. Old-school to the core, Domenico toted a black satchel stuffed with Band-Aids, elastic wrap, and a catch-all spray that was deployed on every wound. Domenico,

Bobby Jones said, "would tell rookies when they came into the locker room the first day of practice, 'Now, if I have to tape your ankles, I'm gonna have to tell the owner that you've got weak ankles.' So he'd get out of having to work." When players limped off the court with sprains during games, Jones claimed that Domenico's efforts consisted of sliding ice bags down the bench. But then, as the season wound to a close, Domenico tended to the players' every bump and bruise so that they would vote him a full share of the playoff profits.

Domenico was the last in a long line of untrained trainers in professional sports. Coaching staffs were bare-bones back then, often little more than a pair of assistant coaches and a trainer who doubled as the traveling secretary and equipment manager. A quick-witted hustler adept at wrapping ankles and booking hotel rooms could stick for decades with a club intent on limiting its payroll. Pasted on Domenico's office walls were headshots of all the Sixers players who'd suited up during his tenure—seemingly a barbed reminder that while players came and went, Domenico was there to stay. The arrival of a professional dancer in 1982–83, however, signaled that change was afoot.

Years earlier, John Kilbourne, a graduate student at UCLA studying dance and its application to sports, had approached Larry Brown, the head coach of the men's basketball team, about testing his theory that dancers and basketball players engaged in similar types of movement and would thus benefit from similar types of conditioning. Recruits to the prestigious collegiate program soon found themselves performing rhythmic aerobics alongside a trained ballerino clad in a leotard and tights. After the first practice, Brown pulled Kilbourne into his office and handed him a uniform and sweatsuit. "I think," Brown said, "things will go much better if you wear this."

Brown soon jumped to the NBA, accepting the head coaching job for the New Jersey Nets. Kilbourne followed but began attracting interest from other professional clubs, including the Sixers. A franchise in cost-cutting mode seemed an unlikely candidate to expand its coaching staff. Malone's contract notwithstanding, Harold Katz had implemented an austerity program when he took over the Sixers. He ditched team buses, rescinded the coaches' company credit cards, and cut ties with a pricey travel agency that Billy Cunningham had recommended because he had a financial stake in it. To persuade the skeptical front office to allocate funds for a conditioning coach, a novel position at the time, Kilbourne framed his services as insurance for the Sixers' priciest investment. "If I can help prevent Moses from missing one game because of injury," he argued, "I'm worth my salary."

Throughout the 1982–83 season, amid a nationwide aerobics craze kick-started by the recent release of Jane Fonda's first home-workout VHS tape, the Sixers converted the start of their practices into a dance studio. While a cassette player blasted upbeat songs by Luther Vandross, Patti LaBelle, Grover Washington, and others, Kilbourne guided the players through twenty minutes of stretching and calisthenics, followed by movement drills in which Erving, Malone, and the others leaped, kicked, and fluttered their arms. At first, some snickered at the sight of professional athletes pirouetting through jazzercise routines. The results, however, spoke for themselves: that season, only the Seattle Supersonics lost fewer players to injury.

But the few injuries the Sixers did suffer late in the season proved to be devastating. The first victim was Erving. While blocking a shot against the Washington Bullets in mid-March, Erving reaggravated a pesky wrist sprain. Unable to rotate his hand, he wore a padded splint for two weeks afterward.

The loss was softened by Andrew Toney. In the first four games that Erving sat out, Toney poured in forty-two points against the Indiana Pacers, thirty-three against the Boston Celtics, twenty-four against the Milwaukee Bucks, and thirty-nine against the Detroit Pistons—all wins for the Sixers. The Pistons game was especially impressive. The Sixers had tussled with a physical Bucks squad the previous evening, stewed in the Milwaukee airport during an hours-long flight delay, then stewed some more as the luggage conveyor belt had malfunctioned in the Detroit airport. It was their fourth game in six nights, all in different cities. Down by a dozen in the final quarter, the sluggish Sixers seemed ready to throw in the towel. But then Toney went berserk. Ten minutes and seventeen Toney points later, the Sixers had chipped the Pistons' lead to one. During a timeout, Cunningham diagrammed a play that called for Toney to drive down the lane and dish off when the defense collapsed on him. Fielding the ball near halfcourt, Toney charged forward as planned but then stopped on a dime and fired a long-range bomb. "I almost died when he took it," Cunningham said of the three-pointer that pushed the Sixers into a late lead. "Did I want him to take it? No."

Cunningham leaned against the locker-room wall, lit a cigar, and sucked in deep. "But that's Andrew," he murmured while exhaling a mouthful of smoke.

Toney just shrugged. "You can't have second thoughts at a time like that."

Nearby, Moses Malone was trying his best to mask his discomfort. He'd labored through a dismal five-for-eighteen shooting night, winding up with a season-low twelve points. At some point, a Pistons defender had banged hard into his right knee. Over the past four seasons, Malone had missed a mere three games, refusing to allow injuries or illnesses to keep him off the court. Shooing away the beat writers, Malone kept the pain to himself, hoping to play through it. Two nights later, against the Knicks in New York, the Sixers put up a measly seventy-six points, a season low. Most concerning was that Malone managed just eight rebounds, roughly half his league-leading average. Over the next week, only once did he tally more than fifteen rebounds, against the Chicago Bulls on March 29.

On that same night, Julius Erving reemerged. Even so, the Sixers struggled to recover the rhythm that had once had them grooving toward seventy wins. His sore wrist still sheathed in a splint, Erving missed fourteen of his twenty-two shots. "I've just gotta get my timing back," he said after the Bulls held on for a two-point win. "I was a little tentative on a few shots. I'm gonna have to concentrate that much harder, shooting with this [padding] on my wrist."

It was the Sixers' twelfth loss and the third in five games, their worst stretch of the season. To win seventy, they'd have to sweep their remaining eleven contests. Reporters quizzed Erving afterward in somber tones. He refused to play along. "This is just one loss," Erving insisted, adding, "Seventy was just a number. It was never a big deal with our players. We never talked about it. The only time it came up was when a reporter asked about it." Echoing the team's captain, Cunningham later called seventy wins "the least important thing in the world." Franklin Edwards claimed that the players had held a meeting earlier about whether they should gun for history or take their foot off the throttle. Ultimately, injuries rendered the decision moot.

As winter gave way to spring, the nightmare scenario of labor strife wiping out the playoffs never came to pass. By the time the April 2 deadline arrived, the league and the players union had put the finishing touches on an unprecedented collective bargaining agreement that would implement a salary cap and avoid any work stoppages. The Sixers, at 60–13, hovered over the rest of the league, ten games ahead of the fading Celtics, six ahead of the Lakers. Their late-season stumbles notwithstanding, the players waved off any notion that they'd peaked too soon. "We set such a high standard that going sixty-six percent sent some antennas up," Erving said about the team's setbacks over the previous month. Their captain was on the mend; the strike had been averted. All the Sixers needed to do was coast into the playoffs.

On April 8, nine days before the season's end, Malone torched the Indiana Pacers with thirty-eight points and twenty-four rebounds, business as usual for someone gliding to his second straight MVP award. On that night, however, Malone did something uncharacteristic: he signaled to Billy Cunningham that he needed a rest. Malone gave no reason why. The answer would reveal itself two days later when Malone showed up hours before the Sixers' next game at the Spectrum with his right knee wrapped in a protective sleeve.

Malone took to the floor against the New York Knicks, but he shot a paltry two for seven and failed to snag a single offensive rebound. The Sixers were saved yet again by Andrew Toney. The Knicks threw four different defenders at him, to no avail. "A player gets into his rhythm, like he did, and then he's not playing a thinking game, he's playing an instinct game," Knicks guard Rory Sparrow said of Toney's forty-point explosion.

With minutes left and the Sixers ahead by double digits, Cunningham asked Malone how his knee was holding up. Malone's response set off alarm bells: "It hurts."

"He never says anything," Cunningham later told reporters, "so for him to say that, I told him he wasn't going to play anymore in that game and that I wanted a doctor to examine him afterward."

Michael Clancy, the team's physician, measured Malone's legs just below the knee and discovered that untreated tendinitis had deteriorated his muscles to such an extent that his right leg was now noticeably skinnier than his left. Clancy's conclusions almost made the Sixers front office wish that a strike had canceled the postseason. "No matter what Moses does or doesn't do," Clancy said, "his injury is not going to totally heal between now and the start of the playoffs." At best, Clancy speculated, through rest and rehabilitation, Malone could get back to 75 percent of his usual self.

Malone didn't join the team on its flight the next day to Atlanta, where they lost to the Hawks on April 12. The following morning, the Sixers flew back to Philadelphia for their final home game. It was Fan Appreciation Night, but fans were in no mood to celebrate. As if rehearsing for an ending they knew all too well, the sellout crowd booed while watching Philadelphia fall behind by nineteen to the Washington Bullets. Months earlier, owner Harold Katz had beefed up the rookie-heavy roster by trading for a pair of veterans—center Clemon Johnson and guard Reggie Johnson—but no one could make up for the absence of Malone, who was said to be going "stir-crazy" on the sidelines, unaccustomed to wearing street clothes in the Spectrum. Without him, the Sixers appeared listless. Even Erving, muddling through a three-for-twelve shooting night, seemed deflated by the sudden turn of events. Enraged, Cunningham informed his players midway through the fourth quarter that practice the next morning would start an hour earlier than usual. Katz tore into them afterward. "I don't mind the losing," he grumbled. "You expect that at this point in the year. But I expect anyone who works for me, in any of my businesses, to work hard. We had eleven players in uniform tonight, and I didn't get that from any of them."

The Sixers recovered two nights later with a narrow victory over the New Jersey Nets but then dropped the final game of the regular season to the Celtics. As the playoffs opened, the team once destined for glory now seemed bruised and beatable. They'd charged to a 50–7 start only to hobble to a 15–10 finish. The lone consolation was that, as the top seed in the Eastern Conference, the Sixers would receive a bye in the first round, granting them an extra week for Malone to round back into shape.

Rather than staying put in Philadelphia, Cunningham intuited that a change of scenery might wash the bad taste from the players' mouths. He scheduled a mini–training camp at Franklin & Marshall College, the same place where their journey had begun seven months earlier. The club arrived in Lancaster on April 19 in the midst of an unseasonable snowstorm. Early the next morning, before his teammates arrived, Malone warmed up alone. Gingerly, his knee still stabilized in a brace, he went through the motions, hesitant about doing too much too quickly. Hours later, while everyone else hit the showers, Malone badgered rookie Mark McNamara, whom one writer dubbed Malone's "favorite tackling dummy," into hanging around so that he could test the limits of his knee. For an hour the two went at each other one-on-one. When prodded afterward for his impressions, McNamara echoed Dr. Clancy's conclusions in less scientific terms. "Today, where he's normally throwing me on the court, [Malone] was only throwing me halfway across the court."

After Malone finally finished his workout, Billy Cunningham caught up to him. "Ready for the playoffs?" he asked.

Wordlessly, Malone nodded.

"How far do you think we'll go?"

George Shirk, the Sixers beat writer for *The Philadelphia Inquirer*, overheard the exchange. He published Malone's answer as "Four, four, four," but every subsequent retelling would render it in the Petersburg native's distinct dialect: "Fo', fo', fo'." It was singular and to the point, brash and sneakily poetic, much like Malone himself. No one else would've claimed, while lugging the sub-.500 Houston Rockets to within two games of an NBA championship, that he and his childhood buddies could've demolished the Boston

Celtics. No one else would've asserted, before having suited up for a single game on a cursed franchise, that seventy wins were forthcoming. And no one else would've dared predict that the Sixers, wracked with uncertainty about Malone's ill-timed injury, would sweep through all three rounds of the playoffs.

There was a supreme irony that on a roster with perhaps the most eloquent spokesperson the league had ever known, it was Malone who conjured up the catchphrase that would forever define the club. If Erving had been asked for his postseason prediction, he likely would've spoken in sculpted paragraphs on challenges and opportunities, injuries and historical baggage, realism and optimism—perfect fodder for newspaper snippets but too wordy and nuanced to stick in the public consciousness. Ultimately, for all his openness and verbal dexterity, Erving left behind a visual legacy—the free-throw line slam, the up-and-under baseline move, the rock-the-cradle stuff—while Malone, the silent superstar, would cement his legacy with one clipped utterance.

Later that night, the Sixers, stuck in a Treadway Inn without cable, reserved a room at a nearby nursing home so they could watch the first-round matchup that pitted the Nets against the Knicks. Whatever hope had permeated the team's locker room following their promising practice dissipated at the viewing party when Malone began complaining about soreness in his knee.

When the pain hadn't subsided by the following morning, Jeff Millman, an equipment manager for the Sixers, rushed Malone back to Philadelphia. The long drive tightened up his knee, and upon opening the car door, he collapsed to the pavement. "I mean, he just about fell flat," Domenico remembered. "He could hardly walk. And I thought, 'Oh, geez, we're this close and now this.'"

Doctors at Temple University Hospital reexamined Malone's right knee and then treated a buildup of fluid in his left knee. Hours later, Malone was back in Lancaster, watching his teammates run through drills. In three days, the Sixers would open their postseason journey at the Spectrum against the winner of the Nets-Knicks series, and their center was sitting immobile on the sidelines in street clothes.

Cunningham was beside himself. "I was a little shocked by it," he muttered. "To have this happen right before the playoffs is very frustrating."

CHAPTER 17

ROLE REVERSAL

The next morning, on April 22, Moses Malone shambled into practice with both legs caked in ice. For hours he stuck to a see-sawing routine imposed by the coaching staff: ten minutes of furious action, ten minutes of forced stillness, his iced knees propped up on an aluminum chair. It was progress, though not as much as Billy Cunningham would've preferred. "I'd feel a lot better if Moses were feeling 100 percent," the Sixers head coach said, his voice pinched with anxiety. "But what are you going to do?"

Earlier, the New York Knicks had fended off the New Jersey Nets. In the closing minutes, a brazen chant had rippled through Madison Square Garden: "We want Philly!" More than a hundred miles away, at a nursing home in the Pennsylvania Dutch Country, Julius Erving had smirked. "You want us?" he'd mumbled to the television. "Well, you got us now."

Returning to Philadelphia, the Sixers staged one final shoot-around. Barely capable of walking two days earlier, Malone managed to remain on the court until the end. What columnist Bill Lyon called the "most-watched legs since Betty Grable" held up. Malone further eased the front office's nerves when he declined ice bags afterward. It had been two weeks since he'd last competed, gritting through thirty-seven uninspired minutes. Malone hadn't been anywhere near full strength then, and as he told reporters now, "I think I can go seventy, seventy-five percent." Even with a damaged center, Erving favored their chances. "We have got the best team in the NBA, and now we simply have to show it," he asserted. "It's there to be found. We are like a panther, lying in the rough, ready to spring upon our prey. We *are* a sleeping giant."

On April 24, 1983, a capacity crowd at the Spectrum buzzed with an even mix of anticipation and dread when the Sixers and Knicks emerged. In the opening minutes, Malone appeared restrained in his movements, testing and probing whether he could withstand the quick starts and sudden stops that the sport demanded. Carrying on at half speed, however, cut against his character. Soon, Malone began barreling full-tilt into the paint, banging his body against the Knicks' big men, his face a mask of scowling indifference to the tremors of pain emanating from his knees. It was perhaps the most emotional performance of his career, with Malone matching his season high of thirty-eight points to go along with seventeen rebounds. As the clock wound down, Philadelphians saluted the effort with a chant of "MO-ses, MO-ses, MO-ses!" Malone acted like he heard nothing.

In good spirits after the Sixers' breezy 112–102 victory, Malone showed rare tolerance for the thicket of microphones hovering near his mouth. "I just like to work, man," he explained. "The harder I work, the less the pain." But then, tiring of question after question about his knees, Malone cut the session short. "You all make it sound like I'm dyin' here," he said, a smile on his face but a glare in his eye. "I told you, everything's gonna be all right." Mark McNamara, who knew just how severe Malone's injury was, marveled at the sudden recovery. "Two days ago, [Malone] was struggling to get around. Four days ago, he couldn't walk. Today he's a god," McNamara said. "He must know someone up there the rest of us don't."

Two off-days ensued, enough time for the Sixers to blunder into further misfortune. Bobby Jones was waylaid by the flu; Andrew

Toney bruised his left thigh during practice. The injury did what few defenders ever could: stopped Toney from shooting. Reeling from the loss of two indispensable players, the shorthanded Sixers tumbled behind by twenty in Game Two. Waving his arms while scurrying up and down the sidelines, Cunningham screamed, "Push it! Push it!" Maurice Cheeks, the roster's lone undamaged star, heeded his coach's directive. Over a fifteen-minute stretch in the second half in which the Sixers ripped through a furious 40–11 run, the unassuming point guard tossed in sixteen points, swiped three passes, and disrupted the Knicks' offense with his quick hands. The Sixers' unlikely 98–91 comeback victory kept Malone's prophecy alive.

Rather than breathing easy after Malone had posted his usual numbers—thirty points, seventeen rebounds—Philadelphians transferred their fears from one superstar to the other. In the first game, Erving had wound up with almost as many turnovers (three) as field goals (four). Midway through the second, Erving had elevated for a signature one-handed stuff, but the ball had clanged off the back rim. More close-range misses had followed. "He missed nine shots within inches of the basket, and that's not a foot or even two feet. We're talking inches," Billy Cunningham said. It wasn't that Erving was terrible; on the contrary, he finished Game Two with a respectable twenty points. It was that, at the worst possible moment, he was beginning to look his age.

The two subsequent contests in New York turned on two plays. Toward the end of Game Three, Bobby Jones, still sick with the flu, deflected a pass; Maurice Cheeks saved the ball from sailing out of bounds; and Malone, seeing open court ahead of him, charged forward. From his courtside seat Harold Katz hollered at the big man to "give up the damn ball," but Malone kept rumbling along, dribbling around four defenders before flipping up a soft runner that nestled into the net. It was, sportswriter Stan Hochman wrote, "like watching a rhino tap dance, and the sight of it drained the color from [Knicks coach] Hubie Brown's mottled face." The Sixers edged out the Knicks by a bucket, 107–105.

The following day, late in the fourth quarter of the fourth game, Knicks guard Rory Sparrow snuck behind Cheeks on the baseline and, in an attempt to break an 85–85 tie, lofted a one-handed floater hoopward. Malone, charging across the lane, snuffed out the shot. The ball caromed to Franklin Edwards, who tossed it downcourt to Erving for a quick-strike layup while getting hacked by a Knicks defender. "That was such a big play," Sparrow said. "They came up with a three-point lead when we should have had a two-point lead." The Knicks' last-ditch hopes of staving off elimination fell short by that exact margin, 105–102.

Despite being a sweep, the series had been tight, one that could have swung the other way were it not for the stark statistical disparity at the center position. Over four games, Malone scored seventy-nine more points and grabbed thirty-nine more rebounds than Bill Cartwright, who'd been a twenty-point scorer for the Knicks as recently as two seasons earlier. "I couldn't stop him," Cartwright said decades later about Malone. "I mean, I did everything, following him, hitting him, but it didn't matter." One writer slapped the ultimate Philadelphia insult on Cartwright, dubbing his performance "Dawkinsesque." No one on the Knicks was stumped about why they'd failed to draw blood against the Sixers. "Moses is the difference," guard Ernie Grunfeld declared.

That Erving, who'd averaged seventeen points on 40 percent shooting, wasn't the difference-maker no longer registered as novel. The Sixers captain seemed unbothered by his uneven performance. "I want to start slow, finish fast. I'm kind of excited, because I know I can do more. The important thing is, through all of this, we're still winning."

Then, with a dash of defiance, Erving issued a warning to future opponents: "I'm feeling like a stick of dynamite, at any time ready to explode."

For the first time in four years, their next opponent wouldn't be their chief rival.

The Sixers' season had, until the last few weeks, unfolded like a dream. The Celtics' was a nightmare. Rumors about the "troubles" in Boston had circulated for months. Each one boiled down to the same root cause: head coach Bill Fitch had worn out his welcome.

Fitch had arrived in Boston in 1979, at the same time as Larry Bird. Both were burdened with the same mandate: revive the vaunted Boston mystique. Fitch played his part by ensuring that no club would be better prepared than his own. In practice, he whipped his players into shape through numbingly repetitive drills. In the locker room, he tested their patience through hours-long screenings of previous games, pointing out every squandered opportunity and defensive lapse. So dedicated was Fitch to his VCR that he was saddled with the nickname "Captain Video." Perfection was what Fitch sought—the pristine play, the flawless half. No matter how effectively his players performed, there was always something they could've done better.

According to center Robert Parish, after the Celtics had defeated the Houston Rockets for the championship in 1981, Fitch interrupted the champagne-soaked celebration by hollering, "Hush, everybody!" Instead of delivering a rousing speech about his pride at having accomplished a shared goal, he rattled off a list of mistakes that each player had committed in the clinching game. "You think that he would've been happy for us!" Parish exclaimed decades later. "That was the first time I ever said 'Fuck you' under my breath to a coach."

Abrasive and unsatisfiable, Fitch dispensed with the niceties and back-patting that other coaches doled out to balance their criticism. "As great as Coach Fitch was at preparing us, one thing he lacked was he had no people skills," Parish said. "I always admired his wife because it's gotta be true love! What else could it be? If you're an asshole, you're an asshole. You can't turn it off." Two years after winning the title, the Celtics had finally had enough. While Fitch fulminated in practice, the players tuned out. Some cracked jokes; others turned their backs. By midseason, the club had lost the plot completely. "Our goal in 1983," forward M. L. Carr admitted, "wasn't to win a championship. It was to get rid of Fitch."

The Celtics collapsed in the playoffs. The Milwaukee Bucks clobbered them by twenty-one points in the first game at Boston Garden, then went on to sweep the series. Only Larry Bird seemed bent out of shape about it. "I just wonder where our damn hearts are," he muttered. For others, the message had been sent. "There was no way that that Milwaukee team was better than we were," Parish said. "We knew that the only way we were going to have a voice with Red [Auerbach] in terms of a coach replacement was to get swept."

The Celtics' early elimination stirred mild disappointment in Philadelphia. "That the 76ers and Boston will not be meeting in the playoffs is regarded in some quarters as like having a World War without Germany," columnist Bill Lyon opined, adding, "Not having Boston around in the spring is like not having mustard for your soft pretzel." The Sixers would've relished nothing more than being the ones who dusted off the Celtics in four. Instead, a franchise that Philadelphia had made a custom of overlooking had gotten the honors.

Role Reversal

Whenever the Sixers took to wallowing in self-pity, the Milwaukee Bucks were there to remind them that it could always be worse. Both clubs were in the midst of seven-year runs of winning fifty or more regular-season games; both felt disrespected by the chattering classes who deemed anything short of a championship a failure during a decade in which the Celtics and the Lakers hoarded titles. Though they were spiritual cousins in coming up short, the Sixers saved face by doing so in the Finals. The Bucks never so much as dabbled in the playoffs' final round in the 1980s. Time after time, Philadelphia blocked their path.

On January 12, during their second matchup of the 1982–83 season at the Spectrum, Bucks head coach Don Nelson had ripped off his sports jacket after a phantom foul was whistled against his side, then hurled the garment across the court. Calmly, Billy Cunningham had retrieved the jacket and, with the timing of a comedian, walked it back to the sidelines "as if it were a dead animal." When the Bucks returned to Philadelphia, in late March, the Sixers had staged a coat-throwing contest using the tattered remains of Nelson's jacket. The winning toss had soared more than forty feet. It was an apt depiction of the power imbalance between the two teams: Nelson had mangled his clothing in genuine frustration; the Sixers, in turn, had made a mockery of the gesture.

The Bucks lumbered into the Eastern Conference Finals sporting a defensive-minded roster evenly stocked with dashing youngsters (Sidney Moncrief, Marques Johnson) and hulking veterans (Bob Lanier, Dave Cowens). Dogged by injuries all year, the Bucks had burned through twenty-three different starting lineups. On the last day of the season, Cowens, the league MVP in 1973, strained some tendons in his right knee, leaving the Bucks a big man short in the playoffs. It was a deficit that the sweep-minded Sixers were eager to exploit.

In the off-week before the third round, Andrew Toney convalesced. For eight hours each day, he submitted to grueling physical therapy sessions. A plan was hatched for the upcoming series: Toney, as the starting shooting guard, would go full bore for short stretches. Then, when he returned to the bench, Al Domenico would hook wires into his aching left thigh, wrapping them in place with gauze and securing the getup with a fiberglass pad and a bulky rubber sleeve. Using a battery pack, Domenico would shoot electric currents through the wires to prevent Toney's leg from stiffening up. The results in Game One were promising: twenty-two points on eleven-of-fifteen shooting. Still, there were kinks to work out. At one point, Toney missed his substitution when Domenico couldn't remove the contraption quickly enough.

It was a game that didn't conform to any preestablished narrative. Erving and Toney fouled out; Malone wore down from wrestling with Bob Lanier, the Bucks long-footed center. Malone's twelve rebounds were offset by an alarming nine turnovers. Forty-eight minutes of bruising basketball settled nothing; the two teams hobbled into overtime knotted at 104.

Foul trouble forced Cunningham to improvise. In the extra period, he leaned on a pair of bench players, Bobby Jones and Clint Richardson. Since coming down with the flu a week earlier, Jones had recuperated with antibiotics that left him winded after minutes on the court. He appeared ripe for the Bucks to attack, which suited Jones just fine. He'd made a career out of duping heftier players into believing that he was a pushover. As he later explained, "I would play a guy who was stronger than me and he'd push me around, and I'd let him push me around. But then, in the fourth quarter when I needed a steal, I'd grab him and hold him and push him off my forearm and get a great deflection. And it would be shocking to him that I was that strong. I wasn't going to challenge him for forty-eight minutes. I challenged him for the last four minutes."

True to form, Jones swiped a Bucks inbounds pass in the final seconds and then twirled in midair while firing a pass to Richardson for a game-winning slam. It was a strange conclusion to a strange game in which Richardson, a steady force off the bench who'd averaged seven points per game in the regular season, scored all seven of Philadelphia's points in overtime to push the Sixers over the top, 111–109.

Whatever relief washed over the Sixers proved short-lived. They arrived at practice the next day to find Erving laid up on the sidelines. For Erving, the opening contest had been a tale of two halves: in the first, he'd racked up seventeen points; in the second, after banging his left knee against a Bucks defender, he'd managed just two more before fouling out. "My expression for it is 'I blew a tire,'" Erving explained. "My knees got sore, and it took away a lot of what I like to do. Mostly, it affected my shot, had me jumping off one leg, reluctant to take any risks. I felt I could play, but some things became sloppy."

By the time Game Two rolled around on May 11, chunky rubber sleeves hugged Erving's knees, stifling his movement. His six points on three-of-eleven shooting marked a career postseason nadir. It was a grueling night not just for Erving. Once, when Andrew Toney broke out on a fast break, Bob Lanier wrestled him earthward by the throat. Shaken, Toney staggered to the sidelines, where Domenico stuck an ice bag to the back of his neck. Malone, too, absorbed beating after beating from a frontline that, one writer noted, clung to him "tighter than the barnacles on the USS

Enterprise." Weathering the punishment, Malone willed the Sixers to an 87–81 win with twenty-six points and seventeen rebounds.

It wasn't Malone whom the press sought out afterward. Reporters instead cut a beeline toward Erving's locker. The barbed questions about whether he could regain his form in time for the Finals washed over Erving in what one reporter characterized as "angry, probing waves." In contrast to his usual levelheaded cool, Erving bristled at the implications behind the grilling. His terse replies mimicked Malone-like speech. "Winning is on my mind," Erving insisted, visibly irritated. "I'm not concerned about individual accomplishments. I feel I'm part of it, even if it's not in a dominating role."

In the third game, three days later in Milwaukee, Erving started sluggishly, as did the Sixers, shackled once again by the Bucks' suffocating defense. But as the pace quickened, Erving perked up. His knees unencumbered by heavy sleeves, Erving darted about in an end-to-end fever, piling up eighteen rapid-fire points after halftime. Their 104–96 win was the seventh in a row for the Sixers.

The locker room remained closed to the media for longer than usual afterward. When the doors finally opened, Erving, showered and clad in red warmups, a gym bag hanging from his shoulder, was already heading out. As reporters shouted questions at him, Erving mumbled, "I'll be back" without glancing their way, his eyes fixed on the exit. It was a brush-off that beat writers had come to expect from Malone, but rarely had they seen it from the player who one reporter claimed "gives more press conferences, and better ones, than most Presidents." An improbable role reversal was underway: as his fo', fo', fo' prophecy edged closer to reality, Malone was all too happy to expound on his favorite subject—winning—while Erving turned into the one dodging prying scribblers.

Erving had little time to stew. The next game took place the following afternoon, and the Sixers, bushed from their pursuit of perfection, finally suffered a letdown. With less than six minutes to go and Philadelphia clinging to a three-point advantage, the players grew colder than a Wisconsin winter. Over the next four minutes, no Sixer so much as sank a free throw, while Milwaukee ran off ten straight points. It was only the third time that season that the 76ers failed to hold a lead that they'd carried into the fourth quarter.

On some level, the 100–94 defeat might've been a blessing in disguise. Malone later admitted that tenured Sixers like Andrew Toney, who were better schooled in the fatalism that afflicted the franchise, had been "all over me, saying I was putting pressure on everybody talking [about a playoff sweep]." Malone attempted to clarify that he didn't necessarily mean that he expected the Sixers to rampage unblemished through each round. "I'm just saying," he said, "if we have an idea of winning the championship, the best thing we can do is win it as fast as we can."

A new angle on their hands, the press poured into Philadelphia's locker room eager for quotes about the snapping of the seven-game win streak. Not only did Erving once again scurry away—"Gotta get to the airport," he murmured while sidestepping questions—but he led an exodus of silent Sixers to their hotel a block away. Ten of twelve players snubbed the media. Only Maurice Cheeks and Clint Richardson stayed behind. It was an extemporaneous show of solidarity with the club's beleaguered captain. As Bobby Jones explained, "I saw Julius leave, and, well, I left then, too."

By the time the Sixers showed up at practice the following afternoon in Philadelphia, it had been seventy-two hours since Erving had last spoken publicly—an eternity by his standards. Reporters approached him with the wariness of someone trying to coax a soundbite out of Malone. Erving, however, signaled a truce. "I needed to cool out," he stated. "I knew it. I did it." Shedding his diplomatic evenhandedness, Erving unloaded his grievances against the narrative being spun about him: "Why must they make a big deal about me scoring six points [in Game Two] after we've beaten Milwaukee for the third straight time? As far as I'm concerned, that's the story, not what I did or didn't do. When I explained how I felt on this point it only led to more bad ink. I figure the best thing I can do is not to add more fuel to the fire."

"It was all B.S.," he concluded, "and the best way to avoid B.S. is not to step in it."

The fifth game seemed a foregone conclusion. The Bucks staged a valiant last stand in the third quarter, narrowing the gap to 63–62, but Erving responded by scoring eleven of the Sixers' next eighteen points. Not even Don Nelson, who, according to one writer, had "coached in this series like a guy trying to ward off an avalanche," could lather himself up into a coat-throwing fury. The Bucks head coach took Milwaukee's elimination to Philadelphia for the third straight season in stride, more resigned than exasperated. "If I owned a farm, I'd bet it on the Sixers," Nelson said after the 115–103 loss. "This is the best team I've seen in ten years."

No champagne was uncorked in the Sixers locker room. Not only was advancing to the Finals nothing new for the core players, but they understood from experience that all they'd managed to do so far was stave off failure. Their probable opponent was a familiar one. Before halftime of the fifth game, the Spectrum crowd already had begun chanting, "We want L.A.! We want L.A.!"

CHAPTER 18

THE FINAL FO'

On the night that the Philadelphia 76ers punched their fourth ticket to the NBA Finals in seven years, the Los Angeles Lakers failed to finish off the pesky Spurs for the Western Conference crown. The series extended to a sixth game in San Antonio, a notoriously unwelcoming city for players not wearing black-and-silver uniforms. A month earlier, during a regular-season matchup between the two clubs, a member of the Baseline Bums, a rowdy gaggle of Spurs loyalists, had held up a placard that read, "A Kareem Abdul-Jabbar Jazz Album" above a fire-melted record.

It was a tasteless jibe at the trauma that the Lakers center had recently endured. On January 31, 1983, one day after the Lakers had been blown out by the Celtics in Boston, Abdul-Jabbar's Bel Air mansion had gone up in flames. After receiving a call from firefighters at 7 the next morning, Abdul-Jabbar boarded a flight to Los Angeles, pulled up to his driveway, and saw nothing but charred walls. He'd lost his Persian rugs, his career mementos, and, most significantly, the three thousand jazz albums he'd accumulated through decades of scrupulous curation. "In an instant," Abdul-Jabbar wrote, "my material world had been reduced to a carry-on bag, and a few things that I had brought with me on the road."

Rather than wallowing in self-pity, Abdul-Jabbar funneled his sorrows into basketball. Jetting to Dallas the next morning, he rejoined the Lakers in time for their game against the Mavericks, in which Abdul-Jabbar missed only two of sixteen shots while netting a season-high thirty-four points. Everywhere he traveled, unfamiliar sounds greeted the announcement of the Lakers starting center: cheers. Fans who'd never warmed to the towering figure whose goggle-shielded facade rarely cracked with emotion embraced him as never before. Despite this heartfelt concern, Abdul-Jabbar remembered it as "a horrific season when injuries abounded."

While injuries had vexed the Sixers in the season's final month, the team had weathered them without losing any key players for the playoffs. The same couldn't be said of the Lakers. In the offseason, they'd upgraded their roster by drafting James Worthy, a sleek forward from North Carolina whose quick slashes to the basket caught defenders off guard. A week before the regular season ended, after the Lakers had all but sewn up the top seed in the Western Conference, Worthy had broken his leg during a meaningless contest against the Phoenix Suns. "James's injury had a big impact on the team psychologically," head coach Pat Riley said. More than throwing their rotation out of whack, it dampened whatever hopes the Lakers had clung to for sneaking past the Sixers for the third time in four years. It didn't help that Bob McAdoo, their super substitute who'd already missed nearly half the year with foot problems, had bruised his thigh in the early rounds of the playoffs.

The Finals came upon the Lakers in a rush. They edged the Spurs by one point on Friday, May 20, flew to Philadelphia on Saturday, and then studied videotape of the Sixers-Bucks series on Sunday while eating breakfast in their hotel. In a nearby conference room, the Lakers coaching staff laid down masking tape across the carpet to replicate a basketball court so that the players, still drained from their battles in Texas, could shuffle through their lines of attack, cramming like dawdling students before an exam for a rematch that was to tip off mere hours later.

The Final Fo'

For once, the Philadelphia 76ers held all the cards: three days of rest and recuperation, an intact roster, and a home arena bursting with rambunctious fans no longer braced for the bottom to fall out. The overwhelming sense among the Sixers was if not now, then never. As always, Moses Malone pared the mission down to its barest elements. "Get the first [game]," he declared, "then you need three more, then it's over."

It wouldn't be so simple. Since Magic Johnson had moved to Los Angeles four years earlier, the Lakers had yet to lose back-to-back games in the playoffs. Despite winning four games across two Finals against the Lakers, the Sixers had never managed to string together any sort of streak. If history were any guide, the final fo' of Malone's original pledge would be the hardest.

Against Philadelphia, the Lakers had abided by an overriding rule: do whatever it took to prevent Julius Erving from igniting the crowd. This time, Pat Riley shifted the focus to stopping Malone from recovering misses. "No rebounds, no rings," Riley reminded his roster in the moments before they took the court for their title defense.

It seemed in keeping with Kareem Abdul-Jabbar's nightmare season that it would conclude with a spate of contests against Malone, his chief tormentor. This time, the task wouldn't be so punishing. To keep Abdul-Jabbar's aging legs fresh, the Lakers often switched him onto Marc Iavaroni. Against Malone, the Lakers rotated a pair of floppy-haired power forwards, Kurt Rambis and Mark Landsberger, whose principal weapons on defense were the six fouls each had to burn. The strategy that the Milwaukee Bucks had employed of pummeling Malone for forty-eight minutes carried over into the Finals, which irritated him to such an extent that he shoved Landsberger in the back midway through the opening game. Landsberger, Malone snarled, was nothing more than "a little gnawing machine at my knees."

Despite featuring two teams traditionally renowned for speed and elegance, Game One was grueling. "There hasn't been so much pushing and shoving since the ticket line opened for *Return of the Jedi*," reporter Jere Longman wrote in *The Philadelphia Inquirer*. At one point, Andrew Toney collided head-on with Lakers guard Norm Nixon, knocking both players out cold. When Nixon came to, Pat Riley asked if he needed a breather. "How about a casket?" Nixon responded. Though he finished the game, Nixon would be rushed to a Philadelphia hospital afterward, where a battery of X-rays cleared him for the following game.

Not even a splitting headache could slow Toney down. Jacking up eighteen shots, he wound up with twenty-five points. Malone and Erving kept pace with twenty-seven and twenty points of their own, respectively. Philadelphia surged ahead by ten in the opening quarter, fell behind by three at halftime, then outscored Los Angeles by nine in the second half to close out a 113–107 win.

Because CBS didn't want to disrupt its regular programming during spring sweeps, the next game wasn't scheduled until four days later. Malone, who would've preferred to plow through the series in consecutive nights, grumbled about the downtime: "I don't want to lay around waiting for the game. I'll be thinking I'm on vacation."

In guarding Abdul-Jabbar, Malone provided a master class in the subtle, often illicit ways in which a defender could aggravate a taller offensive player. His approach was at once legal strategy and subterfuge. On a legitimate level, Malone did everything he could to prevent Abdul-Jabbar from going to his right hand, since he knew that an unblockable skyhook was likely to follow. Forcing Abdul-Jabbar to use his left hand made it more difficult for him to size up his signature shot. More duplicitously, when boxing out, Malone leaned against Abdul-Jabbar while pinning one of his arms down. It threw the Lakers center off-balance just enough for Malone to gain the rebounding advantage. Like a magician using sleight of hand, Malone kept the trick artfully shielded from referees' view. Even though he was one of the league's most physical players, it had been five years since Malone had last fouled out of a contest. When reminded of this, Malone grunted, "I remember the game. Cheap fouls." Charles Barkley would refer to Malone as a wise mentor, someone who tutored him in deceptive practices like stepping on a player's toes the split second he started his shooting motion.

These covert transgressions infuriated Abdul-Jabbar. At one point in Game Two, the Lakers center glared down at Malone's hand, which was clutching his jersey, and waved to the referees. It was a gesture that other Lakers players made fruitlessly all game long. During one crucial stretch, with the Sixers up four, Magic Johnson collided with Andrew Toney in the lane. The ball squirted free, and Maurice Cheeks ran it back for two points. Instead of hustling to the other end, Johnson glowered at the referee, beside himself that no foul had been called. "I've never used so many four-letter words in my life," Pat Riley said after Philadelphia's 103–93 victory. "[The officiating] didn't go both ways."

The final numbers suggested that Riley had a point. The referees whistled sixteen total fouls against the Sixers versus twenty-nine against the Lakers. The Sixers went to the free-throw line thirty-two times while the Lakers shot a mere five foul shots—none in the second half. It was the lowest total ever in an NBA Finals game, a record that would stand for thirty years. So distraught were the Lakers that the team brass discussed filing an official protest, a step that they ultimately decided against.

When asked about the apparent hometown favoritism, Julius Erving, who'd muddled through a six-for-seventeen shooting night en route to fourteen points, had no soundbites at the ready. "That's their problem," he said in reference to the Lakers. Malone, after scoring twenty-four points and snagging twelve rebounds, appeared more worked up about the disrespect Los Angeles was showing him. "I don't understand why they got Rambis checking me," he grumbled. "He can't guard me. I don't know why they got him on me. I don't know what they're gonna do now, but they've never been down 2–0 like this."

Leaving the Spectrum, the Lakers head coach added a touch of levity to an otherwise grim affair. "I guess," Riley told reporters, "we won't spend much time practicing our foul shots." As if the evening couldn't get worse, a fire broke out at the Lakers' hotel after midnight. While alarms blared and smoke billowed out into the hallways, frightened guests instinctively began trailing Magic Johnson to the lobby. Beat writer Steve Springer later said that Johnson told him, "How would I know how to get out of this hotel any more than they would? I've never been in this hotel before, but all of a sudden, this whole long train of people—doctors, lawyers, all these older guys—are following me because I'm Magic. I'll find a way."

Three years earlier, when Kareem Abdul-Jabbar had gone down with an ankle injury during the NBA Finals, Magic had found a way to lead his shorthanded roster out of danger. But now Johnson seemed as directionless as anyone else. In the end, a couple of curtains went up in flames and nothing more, but the incident further underscored the sense that the good fortune that had blessed the Lakers in past matchups against the Sixers had gone missing.

Being in the Finals didn't come with upgrades to the air travel that athletes from that era endured. Rather than jetting directly to Los Angeles, the Sixers first flew commercial to Chicago. While lounging around O'Hare, waiting for a connecting flight, George Shirk of *The Philadelphia Inquirer* caught up with Erving, who'd hardly slept the night before, too amped up by Philadelphia's narrow victory. "I cannot relax now. I cannot relax, or even think about winning a championship, or even how close it is," Erving said with the babbling-brook anxiety of a long-suffering runner-up. "I can't feel good yet, about being ahead, or even about the things we accomplished during the regular season. . . . All I care about is winning four. That's it. Winning four games. And when we do that, all the feelings will come forth then. After the fourth, I can either lay back and cool out or go completely bananas."

Six years earlier, Erving had steamed out to the West Coast hoping to conclude his turbulent first season in the NBA with a ring. By the time he'd returned to Philadelphia, five days later, the Sixers' 2–0 advantage over the Portland Trail Blazers had evaporated. He knew now not to look any further ahead than the next game.

Malone, who'd never let reality shake his rock-hard belief that he and a bunch of schoolyard buddies could whip the NBA's best, had no such hesitation. When asked if he'd rather clinch a championship in California or Pennsylvania, Malone declared, "Hey, I don't care where we get it. I don't care if we get it in Alaska."

With seconds to go in the opening quarter of Game Three in Los Angeles, Kareem Abdul-Jabbar rolled in a layup, pushing the Lakers' lead into double figures. It would be his last bucket until midway through the final quarter. During the thirty minutes in which Abdul-Jabbar went scoreless from the field, Malone hounded the Lakers center. In that stretch, at least, it seemed a transition of sorts, a visual enactment of one reign ending and another beginning.

In his fourteen years in the NBA, Abdul-Jabbar had never finished outside the top ten in MVP voting. He'd been the league's most unstoppable force since Malone was in middle school. But now Malone was challenging his supremacy the only way he knew how: by plowing headlong into it. "I figured I might as well drive to the hoop," Malone stated. "I figured this series, I ain't gonna take no jump shot." The Lakers had no answer to Malone's wrecking-ball approach. "There are a lot of forces in nature you don't stop," Kurt Rambis said. "And [Malone] is one of them." Late in the fourth quarter, with the Lakers still staggering about on their feet, Malone's eight quick points knocked them down for good. His nineteen boards contributed to the Sixers' commanding 54–41 rebounding advantage. Pat Riley's prediction that rebounds led to rings was proving prescient.

Equally key to the Sixers' 111–94 victory was Bobby Jones. In the weeks since coming down with the flu, Jones had shed nine pounds from his already skeletal frame. While sitting on the bench, he appeared weathered from illness, his cheeks sunken, his eyes ringed by dusky circles. But the second he subbed into the action, Jones began slamming his debilitated body into the brawny competition. Jones outscored the Lakers bench on his own in Game Three, amassing seventeen points to their collective sixteen.

With the Sixers enjoying a seemingly insurmountable 3–0 advantage, the media gauged whether Erving, who'd acquitted himself well with twenty-one points and twelve rebounds, would allow himself to believe. "I don't think it's appropriate to talk about it now, because it hasn't happened yet," he insisted. "I mean, I may leave here and get hit by a truck or something." When pressed on whether he could taste the title, Erving smiled. "I don't taste anything but the soda I'm drinking."

But then, to their surprise, he dropped his cautious guise: "We're going to win it. If we don't win it Tuesday [in Game Four], we'll win it the next day." It was as far as he would go. Reporters pestered him about what adding an NBA championship to the two he'd won in the ABA would mean to his legacy. It would mean, Erving growled, "that I wouldn't have to answer questions about not winning an NBA championship."

Sprawled out in the locker room, ice bags affixed to both knees, Malone left no doubt about where he stood: "We didn't lose but two games in a row all season. So how can they win four straight from us now?"

It was a logical statement, hard to argue with on its face, Erving-like in how it projected confidence without disrespecting the opposition. But then Malone punctuated it with a prediction too blunt to be mistaken for anyone else's.

"Ain't no way we don't win it all."

CHAPTER 19

THE ALLIANCE

Billy Cunningham, scarred from watching his club piddle away 3–1 series leads in back-to-back playoffs, couldn't relax. Despite his team's near-perfect romp through the postseason, he was unable to shake the feeling that it could all fall apart in a second. "I am so tired," the Sixers head coach admitted. "I go to bed at 10, but I wake up at 4 or 5, sweating." On May 30, 1983, the off-day before the fourth game, Cunningham delivered a message of urgency to anyone who might've been celebrating prematurely: "We must not allow the Lakers to win even one. We don't want to give them any momentum, any confidence."

This time, panic didn't prevail. Whereas previous iterations of the Sixers would break out fast before fading away, these Sixers eased into playoff games, headed into halftime facing a deficit, then kept their composure in the second half, poised to counterpunch the moment their opponent flagged. It was as if the entire roster had assumed the character of Malone, who gained strength as games wound down. Malone likened the Sixers to a locomotive that revved up gradually, then gathered steam the farther it rolled. Cumulatively through three games, the Lakers had outscored the Sixers by ten points in the first half; the Sixers, in turn, had buried the Lakers by forty-three in the second.

Devoid of momentum and short on players, the Lakers had strained to shift the narrative from the Sixers' coronation—or "exorcism," as columnist Bill Lyon dubbed it—to their own quest to repeat as champions. Whether because of injuries, complacency, or fatigue from the third Sixers-Lakers showdown in four seasons, there was a palpable lack of enthusiasm in Los Angeles. The crowd that filed into the Forum on May 31 harbored few illusions about staging a comeback. The funereal mood was set when actor Jack Nicholson, a stalwart Lakers backer, emerged courtside dressed from head to toe in black, hiding his eyes behind dark shades. Lakers sixth man Bob McAdoo showed up in street clothes, as did guard Norm Nixon, who'd hit just one of six shots in Game Three, still smarting from his collision with Andrew Toney days earlier. At this rate, even if the series were to stretch to its seven-game limit, the Lakers would struggle to field a starting five.

In spite of it all, the Lakers banked on a mix of pride and desperation to avoid the embarrassment of being the first winless team in the Finals since the Washington Bullets were swept by the Golden State Warriors in 1975. In the first two quarters of Game Four, they knocked the Sixers back on their heels, surging ahead by fourteen at halftime, their largest lead of the series. But then, as the second half got underway, Malone sensed a familiar script unfurling. "I could see them tightening up," he said. "They were thinking back to the past. See us comin' again, comin' again. The train was comin' again."

The day before, Malone had lurched into the shootaround clutching his sides in pain. At some point during the previous game, he'd absorbed a sharp elbow to the sternum. He'd shaken it off in the moment but later found himself struggling to exhale. It lent a certain symmetry to his playoff journey: at the start, he could hardly walk; by the end, he could hardly breathe. In both instances,

Cunningham was beside himself. "All I was thinking was, 'We've come this far, we're so close. Oh, no.'"

But if Malone had been able to press through tendinitis on will alone, then a hitch in his breathing seemed unlikely to slow him. It was Malone who brought the Sixers back by duking it out in the trenches in the game's second half. He tipped in missed shots, pestered Kareem Abdul-Jabbar into committing six turnovers, and pulled down more offensive rebounds (eight) than the rebounding total of any individual player on the Lakers. Never satisfied, Cunningham wanted more. During one timeout, he told Malone, "If you get every defensive rebound, we can win," and Malone, undaunted, responded, "Yeah, I can do that." His twenty-three overall rebounds marked the highest number in the Finals since Bill Walton had grabbed twenty-four in 1977. Malone was responsible for over half the Sixers' rebounds, with no one else pulling down more than five. If rebounding was the curse that had kept Dr. J from ascending into the championship circle, Malone single-handedly exorcised it.

Amid this rebounding blitz, Philadelphia's second-tier stars hacked away at the lead. Andrew Toney, undeterred by a tender thigh and a wayward jump shot, piled up twenty-three points, Maurice Cheeks twenty-one. Bobby Jones, for the second straight contest, outscored the entire Lakers bench on his own. Midway through the final period, the Sixers train was chugging inexorably down the tracks.

Only Erving seemed out of sorts. Over the game's first forty-five minutes, he'd drifted through the action, netting a quiet fourteen points. Since his first NBA season, Erving had had to contend with doubts about his ability to rise to the occasion. Year after year, the echoes had grown louder. They'd dogged him when the Sixers had fallen into disarray in the late '70s, when Magic Johnson had powered the centerless Lakers past Philadelphia in 1980, when Larry

Bird had stolen a winnable playoff series in 1981, and when Erving had broken down in tears in 1982. Even now, with the Sixers on the cusp of repaying their long-deferred debt to Philadelphia, the perception was that Malone, the soon-to-be MVP of the regular season and the Finals, was the one shoveling coal into the team's engine.

The closing minutes of Game Four would, once and for all, silence the accusation. It was 106–104, the Lakers in front by a basket. Magic Johnson, who hadn't sat for a second, swung the ball low to Abdul-Jabbar. A quick double-team by Cheeks prompted the Lakers center to look for an open teammate. Reading the play, Erving slashed across the lane, batted Abdul-Jabbar's pass forward, then outraced Michael Cooper to the ball. His two-handed jam from a step inside the free-throw line was classic Dr. J.

A minute later, after a free throw by Johnson had nudged the Lakers back ahead by one, Malone corralled an errant skyhook from Abdul-Jabbar and, in one motion, fired an outlet pass to Cheeks on the break. Normally precise in his passing, Cheeks bounced one too low for Erving. Ricocheting off his right leg, the ball somehow landed in Erving's right hand. Despite his irrepressible forward momentum, Erving still had the muscle memory to flick a twisty playground shot off the glass as Johnson grazed his arm for a foul. For the first time since the opening quarter, the Sixers had recovered the lead.

In the final possessions, both clubs narrowed their focus to their respective superstars. Following a successful free throw by Erving, Johnson dribbled around until his center could establish position in the post. Hacked while lofting another skyhook, Abdul-Jabbar missed a crucial foul shot that would've tied the game. The Sixers soon found themselves with the ball, a one-point advantage, and forty seconds to kill.

As Cheeks flitted about the perimeter, Malone popped out to the right wing, far from where he felt comfortable. Rather than rumbling into the paint, he searched for the team's captain. Erving secured his pass at the top of the key. Magic Johnson was guarding him one-on-one. The rest of the Sixers cleared out. It was Erving's title to win.

For three seconds the two stood there stationary, the past and the future sizing each other up. Between them, they embodied successive stages of the quick-fire evolution that basketball had undergone over the past decade: Erving, the soul of the street game, the legitimizer of playground improvisation, and Johnson, nine years his junior, the face of a new generation, the first to build on the legacy that Dr. J had forged. "He brought in being flamboyant," Johnson said of his idol, "a style that really hasn't been seen before in the organized pro leagues."

Staring at Johnson from above the free-throw line, the ball dangling near his waist, Erving held in his outsized hands the fate not only of his own legacy but also of the league he'd hailed from. Since crossing over to the NBA, Erving had never played on a roster that hadn't carried at least two other former ABA All-Stars. Philadelphia's solution to being stymied twice by Showtime was to double down, teaming together the only two players from the ABA to have won MVPs in the NBA. This Finals would be the last stand of a club infused with ABA talent going against one that didn't have a single player who'd logged a minute in the defunct league.

As the shot clock ticked down, Erving jabbed his right leg forward, rocking Johnson back on his heels. Surprisingly, an off-balance defender didn't trigger Erving's instincts to break toward the basket. Instead, he cocked the ball above his head and let fly.

There was something preordained about the shot, a destiny that mirrored Erving's own. Since attending a family reunion in 1979, Erving had embarked on a spiritual journey, striving to understand the fortune that had blessed his life and the larger forces that had scripted his actions. He spoke about the jumper in similar terms: "I didn't find that shot. It found me." Inevitably, the ball whispered through the net so cleanly that the cords barely budged.

The three consecutive baskets by Erving at the conclusion of Game Four reflected the three separate phases of his career. There was the revolutionary ABA Dr. J, skying over opponents in a shoestring league pulsing with raw athleticism. There was the NBA Doctor, storming into Philadelphia on rumor and promise, fumbling at first but skilled enough to mask his team's sloppiness. And there was the august Erving, slower of foot yet quicker of mind, biding his time behind a balanced roster until the moment arose for redemption.

The Lakers wouldn't score again. At the other end, Cheeks swiped Abdul-Jabbar's dribble and zipped the ball ahead to Malone for a title-punctuating slam. As the buzzer sounded, the silent Sixer once again vocalized what everyone charging onto the court in ecstasy undoubtedly was thinking.

"It was Doc's game!" Malone screamed. "Doc's game!"

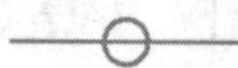

For the ABA veterans—Jones, Malone, Erving, even Cunningham—exhaustion settled in as soon as their long journeys concluded. "I'd never been more tired in my life," Bobby Jones remembered. Reclining on a bench, underweight and ailing, Jones steered clear of the champagne streams. It'd been eight years since he and Erving had faced each other in the ABA Finals, and now the longtime rivals-turned-teammates found each other in the locker room for what Jones called a "spiritual" moment together, "just thanking the Lord for putting us there." Afterward, Jones retreated to the showers, where a group of players gathered in prayer.

While gliding through his postchampionship obligations—shaking Pat Riley's hand and congratulating his staff—Cunningham, pale as milk, barely cracked a smile. There had been rumors that if the Sixers finally won it all, Cunningham would put an end to his perennial springtime suffering. "I was totally consumed by the job," he said decades later. "Even in the summer months, I'd be thinking about the game. My two girls were at an age where I was not being the father I was hoping to be. Even when I was there, I wasn't present." The championship gave him an exit—if his players would allow it. Wrapping his solid arms around his coach's shoulders when Cunningham joined the festivities, Malone asserted, "You're stayin' and we're repeatin'." The final buzzer had sounded less than an hour earlier, and already Malone was prophesying about Philadelphia's future.

Erving, too, basked in the moment mutedly, his demeanor more philosophical than emotional. The tears he'd shed in the same locker room a year before now flowed less profusely. To the media, at least, there was a defensiveness to Erving's posture, an irritation with the very idea that his legacy had been on the line. "I've had three rings [two in the ABA] in twelve years as a pro. So don't get the idea this ring was just for me." He gestured across the locker room. "They needed it more than me."

Erving had little interest in catering to the storyline that beat writers had prewritten. His typically paragraph-length answers were studded with sharp edges. "I never felt that my career would be a failure if I didn't win an NBA title," Erving insisted, adding,

> I guess I'm happier for all the people who wanted this for me than I am for myself. I think people realize that what I do—playing basketball—is not all of what I am. In fact, basketball is only a very small part of my life. I didn't choose it; it chose me. I suppose it's human nature, but people have made it a habit of always dwelling on the negative, of living in the past, with this team. What was always emphasized was our failure and what was overlooked was

> what we accomplished. We have the best record in the NBA over the last seven years. No other team has won as many games. I think we have been a great team, and I don't believe that because we had not won a championship until now that we were failures. I didn't lie awake nights thinking about it, because I knew that I had given my best, and the rest was out of my hands. I could accept that. And now I can accept this title with the same attitude.

Erving was disinclined to engage with the emotional weight that a title carried for the legions of basketball sentimentalists who couldn't stomach the idea of the sport's foremost ambassador retiring without NBA-issued jewelry. Malone happily stepped in. He'd made it known that he'd come to Philadelphia to assist the Doctor in getting over the hump. In the afterglow of that accomplishment, he continued to redirect the spotlight toward the Sixers captain. "This was for the Doc," Malone declared. "I wanted to be able to say that I played on a world championship team with Dr. J."

Slumped on a bench, a paper cup half filled with water in his hands, Malone looked, in one reporter's eyes, like a factory worker who'd just pulled a double shift. And in some sense, his numbers bore that out. In four games, he'd grabbed seventy-two rebounds, more than twice the number that anyone else on the Sixers had collected. No two Lakers had combined for as many boards as Malone had gotten on his own. His twenty-seven offensive rebounds nearly equaled Kareem Abdul-Jabbar's thirty total rebounds. In addition, Malone finished the series as the only player on either team to have accumulated more than one hundred points. He sank more free throws than anyone on the Lakers even attempted. As a whole, the Sixers outrebounded the Lakers by twenty-one, the only time in Erving's four trips to the NBA Finals that his team hadn't suffered a double-digit rebounding deficit. Not coincidentally, it was the only time the Sixers had emerged victorious.

The NBA Finals MVP trophy awarded to Malone vindicated the colossal contract that Harold Katz had drawn up nine months earlier. When asked how it felt to reap such rewards in only his second season as owner, Katz, a man partial to diamonds and sweat and everything else that gleamed, couched his answer in language wholly consistent with his character: "Next to the birth of my children, [winning a championship is] maybe my greatest thrill. I'd equate it to making my first million."

For Malone, the elation of winning soon gave way to enervation. The internal motor that never stopped humming during the season powered down the moment his prediction of a Finals sweep came to pass. "Hey, Moses, look happy, for God's sake," someone suggested, concerned that not even a championship could spread a smile across his face.

"I'm tired. I'm tired, I'm tired. Phew, I'm tired," Malone muttered to himself, too exhausted to shoo the press away.

Some wondered if a championship might raze the impenetrable walls that Malone had constructed around himself, letting in reporters and fans who had been dying to know him better since he was a high schooler. Unable to lie, Malone shook his head. "Gonna be hard." And then he laid out his precise plans for the next two days, followed by his vision for the offseason, one that entailed his customary lapse into silence.

"I'm gonna go to the parade, jump on a float, ride a float, jump on a plane and go home. Moses will be gone."

No sooner did the champagne evaporate off the players' skin than talk of a dynasty ensued. The Sixers' sixty-five regular-season wins were the fifth highest in NBA history to that point; their 12–1 playoff run was unmatched. Even a slight drop-off in subsequent seasons seemed insufficient to dislodge them from the top of the league's heap. The championship reign presaged by Dr. J's arrival in Philadelphia years earlier was finally coming into being. Even Erving, so tight-lipped and conservative in his predictions, allowed himself to believe. "This isn't the end of a long, cumbersome journey," he declared. "This is the beginning."

The celebration that kicked off at the Forum carried over to the Sixers' hotel in Los Angeles. Malone showed up in jeans, a T-shirt, and a gold bracelet with the word "Moses" spelled out in diamonds. Amid dancing and toasts, Malone sank into a cushiony chair, downing glass after glass of orange juice while his bodyguard, a refrigerator-sized man nicknamed "Rugged Road," turned away anyone who approached. One stubborn fan wouldn't retreat until she'd planted a congratulatory kiss on Malone's cheek. "Lady," Rugged Road finally declared, "if you don't back off, I'm going to have to put you on the ceiling." Shielded from the public, exactly as he preferred, Malone doubled over in laughter.

The overnight flight to Philadelphia was a boozy blur. Erving, unable to keep his eyes open while settling into his seat, murmured, "Wake me up when they serve dinner." But when the plane hit cruising altitude, sleeplessness brought Erving to his feet. For hours he roamed the aisles alongside his bubbly teammates, smirking at the "four, four, four" drink orders being hollered out to flight attendants every few minutes. Stuffed into an overhead compartment like a well-traveled suitcase was the championship trophy.

At one point, Malone stopped by Harold Katz's seat and said, "Mr. Katz, you'll be hearing from Mr. Fentress [Malone's agent] in two days." The color drained from Katz's face as fears of renegotiating Malone's contract flashed through his mind. "Of course, we had no intention of doing that," Fentress later said. "Moses was just pulling Katz's leg. Only he could tease the owner like that."

Sleeplessness similarly pervaded Philadelphia. Nearly 1.5 million households throughout northeastern Pennsylvania had tuned in that night, making it the largest local television audience to watch a Sixers game. The second it ended, the city exploded with pent-up energy. Up and down Broad Street, horns blared and firecrackers exploded. Residents surged into Center City on foot, by bicycle, or hanging out of car windows, many of them hoisting brooms and yelling "Sweep! Sweep!" Primed for the moment, vendors popped up hawking hats, pennants, and shirts, including one with a toga-clad Malone descending from a mountain holding tablets that read "Thou art the champs of the world." One buyer dressed the Rocky statue in front of the Spectrum in a red Sixers jersey with Erving's number 6 across the back.

The euphoria was overlaid with relief. No longer could skeptics sneer that the Sixers had been bridesmaids for so long that "they have rice marks on their faces." The championship, one journalist proclaimed, was "a titanic mound of dirt on the graveyard of Philadelphia jokes." It also buried the "We Owe You One" campaign not only for the Sixers but also for the lone player who'd endured each failed stab at the championship over the past seven seasons. "It was a real tear-jerker," one jubilant fan told *The Philadelphia Inquirer.* "Doctor J finally got what he deserved. The king finally was crowned."

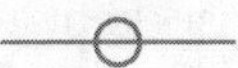

The long, boisterous night gave way to a morning that dawned gray and drizzly. It was the first of June, and some six thousand diehards, skipping work midweek to keep the party going, bunched around a wire-mesh fence outside Philadelphia International Airport.

When TWA Flight 38 touched down later that afternoon, the players descended the aircraft stairs to whistles and cheers from a crowd nearly as big as ones that had sprinkled through games at the Spectrum in recent years. Pressed to deliver a speech, Billy Cunningham, his bloodshot eyes concealed behind dark shades, made a promise no less bold than the "We Owe You One" campaign had been: "We have a group of men who have failed and who were able to pick themselves up and go over the mountain. As Moses said: 'We will repeat. *Repeat!*'"

The following afternoon, office buildings in downtown Philadelphia emptied out as employees flocked to Market and Broad Streets to stake their spots along the parade route. Some climbed atop parked buses; others dangled from the roofs of parking garages. A few intrepid souls huddled high near the bronzed feet of the William Penn statue that crowned City Hall. Some estimates pegged the crowd size in the low seven figures, many of whom showered the players with confetti as their convertibles drove by.

For Erving, the parade carried meaning beyond the adoration. Since coming to Philadelphia, he'd modeled himself as an athlete and a role model whose appeal could bring together a city divided by race and class. And now here he was, donning a white striped sweater and a red hat, his son Cory sitting wide-eyed in his lap, motoring down Broad Street, "seeing all these different people and it was, like, 'Wait a minute—they ain't all from this neighborhood.' A lot of these people crossed the line to celebrate together." Reporters took similar note of the unusual fluidity among revelers who otherwise kept to their own neighborhoods. "Many observers," journalist Gene Seymour wrote in the *Philadelphia Daily News*, "were struck by the sight of black and white strangers throughout Center City making spontaneous, unabashed efforts to merge their celebrations." It was Erving's crossover vision come to life.

There was a competing vision along the parade route, one that resonated more with Erving's counterbalance on the Sixers. General manager Pat Williams recalled the scene forty years later with clarity. During their midday break, a team of high-rise construction workers on South Broad Street hoisted their lunch pails from above when Moses Malone's convertible rolled by below. "It tickled me to death," Williams said, "that these workers up there were so attuned to Malone and how he played."

These two visions attested to the promise of teaming up Erving and Malone. For the Sixers, it was the promise of diametrically opposing personalities and styles of play—the balletic grace and the workmanlike grit, the eloquence and the brusqueness—leading to harmony. As Erving acknowledged in front of the fifty-five thousand fans who filled out Veterans Stadium, the endpoint of the parade, "We have the world championship because after six years of knocking at the door, even though we felt good in our hearts, in our minds, in our souls, we went out and for cold cash we got a hard hat. And we got the final piece of the puzzle that made us complete in every sense of the word." For Philadelphia, it was the promise of bridging, at least temporarily, intractable, historically rooted divisions by bringing together forces often in tension with each other. In its wake, people who rarely mingled—the Main Line elite and the blue-collar ethnics, those who voted for W. Wilson Goode for mayor and those who favored Frank Rizzo—celebrated with one another in the streets.

For that brief moment, the promise held.

EPILOGUE
THE UNRAVELING

And then, just as quickly, it unraveled.

For general manager Pat Williams, it began the moment he received the prize he'd been chasing for a decade. Since 1976, when he'd informed his boss, Fitz Dixon, that the player known as Dr. J was there for the taking, the pressure had mounted for Williams to surround Julius Erving with the complementary pieces that would justify the franchise's multimillion-dollar investment. And now that the championship ring was in his possession—an unassumingly designed piece of jewelry with a diamond in its center and the words "Fo' Five Fo'" along the side—Williams eased up. Sitting at his desk, he would slide the ring on and off his finger, fondle it, hold it up to the light. And before he knew it, a month had slipped by. "I realized," Williams later said, "that the ring was forcing me to focus on yesterday and not today, where you've got to be." So he tucked the ring back in its blue velvet box and locked it away. Over the next forty years, until his death at age eighty-four in July 2024, Williams seldom wore the ring again.

Despite his vow to hole up in Texas over the summer, Moses Malone found himself pulled in a thousand directions. He spent less time at the Fonde Recreation Center than during any other off-season since he'd joined the NBA. He showed up to training camp heavier and out of sorts. "Last summer has got to be the most I ever laid off without playin' ball," Malone said in October 1983. "Seems like every time I looked, someone wanted me to do something. I was flying here and flying there." Injuries, excess weight, and defensive adjustments lowered his averages in points and boards. For the fourth straight year Malone topped the league in rebounds, but the ardor and the intensity of the previous season were missing.

For three months, the Sixers ran neck-and-neck with the Boston Celtics. But then, from mid-January to late February 1984, Philadelphia dropped twelve of seventeen games, nearly as many losses as it had suffered the entire season before. After an early March game in which the Sixers bricked eighteen consecutive shots, Harold Katz aimed his rhetorical fire at the player whom he'd signed to ward off such midseason swoons. "Is Malone worth two million this year?" Katz asked. "No. The answer is absolutely no." Blindsided, Malone responded by not responding at all, withdrawing into himself. The home that he'd forged in Philadelphia suddenly looked no more permanent than any other stop along his ongoing basketball odyssey.

Hoping to reset in the postseason, the Sixers instead got sucker-punched in the first round. The New Jersey Nets blew them out twice in Philly. After the Sixers clawed back even, the two teams battled to a standstill through three quarters in the fifth and final game. Reverting to prechampionship form, Philadelphia floundered in the fourth. A year after guaranteeing a repeat performance, the Sixers suffered a humbling three-point loss to a franchise that hadn't prevailed in a playoff series since Julius Erving had suited up for it the season before the ABA-NBA merger.

There was a cruel inversion for Erving. Eight years earlier, he'd upended a potential Nets dynasty by fleeing to Philadelphia, and now the Nets had upended a potential Sixers dynasty on Philadelphia's home court. In Game Five, Erving hit just five of eleven shots while turning the ball over seven times. Afterward, Nets players voiced what others could see plain as day: Erving and the Sixers had grown abruptly old. No longer oriented toward the future, they seemed, eleven months after running away with a title, a club already fading into the past.

Advancing to the Finals in 1984 were the Los Angeles Lakers and the Boston Celtics. It was a matchup that had been anticipated from the moment that Magic Johnson and Larry Bird had entered the league together, fresh from their faceoff in the 1979 NCAA title game. Their first clash in the NBA Finals, living up to the hype, stretched to the limit, with the Celtics gutting out a seventh-game victory in Boston Garden. The Lakers exacted revenge the following season, then again in 1987. As epic as the Sixers' battles with the Celtics had been in the early '80s, this was the rivalry that would define the decade. More than captivating the nation, it turned the NBA into what it had never before been: buzzy, modish, at the cutting edge of the athletic landscape.

A narrative began to form. Johnson and Bird did more than win eight of ten championships between them in the 1980s; they saved the NBA. They transformed a cash-poor league rife with drug and image issues into one that was profitable and safe for advertisers and TV networks alike. Over time, a clear dividing line formed in NBA history: before Magic and Bird and after.

In June 1984, one week after the first Bird-Johnson Finals concluded with the Celtics clinching their fifteenth championship banner, the Chicago Bulls drafted a skinny guard from North Carolina. Months later, the cover of *The Sporting News* featured Michael Jordan, decked out in surgical scrubs, pressing a stethoscope to a basketball. The accompanying headline said it all: "The Next Dr. J."

From their lithe bodies to their basketball-swallowing hands to their disregard for gravity, Jordan and Erving shared many similarities. In the slam-dunk contest during his rookie season, Jordan demonstrated just how closely he'd studied Erving's career by replicating the free-throw-line jam that had awarded Dr. J the win in the inaugural ABA contest. It was Erving, Jordan said, "who made me dream of flying." Jordan carried forward the path that Erving had cut for inventive leapers partial to playground-refined aerial moves. Unlike Erving, whose youthful in-game flights had gone untelevised in the ABA, Jordan constructed his legend on highlight clips perfectly packaged for nightly newscasts and budding cable channels like ESPN. While Erving had tried and failed to launch a brick-and-mortar shoe boutique, Jordan would make a fortune on a sneaker brand that bore his name. Jordan became, in essence, the ultimate crossover athlete, someone whose fame and admiration spanned not only races but nationalities. Over the next decade, from when the Sixers won the championship in 1983 to when Jordan announced his first retirement in 1993, the NBA went global.

Amid these developments, the Sixers splintered. They were eliminated by the Celtics in 1985, then by the Milwaukee Bucks in 1986. Malone missed the entire playoffs that season after fracturing his right-eye orbital. He was thirty-one years old. His five-year rebounding reign had ended. In 1985–86, Malone didn't even lead his own team in boards. Charles Barkley, a twenty-two-year-old heavyweight whom Malone had taken under his wing, bested his mentor in both total and per-game rebounds.

Unenthusiastic about negotiating a new contract with a player on the downswing, Harold Katz traded Malone to the Washington Bullets for a package fronted by Jeff Ruland, an all-star center beset by foot injuries. Despite having the most to gain by Malone's departure, Barkley was devastated. "Nobody can keep a team loose like he did," he said of Malone. "He's one of the nicest people I've ever played with, one of the few people I know making $2 million a year who isn't a jerk." Erving, too, understood that Malone's value had always extended beyond statistics. "This [trade] creates a void," Erving stated. "Moses was the cog at the center of the wheel. Take him out and it leaves spokes hanging."

For the Sixers, the trade precipitated their decline, the start of a decades-long title drought that one writer dubbed the "curse of Moses Malone." While Malone played well for the Bullets, coasting to his tenth straight All-Star Game, Ruland logged a mere 116 minutes over five games before injuries derailed his career. Bobby Jones retired; Billy Cunningham finally had enough. Even though he'd emerged victorious in nearly 70 percent of the games he'd coached, the highest win percentage for any head coach in NBA history to that point, Cunningham, after his retirement in 1985 at age forty-two, never returned to the profession that had tormented him.

Katz, a savior in 1983, morphed into a villain. The Sixers owner "began treating people like dirt after we won the championship," Clint Richardson later asserted, adding, "I think he ruined the team atmosphere to the point where we really didn't trust each other anymore." He'd alienated his star center to such an extent that Malone vowed never to lose to the Sixers as long as he was in uniform. Malone's wife, Alfreda, said Katz would "come into the locker room with that big cigar in his mouth, criticizing the players. Moses wouldn't take it."

Neither would Andrew Toney. Starting in 1985, Toney struggled to stay on the court amid undiagnosed stress fractures in both feet whose severity Sixers officials doubted. Katz took his complaints public, questioning whether Toney still had the hunger to compete. At one point, the Sixers threatened to suspend Toney unless he played through the pain. Not only would brittle feet sever his relationship with the Sixers, they would cut short Toney's promising career, one that nearly everyone who faced him swore had been pointed toward the Basketball Hall of Fame. Upon retirement, Toney retreated into seclusion. Not until 2012 did he reappear in Philadelphia. Even then, he spurned public ceremonies commemorating the championship club. One of the most dangerous scorers of his era—the guard whom Larry Bird said he'd feared most until Michael Jordan showed up—dropped off the face of the earth.

The 1986–87 season was Erving's eleventh in the NBA, more than twice as long as he'd spent in the ABA. It would also be his last. Everywhere the Sixers traveled, rival teams staged pregame ceremonies, showering Erving with gifts and praise. As he'd often done in the ABA, Erving was called on to address the crowds, to give one last diplomatic speech about basketball's bright future and the legacy he was leaving behind.

The evidence of it was everywhere. An entire generation of acolytes had come of age copying Erving's moves on the playground. Many of the players now bursting into the NBA appeared crafted in Erving's image: creative, entrepreneurial, unapologetically Black, and with style to spare. The best of them reaped the rewards of the commercial opportunities that Erving had opened up during an era when questions continued to abound about whether Black athletes could peddle products to majority-white consumers. Kevin Loughery, Erving's former coach with the New York Nets who later became Malone's coach with the Washington Bullets, asserted that "Doc has done as much for basketball as any other player in the whole history of the game."

When the Sixers swung into Washington, DC, during Erving's final season, Malone was asked if he, too, would want a farewell tour someday. "Naw," Malone said. "I'm going to retire by telephone and ask them to mail in the gifts." At any rate, Malone was in no rush to retire. A basketball nomad no longer in search of a home, he traversed the league for eight more years. He was traded, signed, and sold, ricocheting between Atlanta, Milwaukee,

San Antonio, and even back to Philadelphia for a season. "You name it," Malone said, "it's happened to me." He remains the only NBA MVP who played on nine teams. By the time Malone finally hung up his jersey in 1995, the thirty-nine-year-old was the last man standing from the ABA.

That offseason, Kevin Garnett, a phenom twenty-one years Malone's junior, was drafted straight out of high school, reviving a practice that had gone dormant since the mid-'70s. Over the following decade, adolescent prodigies ranging from Kobe Bryant to Tracy McGrady to LeBron James followed. It was Malone who'd laid the groundwork for the prep-to-pro pipeline that these future Hall of Famers traversed, even though his name was fading from the national consciousness by the time this trend took hold once again.

When he retired, Malone was one of seven NBA players to have won three MVP trophies. The others were Bill Russell, Wilt Chamberlain, Kareem Abdul-Jabbar, Magic Johnson, Larry Bird, and Michael Jordan. Of them, Malone has proven the least prone to hagiographic treatments over time. His face hardly ever graces the montages of past NBA legends that networks cobble together for the playoffs; his style was too workmanlike to lend itself to the YouTube retrospectives that grab the attention of younger generations. He spent his final decades in Houston, patrolling the courts at Fonde Recreation Center to scratch his persistent basketball itch. Up to his untimely death from heart disease in 2015, Malone seldom sat down for in-depth interviews, his indifference to publicity a defining feature to the end. Malone remains the least known basketball superstar because he never cared about making himself knowable.

Darker issues also tarnished Malone's legacy. In 1992, his wife, Alfreda, filed for divorce, accusing her husband of infidelity and physical and emotional abuse. She testified in court that Malone had beaten her, threatened to kill her, and thrown objects at her, including a pair of scissors. Acquaintances backed up Alfreda's allegations, claiming that they'd seen bruises on her at various points. When it was his turn to testify, Moses Malone denied the allegations, stating that he believed his ex-wife was making these claims to harm his future earning potential. In the wake of the divorce, the NBA took no action against Malone. Decades later, the obituaries that ran about him rarely mentioned the allegations.

Marital misdeeds dogged Erving as well, some of which the media brought to light and some of which he himself revealed. In an autobiography published in 2013, Erving wrote about his occasionally stormy marriage to his first wife, Turquoise, including times when he hit her in "self-defense" after he felt that he'd been "attacked." When confronted by Gayle King on *CBS This Morning* about those incidents, Erving stated, "There's no justification—I mean, ever."

If his playing days were a period of ascendance, with his retirement came the fall. There was scandal and there was tragedy. In 1999, Alexandra Stevenson, an obscure tennis prospect, surged into the semifinals of Wimbledon. When a reporter for the *Fort Lauderdale Sun-Sentinel* dredged up a birth certificate that listed Erving as Stevenson's father, he initially denied the allegation, perhaps as a reflexive means of protecting the wholesome image that he'd carefully cultivated, before ultimately confirming that she'd been born of an affair that Erving had had with sportswriter Samantha Stevenson. The following year, Cory Erving, the son who'd ridden on his father's lap during the victory parade in 1983, drove his car into a pond and drowned. His body wasn't discovered for another month, during which time Erving took to the airwaves to plead for information on his whereabouts. Grief and infidelity contributed to the breakup of his marriage to Turquoise in 2003. Shortly thereafter, a sex tape of Erving was leaked. Over the following decade, a risky investment in an Atlanta golf course would drain some of his fortune and largely derail his dreams of business moguldom. An ethereal legend in his youth, graced with class and vision, had become by middle age fallible, blemished—all too human.

Once, when asked which season he'd choose if he could live it all over again, Erving replied, "Maybe one with the Nets. From an individual standpoint, it was my time of greatest creativity and expression as an artist." It was also a time of formation, of discovery, of purity, of putting into practice the lessons learned from a long apprenticeship on the playground; a time before the first-blush dysfunction of the Sixers, before the "We Owe You One" campaign was yoked across his shoulders, before the tears he'd shed after his long, taxing slog through the NBA seemed certain to end titleless.

It is that early iteration of Erving that endures in the popular imagination—the fearless Dr. J of the ABA, his Afro high and his goatee full, leaping over defenders and inventing on the fly, the red-white-and-blue ball mirroring the patriotic stripes of his Nets uniform. It's an image frozen in the '70s yet also timeless, much like the ABA itself. More and more, the NBA has come to resemble the league that it was once disdainful of. The open-floor game and in-air improvisations that had struck basketball fundamentalists as heretical soon became as commonplace as bounce passes. Even so, as of this writing, the NBA has yet to incorporate ABA statistics into its record books. As a result, the ABA remains stuck in a liminal state, remembered more as a colorful curiosity than as a cradle for so much of what has elevated professional basketball into a worldwide phenomenon.

Yet the popular narrative about Johnson and Bird resuscitating a faltering league is incomplete without mention of the ABA and two of its signature players who merged their divergent talents in the NBA to disrupt the decade-long dominance of the Lakers and the Celtics on a team as bold as its boast of sweeping the playoffs.

The legacy of the ABA lives on through the 1983 Philadelphia 76ers, a testament to the beauty and the guts of a league that made the game modern.

Thirty years later, Sixers executives called the player who'd coined the "Fo', fo', fo'" phrase to inform him that they intended to retire his jersey number. Moses Malone refused to let them go forward unless the individual honor was extended to a collective one. The undertaking dragged on past Malone's death. Finally, in 2019, thirty-six years after the last professional basketball championship that Philadelphia has witnessed, a banner etched with the names of every teammate Malone played with during his tenure on the Sixers, from Julius Erving to Andrew Toney, Bobby Jones to Maurice Cheeks, no matter how great or small their role, assumed its rightful place in the rafters.

ACKNOWLEDGMENTS

Heartfelt thanks, first and foremost, to everyone who answered their phones and took the time to chat with me, including Rick Barry, Fran Blinebury, Tommy Bonk, Ron Boone, Junior Bridgeman, Dave Brownbill, Bucky Buckwalter, Bill Cartwright, Harvey Catchings, Billy Cunningham, Earl Cureton, Carroll Dawson, Donald Dell, Randy Denton, Ron Dick, Lefty Driesell, Danny Durso, Franklin Edwards, Julius Erving, Lee Fentress, Bob Ford, Otis Fulton, Neil Funk, John Gabriel, Gerald Govan, Steve Green, Del Harris, Randy Harvey, Lionel Hollins, Marc Iavaroni, Reggie Johnson, Bobby Jones, Gordie Jones, Major Jones, Harold Katz, Greg Kelser, John Kilbourne, Dave Koesters, Kevin Kunnert, Jason Levin, Fred Liedman, Mike Littwin, Timothy J. Lombardo, Jere Longman, Allen Lumpkin, Fred Maglione, Tim Malloy, Cedric Maxwell, Bill Melchionni, Larry Miller, Steve Mix, George Mumford, Calvin Murphy, John Nash, Mike Newlin, Scott Ostler, Robert Parish, Bobby Paschal, Steve Patterson, Mark Piazza, Ron Rabena, Robert Reid, Dave Robbins, Steve Rudman, Bob Ryan, Lou Schneider, Russ Schoene, Jerry Selber, Dan Shaughnessy, Al Skinner, Victor Sonder, Steve Springer, Gary Stromberg, Jack Swope, Stanley Taylor, Bill Walton, Mark Whicker, Pat Williams, and Bernard Wilson.

For help with setting up interviews and providing contacts, I'd like to thank Lia Aliberti, Marc Bona, Stephen Demorest, Michael Dolan, Mike Horan, Rob King, William Lawson, Val Small, Johnny Smith, and John Zannis. Thanks as well to Tricia Gesner for helping me select photos for the insert. A special shout-out goes to Pete Croatto, a fabulous basketball writer whose generosity I hope to repay someday.

Once again, I can't imagine writing a book anywhere in New York City other than the Allen Room at the New York Public Library. This was my second stint there, and I'm eternally grateful to the librarians and administrators for granting me access to this bookish space and its considerable resources. The Schomburg Center for Research in Black Culture is a treasure, a place where I spent weeks immersed in archives. Thank you to the librarians at the Special Collections Research Center at Temple University's Charles Library, the most stunning university library I've ever spent time in. Thank you as well to the librarians at the Houston Public Library who gave me access to their archives.

For keeping me employed and solvent, a huge thank-you to my colleagues at the Random House Publishing Group. I heard so often that being an English major was a surefire route to unemployment, yet here I am, twenty years later, still working on books. It's more than I could have hoped for.

I was uncertain whether I'd ever write another book after my first, *Our Team*. One night, while musing about book topics with my agent, Peter Steinberg, I offhandedly expressed my fascination with the American Basketball Association and its premier player, Dr. J. Walking back to the subway, I felt in my gut that this was a story worth chasing. Thanks to Peter for finding the right home for the book. Thanks to Brant Rumble for taking a chance on it and shepherding it expertly and patiently to completion. And thanks to William Boggess, who once again whipped my lengthy first draft into shape. Albert Tang gave *Moses and the Doctor* the cover of my dreams. Thanks to the entire team at Grand Central: Ben Sevier, Beth DeGuzman, Colin Dickerman, Sean Moreau, Bart Dawson, Staci Burt, Maris Tasaka, and Niyati Patel.

For their support and comfort, thanks to my family: my parents, Jerome and Renee; to the Baima family, Kate, Joe, Olivia, and Ethan; and to the Epplin-Rincker family, Rachel, Thomas, Nathan, and Michael.

It's hard to fathom how much my life has changed over the course of this book's long gestation. I met Jane Healy in January 2022, weeks after I'd settled on the topic. The love she opened up inside me was overwhelming, so intense and profound. By the time I finally got around to writing the proposal, we were inseparable. In May 2023, as I was wrapping up my research, Jane and I got married. Ten months, one mortgage, and half a book later, our daughter, Ava, was born. I finished the second half in a new house alongside the two loves of my life. This book is dedicated to them.

NOTES

Websites, Databases, and Archives

Baltimore Afro-American
Basketball Digest
Basketball Weekly
Black Sports
The Boston Globe
Boston Herald
The Chicago Defender
Ebony
Esquire
GQ
Houston Chronicle
Houston Post
Inside Sports
Los Angeles Times
Newsday
Newspapers.com
New York Amsterdam News
New York Post
The New York Times
The New York Public Library, NYPL.org
Petersburg Progress Index
Philadelphia Daily News
Philadelphia Evening Bulletin
The Philadelphia Inquirer
Philadelphia Magazine
The Philadelphia Tribune
Playboy
Richmond Times-Dispatch

Notes

The Salt Lake Tribune
The Sporting News
Sports Illustrated
Sport magazine
The Washington Post

Prologue: The Speech

xii **"I heard the legend":** Author phone interview with Calvin Murphy, February 20, 2024.

xiii **"My high school coach":** Marty Bell, "Can Dr. J Save the ABA?," *Sport*, March 1975, 22–27.

xiv "**nearly ripped the basket":** Steve Rudman, "Erving-Led Nets Squeeze Past Stars, 95–91," *Salt Lake Tribune*, October 31, 1974, 1-E.

xv **"In two words":** Don Kowet, "Moses Malone: Undergraduate in the ABA," *Sport*, January 1975, 76–77.

xv **"How's my swimming going?":** Author phone interview with Julius Erving, June 17, 2024.

Chapter 1: Call Me the Doctor

3 **Madison Square Garden of playground basketball:** Jonathan Abrams, "A Street Basketball Mecca Gets a Face-Lift," *New York Times*, October 10, 2021.

3 **"thicker than ants":** Peter Vecsey, "If Basketball Is Your High, This Is the Ultimate Trip," *New York Daily News,* August 30, 1971, 38.

3 **The scene, noisy:** For more on the atmosphere of games at Rucker, see Vincent M. Mallozzi, *Asphalt Gods: An Oral History of the Rucker Tournament* (Doubleday, 2003), 18–20.

4 **"Look, if you want":** John Papanek, "I've Always Felt Powerless," *Sports Illustrated*, April 6, 1918. See also Marty Bell, *The Legend of Dr. J: The Story of Julius Erving* (Putnam, 1975), 4–5.

5 **"Just as white":** As quoted in Nelson George, *Elevating the Game: Black Men and Basketball* (HarperCollins, 1992), 76.

6 **"Our game belonged":** Chet Walker, *Long Time Coming: A Black Athlete's Coming-of-Age in America* (Grove Press, 1995), 39.

7 **"Elgin taking the rebound":** Julius Erving with Karl Taro Greenfeld, *Dr. J: The Autobiography* (Harper, 2013), 35.

7 **"Back then," Erving recalled:** Mark Jacobson, "Doctor One and Only," *Esquire*, February 1, 1985.

Notes

7 **"I set no dimensions":** Peter Garry, "The Net-Ripping, Backboard-Shaking, Mind-Blowing Dr. J.," *Sports Illustrated*, December 11, 1972.

8 **"Behind his back":** Jay Searcy, "In School, the Ability Showed Early," *Philadelphia Inquirer*, April 16, 1987, 8.

8 **"Many times when I was":** Bill Rhoden, "The Incredible 'Dr. J.,'" *Ebony*, March 1975.

8 **"If someone had said":** Phil Jasner, *On the Case: His Best Writing on the Sixers, the Dream Team, and Beyond* (Temple University Press, 2017), 148.

9 **tease Erving about carrying:** Joe Gergen, "Erving Comes Home, Where His Heart Is," *Newsday*, August 1, 1973, 92, 89.

9 **"His talents were evident":** Papanek, "I've Always Felt Powerless."

9 **"I don't know why":** Jane Leavy, "Impact of a Superstar," *Washington Post*, May 7, 1982, C1–C2.

9 **"Take that play back":** Phil Jasner, "Dr. J: Basketball Will Endure," *Philadelphia Daily News*, February 11, 1983, 106.

10 **"I was putting limitations":** Steve Jacobson, "More Than a Degree of Success," *Newsday*, June 2, 1983, 135.

10 **"I am trying to practice":** Wayne Embry with Mary Schmitt Boyer, *The Inside Game: Race, Power, and Politics in the NBA* (University of Akron Press, 2004), 199–200.

11 **"I was there":** Author phone interview with George Mumford, June 7, 2023.

11 **"created as much enthusiasm":** Joe Gergen, "Erving Is Eying More Than One Goal," *Newsday*, February 2, 1971, 33.

11 **students would show up:** Author phone interview with Al Skinner, January 10, 2025.

11 **"When Julius got to Massachusetts":** Angelo Cataldi, "At UMass, the Erving Legend Has Grown," *Philadelphia Inquirer*, April 16, 1987, 9.

11 **"hoarse and hysterical":** Cataldi, "At UMass, the Erving Legend Has Grown."

12 **"They tell me he shifted":** John Jeansonne, "Thanks, Doc," *Newsday*, April 19, 1987, 16–17.

12 **"Well, around 1:30 or 2":** Cataldi, "At UMass, the Erving Legend Has Grown."

12 **"It's a shame":** Jim O'Brien, "Leaman Finds Life After the Doctor," *Basketball Weekly*, March 31, 1983, 16.

13 **"I was really brought":** Papanek, "I've Always Felt Powerless."

14 **"Who or what":** Peter Gammons, "Erving, Speed Key to UMass NIT Bid," *Boston Globe*, March 19, 1971.

14 **"Would you be interested":** As quoted in Bob Woolf, *Behind Closed Doors* (Atheneum, 1976), 93.

15 **"I don't have anything left":** Woolf, *Behind Closed Doors.*

15 **"I know they were charging":** Gergen, "Erving Is Eying."

15 **"My god, did you see":** Alexander Wolff, "Julius Erving," *Sports Illustrated*, September 19, 1994.

15 **One writer pointed out:** Robert Brody, "This Hand Is Quicker Than Your Eye," *GQ*, April 1984, 252–255.

15 **"Let's put it this way":** Joe Donnelly, "Erving: 'Have My Basketball Degree,'" *Newsday*, April 6, 1971, 5.

16 **"couldn't get enough of":** Garry, "The Net-Ripping."

16 **"He wouldn't really mean":** Author phone interview with Dave Brownbill, June 15, 2023.

16 **"I could see him creating":** Author interview with George Mumford.

17 **"It's all on instinct":** Author interview with Dave Brownbill.

17 **"You want to outscore":** Garry, "The Net-Ripping."

17 **"The Julius Erving Cult":** Howie Evans, "Sort of Sporty," *New York Amsterdam News*, August 7, 1971, D12.

17 **"Stories of [Erving's] heroics":** Peter Vecsey, "Pro Basketball Rookies…Some Play, Most Don't," *New York Daily News*, November 12, 1971, 95.

17 **"He shocked me":** Jerry Nason, "Bruin Reunion May Not Be…," *Boston Globe*, July 31, 1971, 19.

18 **"Where's the Doctor?":** Author interview with Dave Brownbill.

19 **"no one compares to me":** Peter Vecsey, "Cavaliers' Carr Falls for Fun City," *New York Daily News*, August 5, 1971, 102.

19 **"James Brown, Muhammad Ali":** Evans, "Sort of Sporty."

20 **"Al, we better":** Author phone interview with Mike Littwin, April 3, 2023. This story is also recounted in Terry Pluto, *Loose Balls: The Short, Wild Life of the American Basketball Association* (Simon & Schuster, 2007), 226.

20 **"out of their seats":** Howie Evans, "Sort of Sporty: 'The Doctor and Coach,'" *New York Amsterdam News*, October 2, 1971, D11.

20 **"Look what we found":** Pluto, *Loose Balls*, 226.

Chapter 2: The Prodigy

21 **"I don't ever relax":** Vic Fulp, "Rise of a Prep Cage Star," *Richmond Times-Dispatch*, October 29, 1972, E-12.

21 **"I don't think I'll go":** Vic Fulp, "Stars Help Malone Realize Early Goal," *Richmond Times-Dispatch*, August 30, 1974, C-1, C-3.

22 **"About 20 guys":** Mickey Herskowitz, "Go Up Moses, Rockets Root," *Houston Post*, February 6, 1977, 5-C.

22 **"Kids in the neighborhood":** Ray Didinger, "Moses Makes His Private Life Most Valuable," *Philadelphia Daily News*, May 26, 1983, 96–97, 104.

23 **"Guys hanging":** Didinger, "Moses Makes His Private Life."

23 **Virginian legislators convened:** Robert A. Pratt, *The Color of Their Skin: Education and Race in Richmond, Virginia: 1954–89* (University of Virginia Press, 1992), 3.

23 **the high school closed:** Mike Allen, "The Segregated Reunions of an Integrated School," *New York Times*, August 4, 1996.

23 **still bristled:** Author phone interview with Stanley Taylor, August 1, 2023.

24 **"Before he came":** Thomas Boswell, "Big Moses Malone Has All of Petersburg Saying Amen," *Washington Post*, February 3, 1973, D7.

24 **he couldn't spit out:** David E. Early, "Early Successes Haven't Spoiled Malone," *Minneapolis Star*, April 18, 1974, 13-C.

24 **"He was real quiet":** Fulp, "Rise of a Prep Cage Star."

24 **counselors forbade Malone:** Boswell, "Big Moses Malone Has All."

24 **Petersburg fans started chanting:** Harry Marsh, "Malone Assaults Dinwiddie," *Petersburg Progress-Index*, January 6, 1972, 18.

24 **"I can remember when":** Steven Armstrong, "Peal Can Be Proud of His Former Star," *Petersburg Progress-Index*, October 6, 1974, 29.

24 **"That was the only way":** Author phone interview with Otis Fulton, July 26, 2023.

25 **demand for tickets:** Boswell, "Big Moses Malone Has All."

25 **"Once the Crimson Wave":** John Packett, "Petersburg—Proof for the Cheers," *Richmond Times-Dispatch*, March 5, 1973, B-6.

25 **known affectionately as "Pit Stop":** Dave Kindred, "The Case for Lefty Driesell," *The Athletic*, March 29, 2018.

25 **"There's a God in heaven":** Ken Denlinger, "Malone: His Day Is Here," *Washington Post*, April 17, 1981, E1–E2.

26 **"That guy is the *truth*":** Author phone interview with Lefty Driesell, July 31, 2023.

26 **"Moses Malone is the only":** George Shirk, "Malone Lives by His Instincts," *Philadelphia Inquirer*, February 13, 1983, 1-D, 8-D.

26 **"didn't say three words":** Phil Jasner, "Molding of Man Named Moses," *Philadelphia Daily News*, February 15, 1983, 62.

27 **Only four plays:** Mike Harris, "Petersburg Rode Malone's Wave," *Richmond Times-Dispatch*, December 22, 1996, D8.

27 **he spiked the ball:** Larry Clark, "Wave Sets Stage for Friday Showdown," *Petersburg Progress-Index*, January 10, 1974, 10.

27 **"I'm glad you don't":** Author interview with Otis Fulton.

27 **Sprinkled among:** Bill Cate, "Moses Malone Called Nation's Best Player," *Roanoke Times*, February 17, 1974, C-2.

27 **"Greetings from Petersburg":** Joseph Durso, "It's Easy to Reach for Money If You're Tall," *Shreveport Journal*, January 23, 1976, D5.

27 **holding up a broomstick:** Author phone interview with Dave Koesters, July 26, 2023.

28 **"Answer the bell!":** Author phone interview with Bernard Wilson, July 31, 2023.

28 **college coaches ranging:** Vic Fulp, "Malone 'Shares' His Day," *Richmond Times-Dispatch*, March 23, 1974, B-5.

28 **"Because I don't like it":** David E. Early, "Early Successes Haven't Spoiled Malone," *Minneapolis Star*, April 18, 1974, 13-C.

29 **"A person can ask":** Vic Fulp, "All Available, He Conquered," *Richmond Times-Dispatch*, March 23, 1974, B-5.

29 **"I'd walk out":** Vic Dorr Jr., "In Hot Pursuit," *Richmond Times-Dispatch*, October 5, 2001, M2.

29 **A thriving grift soon:** Frank Deford, "Bounding into Prominence," *Sports Illustrated*, February 19, 1979.

29 **"front-page headlines":** Deford, "Bounding into Prominence."

29 **A television news anchor:** David E. Early, "Recruiting Pressures Pile Up on Star Malone," *Minneapolis Star*, April 19, 1974, 9-B.

30 **"took more punishment":** Sam Lacy, "Instant Millionaire Makes Sense," *Baltimore Afro-American*, September 7, 1974, 9.

30 **"vocal cords are in":** Bill Millsaps, "Wave's Malone Usually Special," *Richmond Times-Dispatch*, December 4, 1973, B-5.

30 **Malone developed a code:** Dwight Chapin, "Malone Makes Experts Eat Their Words," *Des Moines Register*, January 5, 1975, 2D.

30 **"All this stuff":** Chauncey Durden, "The Garbo-ish Malone," *Richmond Times-Dispatch*, May 23, 1974, H-1.

30 **"The recruiters dragged me":** Pat Putnam, "Don't Send My Boy to Harvard...," *Sports Illustrated*, November 4, 1974.

31 **"I rarely talked":** Author interview with Lefty Driesell.

31 **Malone pretended to sleep:** Dorr, "In Hot Pursuit."

31 **"I *told* you!":** Author interview with Lefty Driesell; see also Kindred, "The Case for Lefty Driesell."

32 **"leaped about three":** John Packet, "Sleepy Malone Signs Grant with Terps," *Richmond Times-Dispatch*, June 21, 1974, C-1.

32 **"Don't give me that":** Lawrence Linderman, "*Playboy* Interview: Moses Malone," *Playboy*, March 1984, 53–68.

32 **"it's a big temptation":** Harry Marsh, "Malone Drafted in Third Round by Pro ABA Utah Stars; Kilbourne and Peal Think He Should Attend College First," *Petersburg Progress-Index*, April 18, 1974, 27.

33 **well below the ticket sales:** John Green, "$1 Million Envelops First High School Star to Pass Up College for Pro Basketball," *Pittsburgh Press*, March 19, 1975, 25.

33 **In his first phone conversation:** Dorr, "In Hot Pursuit."

34 **across the orange crate:** Author phone interview with Bucky Buckwalter, July 25, 2023. For more on this meeting, see David Halberstam, *The Breaks of the Game* (Hyperion, 1981), 225–226.

34 **To Buckwalter's astonishment:** Author interview with Bucky Buckwalter.

34 **"The publicity he's going":** Bill Millsaps, "Malone—May Be 'Star' by Now," *Richmond Times-Dispatch*, August 28, 1974, B-5.

35 **"beachball league":** Author interview with Lefty Driesell.

35 **"was giving these wild":** Author interview with Lefty Driesell.

35 **"I tell you what":** Kowet, "Moses Malone," 76–77.

35 **"'I know you guys'":** Author phone interview with Lee Fentress, April 26, 2023.

35 **"I was just looking out":** Author interview with Lefty Driesell.

36 **"All that money":** Rick Telander, *Heaven Is a Playground: A Journey into the Sweet World of Street Basketball*, 5th ed. (Sports Publishing, 2013), 80.

36 **"That inducement to":** Author email exchange with Donald Dell, July 6, 2023.

36 **"flesh-peddler":** Deford, "Bounding into Prominence."

36 **"had a strong disagreement":** Author email exchange with Donald Dell.

37 **"If you are going over":** Harry Marsh, "The Sports Scene," *Petersburg Progress-Index*, August 29, 1974, 27.

37 **"Tonight," she said:** Chapin, "Malone Makes Experts."

37 **"The signing is reprehensible":** Chapin, "Malone Makes Experts."

37 **"The overriding factor":** Chapin, "Malone Makes Experts."

38 **"In an era when":** A. S. "Doc" Young, "Good Morning, Sports! The Malone Caper…," *Chicago Defender*, September 12, 1974, 36.

38 **"whenever a black kid":** Sam Lacy, "Instant Millionaire Makes Sense," *Baltimore Afro-American*, September 7, 1974, 9.

38 **"It don't make no difference":** Deford, "Bounding into Prominence."

Chapter 3: The Red, White, and Blue

40 **on the nose of a seal:** Jackie MacMullan, Rafe Bartholomew, and Dan Klores, eds. *Basketball: A Love Story* (Crown Archetype, 2018), 144.

40 **"making a mockery":** Wayne Embry, *The Inside Game: Race, Power, and Politics in the NBA* (University of Akron Press, 2004), 211.

40 **the Dolgoff Plan:** Adam J. Criblez, *Tall Tales and Short Shorts: Dr. J, Pistol Pete, and the Birth of the Modern NBA* (Rowman & Littlefield, 2017), 172.

41 **"It would take almost five hours":** Joe Gergen, "Traveling Violations in the ABA," *Newsday*, October 27, 1975, 79.

41 **"Govan, you played eight":** Author phone interview with Gerald Govan, June 12, 2023.

41 **"As I went along":** Earl Strom with Blaine Johnson, *Calling the Shots: My Five Decades in the NBA* (Simon & Schuster, 1990), 144.

42 **"beautiful in the same way":** Bill Russell and Taylor Branch, *Second Wind: The Memoirs of an Opinionated Man* (Random House, 1979), 98.

42 **"At times out there":** Al Cohn, "Mild-Mannered Dr. J at Home in Camp," *Miami Herald*, October 27, 1974, 4-DW.

42 **"My overall goal":** Mark Jacobson, "Doctor One and Only," *Esquire*, February 1, 1985, 112–119.

42 **"If you paid":** Author interview with Mike Littwin.

42 **"Last night," Erving replied:** Pluto, *Loose Balls*, 228.

43 **"the good doctor was not born":** Jim Murray, "Dr. J Came to Play," *Los Angeles Times*, August 22, 1975, 3-1, 3-8.

43 **They sparred with owners:** For more on the players' outspokenness and fashion choices, see Theresa Runstedtler, *Black Ball: Kareem Abdul-Jabbar, Spencer Haywood, and the Generation That Saved the Soul of the NBA* (Bold Type Books, 2023), 30.

43 **team rosters in both leagues:** Adam J. Criblez, "White Men Playing a Black Man's Game: Basketball's 'Great White Hopes' of the 1970s," *Journal of Sport History* 42, no. 3 (Fall 2015): 373.

44 **"The question is":** John Papanek, "There's an Ill Wind Blowing for the NBA," *Sports Illustrated*, February 26, 1979.

44 **"I wanted to learn":** Mike Littwin, "He's on the All-Interview Team, Too," *Los Angeles Times*, June 3, 1982, 3-10.

44 **"Did Beethoven have":** Mike Littwin, "Once, He Played Above the Stars," *Los Angeles Times*, June 3, 1982, 3-1, 3-10.

44 **"When I got a platform":** Robert Huber, "Julius Erving Doesn't Want to Be a Hero Anymore," *Philadelphia Magazine*, April 23, 2008.

45 **thousands of families who jammed:** George Vecsey, "Roy Boe Has a Doctor in the House… & Too Many Empty Seats," *Sport*, February 1974, 66–71.

45 **"Wind it up":** Bill Nack, "…With Everyone Playing a Version of the Heavy," *Newsday*, September 23, 1976, 167.

46 **Erving would stroll languidly:** Erving with Greenfeld, *Dr. J*, 187.

46 **"I played year-round":** Phil Jasner, "Still Shining," *Philadelphia Daily News*, February 8, 1986, 39.

46 **he experimented with sleeping:** Erving with Greenfeld, *Dr. J*, 203.

47 **"I am not exaggerating":** Millsaps, "Malone—May Be 'Star.'"

47 **"Moses Will Lead Us":** Didinger, "Moses Makes His Private Life."

47 **"I was sitting in the stands":** Kowet, "Moses Malone," 76–77.

48 **"With all the talent":** Harry Xanthakos, "Moses Malone: No Miracles…Just Victories," *Black Sports*, January 1975.

48 **"What are your thoughts":** Xanthakos, "Moses Malone."

49 **Malone had refused to speak:** Author phone interview with Steve Rudman, September 5, 2023.

49 **Getting Malone to shut up:** Steve Rudman, "Moses Malone Proves Talking Can Be Cool," *Salt Lake Tribune*, January 26, 1975, D1, D6.

49 **"click, he turns it":** Kenneth Denlinger, "Malone Catches Up on His Homework," *Washington Post*, November 24, 1974, C1.

50 **"next time you come in here":** Author phone interview with Bill Melchionni, May 30, 2023.

50 **"Trying to interview Malone":** Rudman, "Moses Malone Proves."

50 **pleaded with his players:** Author interview with Gerald Govan.

50 **"Malone put his warmup":** Rudman, "Moses Malone Proves."

50 **"You're gonna give me":** Author interview with Steve Rudman.

51 **"The people who call Malone":** Didinger, "Moses Makes His Private Life."

52 **"We won fifty straight":** As quoted in Bill Gutman, *Chairmen of the Boards: Erving, Bird, Malone, Johnson* (Ace Books, 1980), 125.

52 **"Sports and society":** *New York Times* news service, "Moses' Journey Through Promised Land," *Chicago Tribune*, November 9, 1976, 51.

52 **"I used to tell":** Paul Attner, "Spirits Are Elevated by Malone's Revival," *Washington Post*, January 20, 1976, D1.

53 **"left-side garbage":** Ray Buck, "Wholly Moses," *Sport*, January 1982.

53 **"meat and potatoes":** Author phone interview with Del Harris, April 27, 2023.

53 **"I heard he could do this":** Tommy Bonk, "Malone Improving with Age," *Houston Post*, October 18, 1978, 2B.

53 **"never learned the basic skills":** George White, "They Skipped Class," *Sporting News*, January 5, 1980, 30.

54 **"I know he's young":** Author interview with Steve Rudman.

54 **"He didn't quit":** Author interview with Gerald Govan.

55 **"Having a superstar":** John Green, "$1 Million Envelops First High School Star to Pass Up College for Pro Basketball," *Pittsburgh Press*, March 19, 1975, 25.

Chapter 4: Dissolution

57 **"I'm going home":** Woodrow Paige, "Moses Finds the Promised Land in Salt Lake," *Sporting News*, May 3, 1975, 47.

57 **"I must have scouted":** Jim O'Brien, "Moses Parted Water for Kids," *Sporting News*, September 6, 1975, 37.

58 **"Foot broke":** Author interview with Del Harris.

58 **"We can't cop":** Curry Kirkpatrick, "And Now the Incredible Shrinking ABA," *Sports Illustrated*, December 15, 1975.

59 **"We have a crisis":** Augie Borgi, "ABA Is Near Crossroads; Scott Given Ax by Pistons," *Newsday*, January 27, 1976, 55.

60 **clutching a bottle:** Author phone interview with Steve Green, November 29, 2023.

60 **"It's a shame that":** Steve Rudman, "Daniels Bails Out as Stars Near End," *Salt Lake Tribune*, December 2, 1975, 19, 21.

60 **when team officials used to dole:** Author phone interview with Randy Denton, November 22, 2023.

60 **"Everybody go down":** *New York Times* news service, "Moses' Journey."

61 **Only two NBA franchises:** Curry Kirkpatrick, "They Run and They Gun—and They're a Mile-High," *Sports Illustrated*, March 29, 1976.

62 **Inspired by the arm-wrestling:** Jim O'Brien, "A Beautiful Show for ABA Fans," *Sporting News*, February 14, 1976, 13, 17. See also Pluto, *Loose Balls*, 25–27.

62 **"the greatest halftime invention":** John Papanek, "Strutting Their Stuffs," *Sports Illustrated*, February 9, 1976.

62 **during clinics for Converse:** MacMullan et al., *Basketball*, 174.

62 **"Now there's three":** Author phone interview with Junior Bridgeman, February 5, 2025.

63 **pantomiming the moves:** Papanek, "Strutting Their Stuffs."

63 **"Doc's in trouble":** Papanek, "Strutting Their Stuffs."

63 **"all the other players":** Jim O'Brien, "'Best Player in Game's History,'" *Sporting News*, April 10, 1976, 49.

64 **"When you got Marvin Barnes":** Author interview with Steve Green.

65 **"Moses didn't need":** Author phone interview with Ron Boone, December 4, 2023.

65 **Malone grunted, "Peeing":** Author interview with Steve Green.

65 **"When you'd watch Malone":** Dick Weiss, "The Sixers' Dawkins and Rockets' Malone—a Tale of 2 Young Centers of Attractions," *Philadelphia Daily News*, May 4, 1977, 75.

65 **"For Moses, as young":** Phil Jasner, "Moses Malone: From 'Superkid' to Superstar," *Basketball Digest*, May 1985, 21–25.

65 **"It was getting kind of":** Author interview with Randy Denton.

65 **"We were all friendly":** Author interview with Steve Green.

66 **"Well, Julius isn't":** John Papanek, "I'll Never Play the Same Old Riff," *Sports Illustrated*, May 17, 1976.

66 **"Hey, look, the guy's killing Doc":** Doug Smith, "Basketball Seminar: Dr. J Tells How to Do It," *Black Sports*, April 1976, 9–14.

66 **nearly four hundred extra:** Jane Gross, "Nets Win at the Buzzer, 120–118, as Erving Hits 15-Foot Jumper," *Newsday*, May 2, 1976.

67 **"I was all over him":** Author phone interview with Bobby Jones, May 25, 2023.

67 **"I want this championship":** Jane Gross, "It's Prime Time for Julius Erving," *Newsday*, May 11, 1976, 80.

67 **"he ended up bringing":** Author interview with Bobby Jones.

67 **"the guy who drove":** Author interview with Al Skinner.

67 **"five-on-one with a helicopter":** Pat Putnam, "The Doctor Opens Up His Medicine Bag," *Sports Illustrated*, May 17, 1976.

67 **"He kept the heat":** Bill Livingston, "Dr. J: Newest Sixer Is Best in the Game," *Philadelphia Inquirer*, October 21, 1976, 1-C, 2-C.

68 **drained champagne bottles:** Don Markus, "Nets Turn Tables to Take ABA Title," *Standard Star* (New Rochelle, NY), May 14, 1976, C-6.

68 **"If this was the last":** United Press International, "Was It ABA's Last Hurrah?," *Kingston Daily Freeman*, May 14, 1976, 13.

Chapter 5: The Start of the Odyssey

69 **would now feature twelve times:** Curry Kirkpatrick, "A Season for All Men," *Sports Illustrated*, October 25, 1976.

70 **"I live by the code":** Tony Kornheiser, "Erving Profits from Agent's Code," *Newsday*, August 2, 1973, 108.

70 **"Weiner comes every year":** Jane Gross, "Roy Boe Gives His Side of Erving's Story," *Newsday*, November 11, 1976, 46T.

70 **"All I asked for":** Jane Gross, "Julius Erving Tries to Adjust to New Team, City," *Newsday*, October 31, 1976.

70 **"The Doctor is guilty":** Dave Anderson, "Doctor J Guilty of Malpractice, Stole the Nets' Heart," *Philadelphia Evening Bulletin*, October 29, 1976, 35.

71 **"just another game":** Dick Weiss and Phil Jasner, "Erving: Best That Money Can Buy," *Philadelphia Daily News*, October 21, 1976, 68.

71 **"brittle bones":** George Cunningham, "Hawks Get Petrie, Hawes," *Atlanta Constitution*, August 6, 1976, 1-D, 6-D.

72 **"he's our property":** Bill Schaefer, "Ramsay Confident He Can Produce a Winner," *Oregon Statesman*, September 20, 1976, 3B.

72 **"exempt from any dealing":** Associated Press, "Blazers Deal Petrie, Hawes to Atlanta," *Longview Daily News*, August 6, 1976, 25.

72 **"I only took half":** Tony Kornheiser, "Rockets Hope Malone Is 'Home,'" *Chicago Tribune*, November 9, 1976, 51.

73 **Malone uttered "foot":** Halberstam, *The Breaks of the Game*, 222.

73 **"Malone should like":** Jim O'Brien, "Gilmore to Rejuvenate the Bulls," *Sporting News*, August 28, 1976, 54.

73 **"[Moses] didn't do anything":** Associated Press, "Blazers Rethink Malone," *Capital Journal*, October 18, 1976, 40.

73 **a gruff "No comment":** Stephen A. Monroe, "Is Moses Braves' Savior?," *Democrat and Chronicle*, October 20, 76, 1D, 3D.

73 **"I'm sure those years":** Didinger, "Moses Makes His Private Life."

73 **"Half a suitcase":** Kornheiser, "Rockets Hope Malone."

74 **"It was kind of like saying":** Pat Williams with Bill Lyon, *We Owed You One! The Uphill Struggle of the Philadelphia 76ers* (Trimark Publishing, 1983), 52.

74 **"We had a significant number":** Author interview with Bill Melchionni.

75 **exotic flowers that were reportedly valued:** Marc Schogol, "Money, Power and Mr. Dixon," *Philadelphia Inquirer*, November 7, 1977, 1-C, 5-C.

75 **"I always wanted to own":** Douglas S. Looney, "That Fitz, He's a Honey," *Sports Illustrated*, November 6, 1978.

75 **"Fitz, we have a chance":** All dialogue in the following paragraphs between Pat Williams and Fitz Dixon is from an author phone interview with Pat Williams on March 14, 2023.

76 **"Not even me":** Jim Barniak, "Dixon Seeks Rebirth of Philly Basketball," *Philadelphia Evening Bulletin*, May 29, 1977.

76 **Williams had to call:** Bill Livingston, "A Diary: How the Sixers Got Dr. J," *Philadelphia Inquirer*, October 31, 1976, 1-E, 6-E.

76 **Caldwell Jones fell to:** Curry Kirkpatrick, "The Doctor Doubled His Fee," *Sports Illustrated*, November 1, 1976.

76 **"With Julius, George McGinnis":** Dick Weiss, "Dr. J Is Ready to Operate," *Philadelphia Daily News*, October 22, 1976, 96, 91.

77 **"Am I allowed to lose":** Skip Myslenski, "Dr. J's Mind, Body Not in Tune," *Philadelphia Inquirer*, October 23, 1976, 1–2C.

77 **"We sold $48,000":** Frank Brady, "Erving to Play in Opener," *Philadelphia Evening Bulletin*, October 22, 1976.

77 **tried to bribe:** Skip Myslenski, "Fastbreak: Fans Keep 76ers' Ticket Office Running," *Philadelphia Inquirer*, December 14, 1976.

77 **plopped his paycheck:** Pete Alfano, "He Learned the Game on the Playgrounds of LI," *Newsday*, October 21, 1976, 174.

77 **"This is not slavery":** Pete Alfano, "Erving's First Showing as a 76er," *Newsday*, October 22, 1976, 132.

77 **"I've stated during the holdout":** Alfano, "Erving's First Showing."

78 **"like President [Gerald] Ford":** Livingston, "A Diary."

78 **"By George, We've Got It":** Ted Green, "George McGinnis: If He Weren't So Real, He Would Seem Unreal," *Boston Globe*, November 7, 1975, 37.

78 **"we're gonna do":** Livingston, "A Diary."

79 **"My mind felt I could":** Kirkpatrick, "The Doctor Doubled."

79 **"We were all so happy":** Bill Livingston, "76ers Get Their Act Together," *Philadelphia Inquirer*, October 27, 1976, 1–2C.

80 **"I wasn't going to placate":** Stephen A. Monroe, "Surprising Braves Trade Malone," *Democrat and Chronicle*, October 26, 1976, 1D, 3D.

80 **"[Moses] was happy happy":** *New York Times* news service, "Moses' Journey."

81 **"in a bad way":** Kornheiser, "Rockets Hope Malone."

81 **"he could be a hero":** George White, "Ray Patterson: Rocket GM Weathered Dark Days Because Faith in City Didn't Waver," *Houston Chronicle*, March 6, 1978, 3-1, 3-8.

81 **"Mo, now you're home":** Kornheiser, "Rockets Hope Malone."

Chapter 6: The Philadelphia Monster

85 **suspend traveling violations:** Rudy Tomjanovich with Robert Falkoff, *A Rocket at Heart: My Life and My Team* (Simon & Schuster, 1997), 72.

85 **"little traveling band":** Author phone interview with Tommy Bonk, July 10, 2023.

85 **"like over at NASA?":** Author phone interview with Steve Patterson, June 14, 2023.

86 **burned through ten thousand:** George White, "Philadelphia's $6 Million Julius Erving Here Tonight," *Houston Chronicle*, October 27, 1976, 6-1.

86 **"A lot of the reason":** Frank Brady, "Doctor Dunks Seven, Mac Also 'Awesome' in Sixers' Triumph," *Philadelphia Evening Bulletin*, October 28, 1976.

86 **"Just another move":** Brady, "Doctor Dunks Seven."

87 **"[The 76ers] aren't polished":** George White, "Rockets Bystanders to Sixer Circus Act," *Houston Chronicle*, October 28, 1976, 3-1.

87 **"the world's in trouble":** Jerry Wizig, "Murphy Warns World's in Trouble with Dr. J," *Houston Chronicle*, October 28, 1976, 3-5.

88 **"he might have gone down":** Author phone interview with Neil Funk, June 11, 2023.

88 **"He was never a hard worker":** Bruce Newman, "Oh, What Might Have Been," *Sports Illustrated*, March 1, 1982.

88 **"He was six eleven and chiseled":** Author phone interview with Harvey Catchings, October 16, 2024.

89 **"one guy would be smoking":** Dave Wohl, "The Extremely High Bar Set for NBA Manchild Darryl Dawkins," *Sports Illustrated*, April 11, 1988.

89 **"I thought I was on tour":** Samantha Stevenson, "Dr. J. Playing a New Game," *New York Times*, April 23, 1978.

89 **"We're an experience":** David Casstevens, "Putting a Cork on Sixer Speed," *Houston Post*, May 10, 1977, 1C.

89 **"The Philadelphia Monster has been":** Leigh Montville, "But, Can the Doctor Help a Monster?," *Boston Globe*, October 26, 1976, 29.

90 **"a line at a delicatessen":** Bud Shaw, "Big Mac Deserves Break Today," *Philadelphia Daily News*, April 3, 1981, 82.

90 **The next game opened:** Mark Heisler, "76ers' Troubles Clog Victory Trail," *Philadelphia Evening Bulletin*, January 2, 1977, 7.

90 **"I always felt I never":** Ted Green, "76ers Mostly Talk So Far," *Newsday*, November 11, 1976, 126, 117.

90 **"What I could bring":** Author interview with Julius Erving.

90 **"Here I was":** Curry Kirkpatrick, "Hey, What's Up with the Doc?," *Sports Illustrated*, March 26, 1979.

91 **"The ABA was a minor league":** Papanek, "I've Always Felt Powerless."

91 **"New York was my first":** Jim O'Brien, "Philly No Paradise, Says Dr. J," *Sporting News*, January 15, 1977, 35.

91 **"The ABA was one for all":** Author interview with Julius Erving.

91 **"If I were with the Nets":** Bill Livingston, "Dr. J Starting to Display Old Tricks as 76er," *Sporting News*, February 12, 1977, 3.

92 **"All I do is sit":** Mark Heisler, "Sub Asks to Play or Leave," *Philadelphia Evening Bulletin*, December 16, 1976.

92 **"I'm tired of being insulted":** Mark Heisler, "76ers' Free Raps Shue, Asks Trade," *Philadelphia Evening Bulletin*, March 14, 1976.

92 **"Players being unhappy":** Curry Kirkpatrick, "Good, but Why Not the Best?," *Sports Illustrated*, March 21, 1977.

93 **"No one here respects":** Turquoise Erving, "The Regrets of a Player's Wife," *New York Times*, March 13, 1977.

93 **"an attention span":** Mickey Herskowitz, "Freelance Sixers Have Talent Edge," *Houston Post*, May 22, 1977, 8C.

93 **"We've been like a wagonload":** John Papanek, "The Sixers Do the Hustle," *Sports Illustrated*, May 16, 1977.

93 **"Moses showed up":** Author interview with Steve Patterson.

94 **"spark of intensity":** Kornheiser, "Rockets Hope Malone."

94 **Kunnert complained about:** Author phone interview with Kevin Kunnert, August 7, 2023.

94 **"defy a lot of":** George White, "Rockets Flout NBA Theory," *Houston Chronicle*, May 3, 1977, 6-3.

95 **"your basic fight":** George White, "76ers Disparage Rockets Defense, Lack of Speed," *Houston Chronicle*, May 7, 1977, 3-2.

95 **"One would've thought Moses":** Tommy Bonk, "Sixers Outrun Rockets," *Houston Post*, May 6, 1977, 1F, 10F.

96 **"I'm not going to talk":** Mark Heisler, "Can Rockets Slow Pace?," *Philadelphia Evening Bulletin*, May 8, 1977.

96 **The session got so heated:** David Casstevens, "76ers Take It Easy as Confidence High After Thursday Win," *Houston Post*, May 7, 1977, 2D.

96 **"the warm bodies":** Frank Dolson, "All Over but the Shooting," *Philadelphia Inquirer*, May 9, 1977, 1-C, 3-C.

96 **"won one more":** Bill Livingston, "Rockets Blast 76ers by 118–94," *Philadelphia Inquirer*, May 12, 1977, 1-C.

96 **"Can't shoot if you ain't":** Livingston, "Rockets Blast 76ers."

97 **"[Malone] doesn't play anybody":** George White, "Crowding Dr. J in Second Half Paid Dividends," *Houston Chronicle*, May 16, 1977, 2-4.

97 **"If Mo says":** White, "Crowding Dr. J."

97 **"[Steve] Mix, he don't":** Frank Dolson, "Rockets Talk with Basketball," *Philadelphia Inquirer*, May 16, 1977, 1-C, 5-C.

97 **"How does he know":** Frank Brady, "War of Words Escalates with Steve Mix's Remarks," *Philadelphia Evening Bulletin*, May 16, 1977.

97 **"They threw that stuff":** Tommy Bonk, "Shootout: Believing Rockets Go for Series Tie Tonight," *Houston Post*, May 17, 1977, 1D, 4D.

98 **"looked like fall registration":** David Casstevens, "A Love Affair with Rockets," *Houston Post*, May 17, 1977, 1D, 4D.

98 **"They'd get down there":** Skip Myslenski, "Foul Call Was Foul—Rockets," *Philadelphia Inquirer*, May 18, 1977, 1-D, 3-D.

99 **"We had a timeout":** Author interview with Calvin Murphy.

99 **"I don't ever say":** Author phone interview with Mike Newlin, February 5, 2024.

99 **"I felt completely empty":** Robert Falkoff, "Mo's Low Long Gone," *Houston Post*, May 3, 1981, 1C, 10C.

Chapter 7: Individual Versus Team

101 **by lofting balls skyward:** Jack Scott, *Bill Walton: On the Road with the Portland Trail Blazers* (Crowell, 1978), 226.

Notes

101 **"We've been consistent":** Dick Weiss, "It's All Over for Sixers," *Philadelphia Daily News*, June 6, 1977, 60, 58.

101 **"incredible study in intensity":** Bill Livingston, "Mix's Sprain Strains 76ers' Title Hopes," *Philadelphia Inquirer*, May 21, 1977, 1-2C.

102 **"are the medium":** Jack Ramsay with John Strawn, *The Coach's Art* (Timber Press, 1978), 48.

102 **"ran the system so well":** Author phone interview with Lionel Hollins, January 15, 2025.

102 **"a non-team":** Bill Lyon, "Sixer System: Yes, It Exists," *Philadelphia Inquirer*, February 26, 1978.

102 **"is preached so much":** Curry Kirkpatrick, "A Fever Called Blazermania," *Sports Illustrated*, October 31, 1977.

102 **"teamwork, character, and a little":** Wayne Thompson, "Disciplined Blazers Buy Ramsay's Tough System," *Sporting News*, March 25, 1978, 5.

103 **"All season, we've been":** Mark Heisler, "Dr. J Turns It On," *Philadelphia Evening Bulletin*, May 29, 1977.

103 **"most of white America":** Newman, "Oh, What Might Have Been."

103 **"see the old Dr. J?":** Alex Sachare, "Jones Should Enable Dr. J to Make More House Calls," *Philadelphia Evening Bulletin*, August 20, 1978.

103 **"Lots of times we run":** Mark Heisler, "Dr. J: Carefree Practices May Hurt 76ers," *Philadelphia Evening Bulletin*, April 22, 1977.

104 **"If a black player":** Darryl Dawkins, *Chocolate Thunder: The Uncensored Life and Times of Darryl Dawkins* (Sport Media Publishing, 2003), 76.

104 **white team basketball:** For more on this point, see Adam J. Criblez, "White Men Playing a Black Man's Game: Basketball's 'Great White Hopes' of the 1970s," *Journal of Sport History* 42, no. 3 (Fall 2015): 374.

105 **"I don't have anything":** Skip Myslenski, "2 Streaks Soar to the Occasion," *Philadelphia Inquirer*, May 23, 1977, 1-C, 3-C.

106 **"had hit a junkyard":** Curry Kirkpatrick, "There's No Place Like Home Court," *Sports Illustrated*, June 6, 1977.

106 **"What was Doc doing":** Dawkins, *Chocolate Thunder*, 79.

106 **"When Doc sat at halfcourt":** Author interview with Harvey Catchings.

107 **"A disaster, isn't it?":** Frank Dolson, "Ambush on the Oregon Trail," *Philadelphia Inquirer*, June 1, 1977, 1-D.

107 **"I looked around":** Stan Hochman, "Erving: Fix Air Conditioned Heads," *Philadelphia Daily News*, May 15, 1979.

107 **"Dr. J out of the closet":** Bill Lyon, "Playoffs Proved the Erving Legend," *Philadelphia Inquirer*, June 7, 1977, 1-D, 3-D.

107 **"Unless somebody else":** Lyon, "Playoffs Proved the Erving Legend."

108 **"resembled a guy pulling":** Stan Hochman, "Bobby Gross Won't Read This, but He's Quite a Player," *Philadelphia Daily News*, June 4, 1977, 39.

108 **"Who the hell is Bobby Gross?":** Author interview with Neil Funk.

108 **"What went wrong":** Mark Heisler, "Mac Took Too Long to Find Shot," *Philadelphia Evening Bulletin*, June 7, 1977.

108 **"The Blazers fly United":** Wayne Thompson, "Discipline Puts Crown in Blazers' Showcase," *Sporting News*, June 18, 1977, 45.

109 **"a blind man searching":** Curry Kirkpatrick, "All for One Sure Beats One for All," *Sports Illustrated*, June 13, 1977.

109 **"You dumbass, I just":** "He's Worth Every Penny," *Philadelphia Evening Bulletin*, October 16, 1977.

109 **"If we won":** Ray Didinger, "Sixers' Style Nos," *Philadelphia Evening Bulletin*, June 6, 1977.

109 **"It's OK," Erving murmured:** Ray Didinger, *Finished Business: My Fifty Years of Headlines, Heroes, and Heartaches* (Temple University Press, 2021), 198–199.

110 **"victory is only defeat":** Author phone interview with Jere Longman, May 17, 2023.

110 **"The prevailing feeling":** Author phone interview with Jerry Selber, April 25, 2023.

111 **"you fans have a right":** Author interview with Jerry Selber; author phone interview with Victor Sonder, April 25, 2023.

111 **"Where did we screw up":** Mark Heisler, "Sixers Don't Owe Anybody," *Philadelphia Evening Bulletin*, September 22, 1977.

Chapter 8: Rise and Drift

113 **"You went down to Fonde":** Author interview with Calvin Murphy.

113 **"If you didn't win":** Author phone interview with Major Jones, January 7, 2025.

113 **losing players slipped:** George White, "Fonde Center: 'The Best Little Basketball Gym in Texas,'" *Houston Chronicle*, June 4, 1979, 2-2.

114 **"On Monday, [Malone] would":** Author phone interview with Robert Reid, April 22, 2023.

114 **"Talk to Lee":** Author interview with Steve Patterson.

114 **"Moses loves to":** Phil Jasner, "Despite Need, Sixers Forget McHale," *Philadelphia Daily News*, December 31, 1982, 76.

114 **"All I do is play":** Linderman, "*Playboy* Interview."

115 **"I measure my words":** Stan Hochman, "Everything's A-OK When the Doctor Gets to Visit," *Philadelphia Daily News*, February 2, 1982, 64–65.

115 **"I would take Darryl":** George White, "76ers Disparage Rockets Defense, Lack of Speed," *Houston Chronicle*, May 7, 1977, 3-2.

115 **"You can't understand him":** Peter Vecsey, "A New Day for the NBA," *Sport*, November 1983.

115 **"Moses will be like Bill Russell":** "Insiders Say," *Sporting News*, May 28, 1977, 4.

116 **called reporters "janitors":** Author phone interview with Marc Iavaroni, October 18, 2024.

116 **"I don't talk on Tuesdays":** Author interview with Tommy Bonk.

116 **"I've always been happy":** Ronald O. Howell, "Moses Malone: Basketball's Million-Dollar Baby," *Ebony*, January 1980, 38–42.

116 **"You play with teammates":** George White, "Moses Reaches NBA's Promised Land at 23," *Sporting News*, February 3, 1979, 3.

117 **"You can't talk defense":** Jerry Wizig, "Henderson, Leavell Melt Spurs' Iceman," *Houston Chronicle*, April 3, 1980, 2-9.

117 **"I think I have":** Buck, "Wholly Moses."

117 **"People would think":** Linderman, "*Playboy* Interview."

118 **"Anybody can shoot":** Bill Lyon, "Malone Alone: The Last Dinosaur," *Richmond Times-Dispatch*, December 5, 1993, D12.

118 **"Basketball at this level":** George White, "Intense Mo & Co. Blast West in OT," *Houston Chronicle*, February 4, 1980, 2-1, 2-6.

118 **"It's very rare":** George White, "Malone at 23," *Houston Chronicle*, January 12, 1979, 2-1, 2-5.

118 **"That second jump was":** Author phone interview with Bill Cartwright, July 23, 2023.

118 **"He spends every single":** White, "Moses Reaches NBA's Promised Land."

118 **"going after every rebound":** Ron Reid, "Sports People," *Philadelphia Inquirer*, May 12, 1983, 2-C.

119 **"couldn't shoot a lick":** Author interview with Bucky Buckwalter.

119 **"Moses didn't play basketball":** Author interview with Mike Newlin.

119 **"I couldn't have done it":** "Insiders Say," *Sporting News*, June 16, 1979, 4.

120 **"as much lateral movement":** Dawkins, *Chocolate Thunder*, 70.

120 **"I wasn't enjoying myself":** Greg Logan, "It Isn't Easy to Be Dr. J," *Basketball Digest*, March 1983.

120 **"There was an emptiness":** Logan, "It Isn't Easy to Be Dr. J."

120 **twenty different envelopes:** Author phone interview with Mark Whicker, June 14, 2023.

121 **comedians could open:** Lindsey Gruson, "About Philadelphia, Jokes Still Go for the City's Jugular," *New York Times*, December 22, 1986.

122 **The team that captured:** For more on the blue-collar ethos that Philadelphia imagined for itself, see Timothy J. Lombardo, *Blue-Collar Conservatism: Frank Rizzo's Philadelphia and Populist Politics* (University of Pennsylvania Press, 2018), 9, 159–160.

122 **"The most laborious":** Bill Livingston, "Why Doesn't Phila. Love the 76ers?," *Philadelphia Inquirer*, May 8, 1977, 1-F.

122 **racial tensions flared:** Ryan A. Swanson and David K. Wiggins, eds., *Philly Sports: Teams, Games, and Athletes from Rocky's Town* (University of Arkansas Press, 2016), 153–154.

123 **"some nightmare sheriff":** Walker, *Long Time Coming*, 169.

123 **roughly 75 percent of players:** Papanek, "There's an Ill Wind."

123 **"This is not to sound":** As quoted in Joshua Mendelsohn, *The Cap: How Larry Fleisher and David Stern Built the Modern NBA* (University of Nebraska Press, 2020), 124.

124 **Dawkins claimed that:** Dawkins, *Chocolate Thunder*, 100–101.

125 **"His style of play did not":** Author interview with Al Skinner.

125 **"I love America":** Erving with Greenfeld, *Dr. J*, 124.

125 **"'Crossover' became an important":** As quoted in Larry Platt, *New Jack Jocks: Rebels, Race, and the American Athlete* (Temple University Press, 2002), 146.

126 **Converse executives claimed:** Phil Jasner, "Erving, Bird Team Up for Ad," *Philadelphia Daily News*, December 18, 1981, 96.

126 **"I was restless":** Jay Searcy, "Erving Wants to Find Life After the NBA," *Post-Standard* (Syracuse, NY), April 20, 1987, C-2.

126 **a reunion was planned:** Fran Blinebury, "Dr. J Finds His Roots," *Philadelphia Journal*, October 10, 1979.

126 **On a scroll:** Marc Markowitz, "A Sense of Awareness on and off the Court," *Morning Call* (Allentown, PA), October 11, 1979, C10.

127 **"A long time ago":** Searcy, "Erving Wants to Find."

127 **"I started thinking about destiny":** Dick Weiss, "Erving Gets to His Roots," *Philadelphia Daily News*, October 10, 1979, 62.

127 **"I divided my life":** Papanek, "I've Always Felt Powerless."

Chapter 9: The Philadelphia Reboot

129 **"He looked so good":** Ray Didinger, "A 'New' Erving Leaps into Leadership," *Philadelphia Evening Bulletin*, April 15, 1980.

129 **"He looks soft":** Bob Quincy, "Billy Cunningham: The Cougars MVP," *Basketball Digest*, December 1973, 45–46.

130 **"more popular in Philly":** Curry Kirkpatrick, "Storms over the Atlantic," *Sports Illustrated*, November 21, 1977.

130 **he hurled clipboards:** Scott Ostler, "Now, Just Call Him Billy Cool," *Los Angeles Times*, May 31, 1982, 3-1, 3-4.

130 **"He'd be busting":** Phil Jasner, "Cunningham Was an Instant Hero," *Philadelphia Daily News*, October 19, 1976, 56.

131 **"We trimmed out":** Author interview with Pat Williams.

131 **"Anyone who cursed":** Charles Barkley, *Outrageous! The Fine Life and Flagrant Good Times of Basketball's Irresistible Force* (Simon & Schuster, 1992), 132.

131 **"That's why I'm glad":** Woodrow Paige Jr., "Mr. Clean Does Denver's Dirty Work," *Sport*, June 1978.

131 **the flavor of the gum:** Bill Lyon, "'Stork' Delivers When Necessary," *Philadelphia Inquirer*, May 29, 1983, 7-D.

131 **"I quickly figured out":** Author interview with Bobby Jones.

132 **"Bobby Jones gives you":** Bill Lyons, "Bobby Jones: Uncalled Upon," *Philadelphia Inquirer*, November 19, 1981, 1-E, 4-E.

132 **"always has combined":** Mark Whicker, "Jones Discovers Joys of Success," *Philadelphia Daily News*, June 1, 1983, 74.

132 **"If you have five guys":** Author interview with Bobby Jones.

132 **"Nobody was stabbing":** Phil Jasner, "Steve Mix Takes a Hard Look at His Sport," *Philadelphia Daily News*, October 9, 1980, B-10–B-12.

132 **"'How are you trading'":** Author phone interview with Billy Cunningham, July 14, 2023.

133 **"This kid better be":** Ray Didinger, "This One's for You, Jack McMahon," *Philadelphia Daily News*, June 2, 1983, 102.

133 **"as insistent and consistent":** Mark Whicker, "Cheeks Rates a Star," *Philadelphia Daily News*, January 22, 1983, 43.

134 **Cheeks flushed it through:** Alan Greenberg, "And Then Sometimes He's the Open Man," *Los Angeles Times*, May 10, 1980, 3-1, 3-8.

134 **Blindfolded, Cheeks nibbled:** Stan Hochman, "Mo Lets Chips Fall Where They May," *Philadelphia Daily News*, February 11, 1981, 64, 63.

134 **"Not being a vocal":** Author phone interview with Franklin Edwards, June 7, 2023.

134 **"I remember during timeouts":** Author interview with Bobby Jones.

135 **"If you try to rev":** Bill Lyons, "In Every Game, Dr. J Reaches for the Stars," *Philadelphia Inquirer*, November 5, 1981, 1-C, 5-C.

135 **"leaning against a block":** Ray Didinger, "Don't Rock the Doc," *Philadelphia Evening Bulletin*, April 24, 1980.

135 **"like a mackerel":** Ray Didinger, "The Doctor Puts a Ballgame in His Bag," *Philadelphia Evening Bulletin*, April 7, 1980.

135 **"high tide on the Jersey Shore":** Rusty Pray, "Why Sixers Don't Draw Fans at Home," *Courier-Post* (Camden, NJ), February 17, 1980; Mark Whicker, "Sixers Haven't Caught the Fans' Fancy," *Philadelphia Evening Bulletin*, January 5, 1979.

137 **"His hair is as ruly":** Tom Callahan, "The Best the Game Offers," *Time*, May 24, 1982, 89.

138 **"The Sixers of two":** Ray Didinger, "The Swagger Is Gone," *Philadelphia Evening Bulletin*, April 28, 1980.

138 **"So we went to Julius":** Author phone interview with Greg Kelser, March 5, 2024.

138 **"Forget everything":** Larry Bird and Earvin "Magic" Johnson Jr. with Jackie MacMullan, *When the Game Was Ours* (Houghton Mifflin Harcourt, 2009), 64–65, 81.

139 **"He helped me to become":** Author interview with Greg Kelser.

139 **"an ear-to-ear grin":** Jim Murray, "Oh, the Magic of a Smile Can Really Be Contagious," *Los Angeles Times*, June 6, 1982, 3-1, 3-6.

140 **"get a big book":** Author phone interview with Steve Springer, April 17, 2023.

140 **"All the attention":** Kareem Abdul-Jabbar with Mignon McCarthy, *Kareem* (Random House, 1990), 3.

141 **The two had sized each other:** Abdul-Jabbar with McCarthy, *Kareem*, 81.

141 **"Don't let the Doctor":** Ted Green, "Lakers to Stay with Plan A: Shut Down Dr. J," *Los Angeles Times*, May 9, 1980, 3-1, 3-6.

141 **"I'm the bait":** Jim Murray, "Dr. Discovers the Cure," *Los Angeles Times*, May 11, 1980, 3-1, 3-9.

142 **"I figured Darryl":** Mark Heisler, "That Big Reverse Layup by Dr. J Won't Go Away," *Los Angeles Times*, May 15, 1980, 3-1, 3-11.

142 **"I know that's a play":** Author interview with Mike Littwin.

142 **"Kilimanjaro a goosebump":** Gary Smith, "Doc Leaves 'Em Dumbstruck," *Philadelphia Daily News*, May 12, 1980, 78.

143 **"Have no fear!":** As quoted in Jeff Pearlman, *Showtime: Magic, Kareem, Riley, and the Los Angeles Lakers Dynasty of the 1980s* (Avery Publishing, 2014), 98.

143 **"our poorest game":** Dick Weiss, "Another 76ers' IOU," *Philadelphia Daily News*, May 17, 1980, 40, 39.

144 **"Rebounding is an area":** Dick Weiss, "Sixers Seek 'Magic' Moment," *Philadelphia Daily News*, October 9, 1980, B-3, B-5.

Chapter 10: Collision Course

145 **"How the hell does":** Author phone interview with Carroll Dawson, July 6, 2023.

146 **"'CD, 'round here'":** Author interview with Carroll Dawson.

146 **"I ain't doing it":** Author interview with Steve Patterson.

146 **"I don't dig superstar":** Howell, "Moses Malone: Basketball's Million-Dollar Baby."

146 **"'It's us. It ain't'":** Author interview with Major Jones.

146 **The T-shirts that comprised:** George Shirk, "Rockets' Moses Malone: The Giant That Practically Nobody Knows," *Philadelphia Inquirer*, May 5, 1981, 1-D, 6-D.

146 **"I said, 'Man'":** Author interview with Gerald Govan.

147 **"probably the most talented":** Author interview with Rick Barry, February 24, 2024.

147 **"has three speeds":** Bob Ryan, "Rockets Get Even with Celtics," *Boston Globe*, May 8, 1981, 35.

147 **"tough individual defense":** George White, "Ugly Is Beautiful in Rocket Leveler," *Houston Chronicle*, May 11, 1981, 2-1, 2-6.

148 **When they unveiled their:** Author interview with Rick Barry.

148 **"Ray just totally clobbered":** Author interview with Tommy Bonk.

148 **"You don't make thoroughbreds":** Author interview with Calvin Murphy.

148 **"We never had any margin":** Phil Jasner, "Moses Malone: From 'Superkid' to Superstar," *Basketball Digest*, May 1985, 21–25.

148 **"Any time Moses takes":** United Press International, "Rockets Earn the Right to Brag," *Philadelphia Daily News*, April 30, 1981, 74.

149 **"When I scout":** Phil Jasner, "Toney: 76ers Factor Worth Multiple Gains," *Philadelphia Daily News*, December 21, 1981, 72.

149 **"you would just fall off":** Author interview with Bobby Jones.

149 **"Andrew had the mentality":** Author interview with Franklin Edwards.

150 **"Ain't you first-team":** Author interview with Lionel Hollins.

150 **Paschal remembered rolling:** Author phone interview with Bobby Paschal, May 25, 2023.

150 **"Close the gym":** Alan Greenberg, "Toney Puts the 76ers in Command," *Los Angeles Times*, May 17, 1982, 3-2.

150 **"At some point in every":** Author interview with Bobby Paschal.

151 **"I know I can't make 'em":** Ray Didinger, "Moses Takes Sixers One Step Beyond," *Philadelphia Daily News*, June 2, 1983, 94–96.

151 **"When Andrew gets that":** Ray Didinger, "Bucks Are Victims of Toney's Rhythm," *Philadelphia Daily News*, May 19, 1983, 85.

151 **"I want to move away":** Littwin, "Once, He Played Above the Stars."

151 **"What do Salvatore":** Advertisement in the *Philadelphia Inquirer*, September 12, 1980, 12-A.

152 **"I have that feeling":** Stan Hochman, "Julius Erving: A Man for All People," *Philadelphia Daily News*, February 13, 1981, 85.

153 **"stirs fans across":** Bill Livingston, "Sixers Are Running Out of Time," *Philadelphia Inquirer*, May 5, 1981, 1-D.

153 **"Because they hear noise":** Bill Lyons, "Rare Welcome for the Sixers," *Philadelphia Inquirer*, February 5, 1981, 1-C, 7-C.

153 **"It was a team":** Author interview with Billy Cunningham.

153 **"He was a bad symbol":** Author phone interview with Lou Scheinfeld, March 23, 2023.

154 **"You can't be like Nero":** Author interview with Lou Scheinfeld.

154 **Jones had stuck around:** Chuck Newman, "Baker Games: Empty Seats and Memories," *Philadelphia Inquirer*, July 20, 1981, 1-C, 7-C.

155 **"feared for their lives":** Gil Spencer, "What Does It Take to Make a Championship?," *Philadelphia Inquirer Magazine*, May 25, 1980, 15–25, 34.

155 **"I would like to say":** Ray Didinger, "Lost in City of Winners," *Philadelphia Daily News*, December 5, 1980, 83.

155 **"They have broken hearts":** Larry Whiteside, "Fans Aren't Flocking," *Boston Globe*, April 24, 1981, 35, 40.

156 **When Buss greeted him:** Author interview with Steve Springer.

156 **"a hand ride":** Author interview with Scott Ostler, April 6, 2023.

157 **they'd flash the matchbooks:** Author interview with Steve Springer.

157 **"Kareem is probably":** Author interview with Del Harris.

157 **"just wanted to play":** Author interview with Scott Ostler.

158 **"When I'm scoring and rebounding":** George White, "Rockets Stun World Champion Lakers 111–107," *Houston Chronicle*, April 2, 1981, 2-1, 2-5.

158 **"You know when":** Author interview with Mike Littwin.

158 **"They think I hog":** Mike Littwin, "Johnson Feels Some Lakers Are Resentful," *Los Angeles Times*, April 4, 1981, 3-1, 3-8.

158 **"I didn't really say":** Pat Riley, *Show Time: Inside the Lakers' Breakthrough Season* (Smithmark, 1988), 7.

158 **"The Lakers wanted to get out":** Author interview with Major Jones.

159 **"Magic got into the lane":** Author interview with Mike Littwin.

159 **"We don't care nothing":** George White, "A Beautiful Rockets' Win," *Houston Chronicle*, April 6, 1981, 2-1, 2-7.

159 **"I would so blatantly":** "Rockets' Upset Pleases Sixers," *Philadelphia Daily News*, April 4, 1981, 80.

160 **"What he did night in":** Author interview with Al Skinner.

161 **"the Spectrum the texture":** Stan Hochman, "The Sixers' Pied Piper," *Philadelphia Daily News*, April 24, 1981, 91.

161 **"It looks like we've":** Tom Cushman, "The Other Side of Julius Erving," *Philadelphia Daily News*, April 20, 1981, 71.

161 **"It was a helluva game":** Peter Vecsey, "Fans Owe One to Sixers," *New York Post*, April 20, 1981.

161 **"We get more people":** Frank Dolson, "76ers Look Past the Empty Seats," *Philadelphia Inquirer*, April 20, 1981, 1-C, 4-C.

161 **"like cornering a Battle":** Cushman, "The Other Side."

Chapter 11: The Boston Mystique

163 **Only the Celtics possessed it:** For more on the Boston Celtics and tradition, see Halberstam, *The Breaks of the Game*, 358.

164 **"I didn't get ulcers":** Hal Lundgren, "Auerbach: Celts' President, GM Had Hand in 13 Titles," *Houston Chronicle*, May 11, 1981, 2-1, 2-9.

164 **"One hundred twenty degrees":** Bill Livingston, "Some Arenas Are Clinics for the NBA's Spring Fever," *Philadelphia Inquirer*, April 24, 1983, 11-E.

164 **"What makes the Celtics":** Bill Livingston, "Family Feeling Makes Celtics a Special Team," *Philadelphia Inquirer*, November 5, 1982, 1-C, 7-C.

165 **"about as important":** Robert Gluck, "Jews on the Ball," *Jerusalem Post*, November 29, 2012.

167 **"There was a reaction":** Ken Berger, "Dr. J: Wilt Paved the Way for Me," *Times-Tribune* (Scranton, PA), October 15, 1999, 25.

168 **"Perhaps the biggest thing":** Larry Bird with Bob Ryan, *Drive: The Story of My Life* (Doubleday, 1989), 83.

168 **"I'm not into that, man":** Frank Brady, "Celtics Are Finding It Hard to Overlook Andrew Toney," *Philadelphia Evening Bulletin*, April 26, 1981.

168 **"Getting my yard mowed":** Danny Robbins, "A Machine Named Bird Does the Job," *Philadelphia Inquirer*, April 23, 1981, 1-D, 4-D.

168 **"I hate to show":** Bud Shaw, "Celts Ride Bird's Non-Stop Flight," *Philadelphia Daily News*, April 23, 1981, 64.

169 **"Plop plop, fizz fizz":** Bill Livingston, "B. Jones Saves It for 76ers," *Philadelphia Inquirer*, April 27, 1981, 1-C, 6-C.

169 **"That fourth win":** Mark Whicker, "The Celtics' Rise and Sixers' Fall...," *Philadelphia Evening Bulletin*, October 11, 1981, 4–5.

170 **"I remember that night":** Author interview with Pat Williams.

170 **"a team of character":** Michael Madden, "The Comeback Begins...," *Boston Globe*, May 18, 1981, 64.

170 **"They get 10,000":** Phil Jasner, "Believe It—Boston Does," *Philadelphia Daily News*, May 2, 1981, 35.

170 **"A man runs into":** Bill Livingston, "Sixers Squander Lead, Lose to Boston," *Philadelphia Inquirer*, May 2, 1981, 1C.

170 **"It was just the emotions":** Author phone interview with Cedric Maxwell, October 30, 2024.

171 **"Each stampede to":** Peter Vecsey, "Game 6: Only the Strong Survived," *New York Post*, May 2, 1981.

171 **"Doc was struggling":** Author interview with Billy Cunningham.

171 **"I'm our best offensive player":** Joe Klein, "O, What a Lovely War," *Inside Sports*, May 1982.

173 **"One point?":** Ray Fitzgerald, "For the Doctor, Frustration...," *Boston Globe*, May 4, 1981, 36.

173 **"put their whistles":** Author phone interview with Bob Ryan, April 7, 2023.

173 **tossed through a windshield:** Erving with Greenfeld, *Dr. J*, 340.

173 **"all-out war":** Bird with Ryan, *Drive*, 91.

173 **"It looked like every":** John Papanek, "The Worth of a Bird in Hand," *Sports Illustrated*, May 11, 1981.

173 **"half of Eastern Massachusetts":** Author interview with Bob Ryan.

174 **"no autopsy, no foul":** Peter Vecsey, "Too Late, Dr. J Learns Valuable Lesson," *New York Post*, May 7, 1981.

174 **"Don't choke":** Whicker, "The Celtics' Rise and Sixers' Fall."

174 **"victims of the gremlins":** Harvey Araton, "Once Again, the Sixers Can't Answer the Question," *New York Post*, May 4, 1981.

174 **"OK, we're going!":** Phil Jasner, "Memories Behind, 76ers Meet Celtics Again," *Philadelphia Daily News*, December 4, 1981, 114.

175 **"All right, is Rodney":** Robert Falkoff, "Writers, Fans Not Sold on Rockets," *Houston Post*, May 7, 1981, 1D, 4D.

176 **"a bit like Lawrence Welk":** Michael Madden, "Did You See That Play by Bird?," *Boston Globe*, May 18, 1981, 67.

176 **"We never had a jinx":** Leigh Montville, "Funny, They Don't Act Like Losers," *Boston Globe*, May 8, 1981, 35.

176 **"Trying to get up":** Bob Verdi, "Celtics One Game Away from Ending Pointless Series," *Chicago Tribune*, May 13, 1981, 4-1, 4-2.

176 **"Ain't nothing going to change":** Malcolm Moran, "Moses Malone at Center Stage," *New York Times*, May 3, 1981.

176 **"I always talked around":** Author interview with Del Harris.

177 **"You'd hate to be behind":** Verdi, "Celtics One Game Away."

178 **"They ain't that good":** Bill Livingston, "Celtics' Speed Buries Rockets, 109–80," *Philadelphia Inquirer*, May 13, 1981, 1-C, 7-C.

178 **"He said it to be funny":** Author interview with Calvin Murphy.

178 a **"polite F-U":** Author interview with Steve Patterson.

178 **"We are all so sick":** George White, "Two Mysteries," *Houston Chronicle*, May 14, 1981, 2-1, 2-5.

179 **"There was no way":** Dick Weiss, "Celts' Bird of Paradise," *Philadelphia Daily News*, May 15, 1981, 92.

179 **"Moses, you better get":** Author interview with Cedric Maxwell.

179 **"The Celtics are still chumps":** George White, "Celtics Punish Rockets, Take 3–2 Series Lead," *Houston Chronicle*, May 13, 1981, 2-1, 2-2.

179 **"eat some of those":** Peter Vecsey, "Winning Is Child's Play," *New York Post*, May 13, 1981.

179 **"Oh yeah, we'd take 'em":** Michael Madden, "Malone Stands Firm: 'Sixers Are Better,'" *Boston Globe*, May 15, 1981, 65.

180 **"After all the hollering":** Chronicle News Services, "Bird Apologizes for Profane Remark Made About Moses," *Houston Chronicle*, May 19, 1981, 2-1.

Chapter 12: Of Rebounds and Planets

181 **"The 76ers were like a toy":** Author phone interview with Ron Rabena, January 16, 2025.

181 **"That doesn't mean":** Phil Jasner, "The Life and Times of Julius Erving," *Philadelphia Daily News*, October 7, 1981, 64.

182 **$10 million in losses:** Phil Jasner, "Brave New Worlds for Fitz and Harold," *Philadelphia Daily News*, September 25, 1981, 88.

182 **"It's impractical for me":** Bill Lyon, "Celtics Bring Out Best in the Fans and Sixers," *Philadelphia Inquirer*, April 25, 1981, 1-C, 5-C.

182 **"Stuttering made me":** Bill Lyon, "Harold Katz: Tales of Ambition," *Philadelphia Inquirer*, March 27, 1983, 20–24.

184 **"Many people have called me":** Stephen J. Morgan, "Harold Katz, a Diet-Center Entrepreneur Hungry for an NBA . . . ," UPI Archives, July 9, 1981.

184 **"Fire everybody":** Author phone interview with Harold Katz, November 28, 2023.

184 **"In case you don't know":** DD Eisenberg, "The Zink Glad to Be Back in Sixers' Fold," *Philadelphia Evening Bulletin*, August 8, 1981.

185 **"the invention of electric":** Alan Greenberg, "When Zink Talks, Even CBS Listens," *Los Angeles Times*, May 16, 1980, 3-2, 3-10, 3-12.

185 **"So there was a competition":** Author phone interview with Jack Swope, January 17, 2025.

185 **"The whole charisma":** Author interview with Mark Whicker.

186 **"I think these people here":** George White, "Malone Stops Celtics, Taunts," *Houston Chronicle*, November 19, 1981, 2-1, 2-9.

186 **"I think some smart man":** Leigh Montville, "Celtics Fans Forced to Eat Crow," *Boston Globe*, November 19, 1981, 65.

186 **"had been treated as if":** Montville, "Celtics Fans Forced to Eat Crow."

187 **"to try and sell oil":** Stan Hochman, "Dawkins Is Center of Praise from Teammates," *Philadelphia Daily News*, April 22, 1982, 91.

188 **"His size told me":** Author interview with Harold Katz.

188 **"I'm an entertainer":** Barry McDermott, "Now You See Him, Now You Don't," *Sports Illustrated*, February 11, 1980.

188 **"He just let his imagination":** Author phone interview with Fran Blinebury, April 27, 2023.

189 **"Well, I've got a name":** Author interview with Fran Blinebury.

189 **"The number one subject":** Bill Livingston, "Dawkins Waits for His Day," *Philadelphia Inquirer*, April 21, 1982, 1-D, 4-D.

189 **wrap Dawkins in a bear hug:** Scott Ostler, "Chocolate Thunder or Chocolate Souffle," *Los Angeles Times*, June 7, 1982, 3-1, 3-8.

190 **"Darryl, until you get":** Author interview with Harold Katz.

190 **"Don't expect that":** Author interview with Billy Cunningham.

190 **"Why are you going":** Author interview with Lionel Hollins.

190 **"one of the leading":** Frank Brady, "Mix, Erving: Words to the Wise," *Philadelphia Evening Bulletin*, October 8, 1981.

190 **Dawkins stuck out:** Dave Wohl, "The Extremely High Bar Set for NBA Manchild Darryl Dawkins," *Sports Illustrated*, April 11, 1988.

191 **"How many did Moses":** Harvey Araton, "Meeting Houston's Boy Owner," *Basketball Weekly*, January 21, 1982, 20.

191 **"it would've worked out":** Author interview with Major Jones.

191 **"If we start next year":** Ed Fowler, "Moses Malone: Houston's Personal Property," *Houston Chronicle*, February 13, 1982, 4-1.

191 **"I have never, ever":** Fran Blinebury, "Mo Speaks Out," *Houston Chronicle*, June 16, 1982, 2-1.

192 **"Moses had no flair":** Author interview with Greg Kelser.

192 **"Rest? I can rest":** Author interview with Major Jones.

192 **"In 1982, the deal":** Author interview with Fran Blinebury.

192 **staging a mutiny:** Robert Falkoff, "Rocket Policy Clouds Harris' Status," *Houston Post*, February 14, 1983, 1C, 6C.

193 **"That's why the next year":** Author interview with Calvin Murphy.

193 **"I never wanted":** Fran Blinebury, "The $13,000,000 Man," *Houston Chronicle*, September 3, 1982, 2-1, 2-5.

193 **"I'll bet this is the first time":** Blinebury, "The $13,000,000 Man."

193 **"How do you win":** Phil Jasner, "Sixers Falter in Leading Role," *Philadelphia Daily News*, April 12, 1982, 80.

194 **"Our guys are too nice":** Bruce Newman, "The 76ers: Bridesmaid Revisited," *Sports Illustrated*, April 12, 1982.

194 **"I know it's off the wall":** Phil Jasner, "Are 76ers Really Wilting?," *Philadelphia Daily News*, January 19, 1982, 62, 64.

194 **"Either we get":** George Sirk, "Celts Rule the Boards, Top Sixers in Overtime," *Philadelphia Inquirer*, April 12, 1982, 1-D, 6-D.

194 **"I try to play":** Bill Lyon, "Sixers Seeking a New Tradition," *Philadelphia Inquirer*, May 9, 1982, 1-E.

Chapter 13: The End

197 **"This is the first year":** Littwin, "Once, He Played Above the Stars."

197 **"We're proud, but":** Phil Jasner, "Sixers Kings of the Road," *Philadelphia Daily News*, December 2, 1981, 80, 76.

197 **"If I have to go":** Phil Jasner, "For 76ers, Best Is Yet to Come," *Philadelphia Daily News*, April 27, 1982, 88, 86.

198 **"as unpredictable as":** Steve Hershey, "Unpredictable 76ers Bounce Back," *Sporting News*, June 7, 1982, 46.

198 **"Three to one, Billy!":** Bill Lyon, "... But Never on Sunday," *Philadelphia Inquirer*, May 20, 1982, 1-C, 7-C.

198 **two Rolaids taped inside:** Mary Flannery, "Sondra Cunningham Handles the Pressure," *Philadelphia Daily News*, May 28, 1982, 126.

198 **"See you on Sunday!":** Phil Jasner, "Sixers Say End Is Here," *Philadelphia Daily News*, May 21, 1982, 128, 126.

199 **"The coffin lid":** Bill Lyon, "Bird: Green Machine to Shift into High Gear," *Philadelphia Inquirer*, May 21, 1982, 1-C, 4-C.

199 **"So here we go":** Bill Lyon, "Close to the Edge," *Philadelphia Inquirer*, May 22, 1982, 1-C, 4-C.

199 **"You could look at":** Phil Jasner, "Sixers Still in Haunt," *Philadelphia Daily News*, May 22, 1982, 48, 46.

199 **searching for Toney's jumper:** Phil Jasner, "76ers Have Final Say," *Philadelphia Daily News*, May 24, 1982, 92, 90.

200 **"they might as well":** Bob Ryan, "The 76ers Responded, and the Ghosts Are Gone," *Boston Globe*, May 24, 1982, 1, 36.

200 **"Philadelphia will disown":** Dave Sims, "One Man's Prediction: Sixers Will Still Win It," *Daily News*, May 23, 1982, 79.

200 **"For the same reason":** Bill Lyon, "A Death March in Double Time," *Philadelphia Inquirer*, May 23, 1982, 1E.

200 **"You know what I wanna do?":** Author interview with Billy Cunningham.

200 **"Man, the coaches left":** As quoted in Erving with Greenfeld, *Dr. J*, 355.

201 **"That's when I got scared":** Anthony Cotton, "Banishing the Green Ghosts," *Sports Illustrated*, May 31, 1982.

201 **Erving roused the roster:** Author interview with Ron Rabena.

201 **"The way I figured":** Leigh Montville, "The 76ers Responded, and the Ghosts Are Gone," *Boston Globe*, May 24, 1982, 1, 36.

201 **"Kick Their Ass":** Mark Whicker, "Sixers No Longer Need a Character Reference," *Philadelphia Daily News*, May 24, 1982, 89.

201 **"We both were almost":** Author interview with Bobby Jones.

202 **"There's not many players":** Author phone interview with Robert Parish, July 19, 2023.

202 **"Then they'd get to":** Author interview with Cedric Maxwell.

202 **"I would just do":** Bill Lyon, "Dr. J: Skywalking into Phase II," *Philadelphia Inquirer*, April 4, 1982, 16–22.

202 **"We were overconfident":** Author interview with Cedric Maxwell.

203 **"I'm going to be real quick":** Jasner, "76ers Have Final Say."

203 **"Of all the people":** Author interview with Billy Cunningham.

203 **"So it has become":** Stan Hochman, "Erving Brings Profound Touch to Sixer Camp," *Philadelphia Daily News*, May 25, 1982, 92, 91.

203 **most important game:** Erving with Greenfeld, *Dr. J*, 356.

203 **"we got so caught up":** Author phone interview with Earl Cureton, April 5, 2023.

204 **"There were times when":** Author interview with Steve Springer.

204 **"Cattle stampedes":** Bill Lyon, "76ers Victims of Hit and Run," *Philadelphia Inquirer*, May 28, 1982, 1-C, 8-C.

205 **"Rebounding, or the lack":** George Shirk, "2d Round May Be Sixers' Cup of Tea," *Philadelphia Inquirer*, June 27, 1982, 1-D, 14-D.

205 **"the eternal Don Quixote":** Bill Lyon, "Sixers' Death Comes in a Blaze of Glory," *Philadelphia Inquirer*, June 9, 1982, D1, D4.

206 **"It takes ten or fifteen":** Jan Hubbard, "76ers' Erving Shows Class in Loss to Lakers," *Fort Worth-Star-Telegram*, June 10, 1982, E1.

206 **"When you lose":** As quoted in Williams with Lyon, *We Owed You One!*, 183.

207 **"After my brother died":** James McBride, "Dr. J Is Not an Ordinary Superstar," *The Courier* (Waterloo, IA), May 23, 1982, E8.

207 **"I don't know what it would take":** Marty Bell, "Julius Erving's Rise from Obscurity," *Philadelphia Daily News*, October 23, 1976, 61.

207 **"I kept thinking of Doc":** Don Benevento, "Sixers Keep Katz Awake; but Big Changes Not Planned," *Courier-Post*, June 10, 1982, C1–2.

207 **"I feel much more":** Thom Greer, "The Doctor Feels Deep Pain but Sees Another Tomorrow for the Game Sixers," *Philadelphia Inquirer*, June 9, 1982.

207 **"Maybe there will be":** Bill Handleman, "Latest Episode Was Cruelest Blow of All to Erving, Sixers," *Asbury Park Press*, June 10, 1982, C1.

Chapter 14: The Unanticipated Suitor

211 **"I'm twenty-seven":** Fran Blinebury, "Mo Speaks Out," *Houston Chronicle*, June 16, 1982, 2-1.

211 **"I don't want to have":** Blinebury, "Mo Speaks Out."

211 **"Start the bidding":** Harvey Araton, "Back Up the Brinks Truck, Here's Moses," *Basketball Weekly*, June 15, 1982, 10–11.

212 **"I never met him":** Phil Jasner, "Sixers' Season Should Be Savored," *Philadelphia Daily News*, February 3, 1983, 68.

213 **"absolutely crazy":** Fran Blinebury, "Katz: Malone Offer Is 'Crazy,'" *Houston Chronicle*, June 7, 1982, 2-1, 2-6.

213 **"running a grocery store":** Frank Dolson, "Katz Changes His Fiscal Tune," *Philadelphia Inquirer*, September 3, 1982, 1-C.

213 **"Would Moses help":** Phil Jasner, "With Moses on Board, Cunningham, Katz Have High Hopes," *Philadelphia Daily News*, October 28, 1982, B-6–7.

214 **"General managers didn't want":** Author phone interview with Steve Mix, April 26, 2023.

215 **was a done deal:** George Shirk, "Malone Lives by His Instincts," *Philadelphia Inquirer*, February 13, 1983, 1-D, 8-D.

216 **Cunningham dropped his clubs:** Author interview with Billy Cunningham.

216 **"We're all there except Billy":** Author phone interview with John Nash, April 30, 2023.

216 **"I just took a freaking":** Author interview with Billy Cunningham.

216 **"Hey, I'm no dummy":** Shirk, "Malone Lives by His Instincts."

217 **"I'm just here to help Doc":** Author interview with Pat Williams.

217 **"No 'ferred":** Author interview with Harold Katz.

217 **The total was more:** For further details, see Mendelsohn, *The Cap*, 186.

217 **"If you could have any":** Ray Didinger, "At Any Price, Malone Is a Hard Worker," *Philadelphia Daily News*, September 3, 1982, 119.

218 **Malone had promised Mitchell:** Didinger, "At Any Price, Malone Is a Hard Worker."

218 **"There hasn't been such":** Ed Fowler, "Pulling the Old 'Wool-over-the-Eyes' Caper," *Houston Chronicle*, September 3, 1982, 2-2.

218 **"Christ, Ray":** Author interview with Steve Patterson.

219 **questioned how small-market:** Mendelsohn, *The Cap*, 187.

219 **"push the NBA":** "Our Opinion: Up, Up and Away in NBA," *Sporting News*, September 27, 1982, 6.

219 **"I know there are people":** Bill Lyon, "Will Moses Lead Them?," *Sporting News*, November 1, 1982, 3.

219 **"I looked at Moses":** Author interview with Bobby Jones.

200 **"If we didn't get":** Neil Hohlfeld, "Rocket Owner Never Wavered in 76er Talks," *Houston Chronicle*, September 16, 1982, 2-10.

221 **"With Malone, we were going":** Robert Falkoff, "Rockets Deal All-Pro Malone to 76ers," *Houston Post*, September 16, 1982, 1C, 8C.

221 **"Somebody [on the Rockets]":** Ray Buck, "No Respect," *Houston Post*, October 14, 1982, 1B, 7B.

221 **"Have you ever seen":** Bill Lyon, "High-Priced and Worth It," *Philadelphia Inquirer*, January 14, 1983, 1-D.

222 **"Doc'll still be the show":** Phil Jasner, "Sixers Part Red Tape for Moses," *Philadelphia Daily News*, September 16, 1982, 92, 90.

222 **"He's got a lot of talent":** Stan Hochman, "Malone Saving His Fireworks for on the Court," *Philadelphia Daily News*, September 16, 1982, 91.

222 **"They wouldn't have paid":** Bill Livingston, "Inner Fire," *Philadelphia Inquirer*, September 16, 1982, 1-D, 6-D.

222 **"Good for you, Charlie":** Robert Falkoff, "Good for You, Charlie Thomas," *Houston Post*, September 19, 1982, 2C.

223 **"I could walk down":** Details in the previous three paragraph from George Shirk, "Moses Malone: What You See Is What You Get," *Philadelphia Inquirer Magazine*, May 8, 1983; author phone interview with Tim Malloy, May 15, 2023; Pete Croatto, "The Year We Won It All: A Behind the Scenes Oral History of the 76ers' Epic 1983 Championship," *Philadelphia Magazine*, April 22, 2023.

Chapter 15: Perfectly Mismatched

225 **"Four rookies and *five*":** George Shirk, "Thinking Young," *Philadelphia Inquirer*, October 29, 1982, 1-D, 4-D.

225 **"Moses will take a day":** Phil Jasner, "Malone's Turf Staked Out as Land of a Giant," *Philadelphia Daily News*, October 6, 1982, 79.

226 **"The players were not ecstatic":** Author interview with Billy Cunningham.

226 **"We are going to win":** George Shirk, "Sixers Search for Perfect Mix on Club Transformed in Off-Season," *Philadelphia Inquirer*, October 25, 1982, 5C.

226 **"He talked about it":** Author interview with Franklin Edwards.

226 **"Moses didn't have that attitude":** Author phone interview with Russ Schoene, July 17, 2023.

226 **"Where have all our":** Phil Jasner, "How's This for Openers," *Philadelphia Daily News*, October 30, 1982, 44, 42.

227 **"Caldwell was a sacrificial":** Author interview with Julius Erving.

227 **"If I can't play with one Jones":** Author interview with Major Jones.

227 **"One of the reasons I came":** Author interview with Pat Williams.

227 **"With CJ, Moses":** Phil Jasner, "Julius Erving: It's His Nature to Be a Leader," *Philadelphia Daily News*, October 28, 1982, B-2–B-3.

227 **"I never thought the NBA":** Dick Weiss, "Relaxed Malone Finally Opens Up," *Philadelphia Daily News*, June 8, 1983, 90.

228 **"I'm only a human being":** Bill Livingston, "Dandy Debut," *Philadelphia Inquirer*, October 30, 1982, 1-D, 6-D.

228 **"Seventeen rebounds would have":** Mark Whicker, "76ers Show Tip of the Iceberg," *Philadelphia Daily News*, October 30, 1982, 43.

229 **"Seventeen boards is":** Livingston, "Dandy Debut."

229 **"On the court, Boston":** Phil Jasner, "Round 1: Sixers, Celtics Singing the Bruise," *Philadelphia Daily News*, November 8, 1982, 82.

230 **"the missing link":** Phil Jasner, "Sixers Thunder Past Lakers," *Philadelphia Daily News*, December 6, 1982, 88, 86.

230 **"stunned. Shellshocked":** George Shirk, "Boards Help Sixers Pass the Big Test," *Philadelphia Inquirer*, December 7, 1982, 1-D.

231 **hit that number once:** George Shirk, "'Tis the Season to Evaluate the New, Improved Sixers," *Philadelphia Inquirer*, December 12, 1982, 8-E.

231 **"It's amazing what":** Shirk, "Boards Help Sixers."

232 **"I'm a so much better":** George Shirk, "Malone Dominant as Sixers Triumph," *Philadelphia Inquirer*, December 6, 1982, 1-C, 8-C.

232 **"There are times for":** Bill Lyon, "Erving Doesn't Mind Taking a Back Seat," *Philadelphia Inquirer*, May 3, 1983, 1-C, 7-C.

232 **"Moses keeps batting":** Lynn Darling, "Moses: Opulent Life in a Fishbowl," *Washington Post*, November 28, 1982, D1, D3.

232 **"I ain't out there":** Dan Barreiro, "Moses Makes the Difference," *Miami News*, June 2, 1983, 1B.

232 **"We used to be a pretty team":** Bruce Newman, "Thou Shalt Rejoice, Said Moses," *Sports Illustrated*, June 13, 1983.

233 **"My entire generation idolized":** Author interview with Earl Cureton.

233 **"The other players on the team":** Barkley, *Outrageous!*, 155.

233 **"made Julius more":** Author interview with Franklin Edwards.

234 **"You remind me a lot":** Author interview with Russ Schoene.

234 **"picking teams and talking":** Author interview with Russ Schoene.

234 **"I would always lose":** Author phone interview with John Kilbourne, March 10, 2023.

234 **"Moses was known":** Author interview with Steve Green.

235 **"His body was built":** Author interview with Franklin Edwards.

235 **"So many other things":** Stan Hochman, "He's Not Getting Older...," *Philadelphia Daily News*, February 24, 1983, 79.

235 **instructed Maglione to invite:** Author phone interview with Fred Maglione, April 17, 2023.

236 **use the Lord's name:** Author interview with Bobby Jones.

236 **At a fundraising dinner:** Robert Falkoff, "Malone Filming Sequel to 'Moses, MVP,'" *Houston Post*, November 18, 1979, 4C.

236 **"I was always petrified":** Author interview with Fred Maglione.

236 **Each time, Malone declined:** Shirk, "Moses Malone."

236 **hurtling over curbs:** Shirk, "Moses Malone."

237 **"tremendous racial separation":** Larry Platt, "The Graying of Dr. J," *Philadelphia Magazine*, May 1993, 77–79, 121–123.

238 **"Hold that cliché, Doc":** Papanek, "I've Always Felt Powerless."

238 **"You didn't have people":** William Robbins, "Election of Black Mayor in Philadelphia Reflects a Decade of Change in City," *New York Times*, November 10, 1983.

238 **"they want a brawler":** As quoted in Platt, *New Jack Jocks*, 110.

239 **"offered redemption to":** Lombardo, *Blue-Collar Conservatism*, 161.

239 **served as a racial code:** For more on the "blue-collar" label, see Jeffrey Lane, *Under the Boards: The Cultural Revolution in Basketball* (University of Nebraska Press, 2007), 115–120.

240 **"wear a football helmet":** Scott Ostler, "Now It's Moses Doing Surgery—on L.A.," *Los Angeles Times*, May 30, 1983, 3-1, 3-9.

240 **"You can do a 360":** Anthony Cotton, "Blood, Sweat and Cheers," *Sports Illustrated*, October 31, 1983, 46–52.

240 **For hours he pedaled:** Author interview with Bobby Jones.

240 **an extra employee:** Phil Jasner, "Just Another Day at the Gym," *Philadelphia Daily News*, May 3, 2001, 111.

240 **"I wanna see *tension*":** Linderman, "*Playboy* Interview."

240 **"You can't just *play*":** Alan Goldstein, "Moses Malone: The Bullets' Big Man Shoots for Revenge," *Basketball Digest*, February 1987, 19–24.

241 **"His factory is":** Shelby Strother, "Malone Earns His Keep," *Florida Today*, May 12, 1981, 1C.

241 **matched their box-office:** Bill Lyon, "Sixers Buck Financial Trend," *Philadelphia Inquirer*, November 2, 1982, 1-D.

241 **"That's the guy":** Author interview with Bob Ryan.

241 **"You can be rich":** Lynn Darling, "Moses: Opulent Life in a Fishbowl," *Washington Post*, November 28, 1982, D1, D3.

242 **"Sixers fans who shout":** Jim Davis, "76ers Owner 'Slam Dunks' in Our Face," *Philadelphia Tribune*, February 11, 1983, 5.

Chapter 16: The Philadelphia Machine

243 **Iavaroni had nightmares:** Author interview with Marc Iavaroni.

244 **"I knew they were good":** George Shirk, "Streak at 14 as 76ers Beat SuperSonics," *Philadelphia Inquirer*, January 22, 1983, 1-C, 6-C.

244 **"It's all very business-like":** Phil Jasner, "Sixers Streak as Bulls Doze," *Philadelphia Daily News*, January 20, 1983, 80, 78.

244 **"The center by committee":** Author interview with Julius Erving.

245 **"didn't do dumb things":** Author interview with Mark Whicker.

245 **"All I want to do":** George Shirk, "At Midseason, Sixers Are Cream of the NBA Crop," *Philadelphia Inquirer*, January 30, 1983, 1-E, 12-E.

245 **"once the ball goes in":** Author interview with Bobby Jones.

245 **"Every time we walk":** Bruce Newman, "This May Be One for the Books," *Sports Illustrated*, February 28, 1983.

245 **"If you don't get us":** Bill Lyon, "Fast-Finishing Sixers Now Own This Series," *Philadelphia Inquirer*, May 30, 1983, 1-D, 4-D.

246 **"Being in the spotlight":** Jayson Stark, "Unveiled," *Philadelphia Inquirer*, February 27, 1983, 1-D, 12-D.

246 **"I was starting every":** Author interview with Marc Iavaroni.

247 **"Why not just take":** George Shirk, "Toney Added to All-Stars by Coaches," *Philadelphia Inquirer*, February 4, 1983, 1-C, 6-C.

247 **"I never play it":** Stan Hochman, "The Sixers' Pied Piper," *Philadelphia Daily News*, April 24, 1981, 91.

248 **their middle fingers:** Author interview with Cedric Maxwell.

248 **dry-cleaning costs:** Michael Madden, "It's Welcome (?) to the Spectrum," *Boston Globe*, May 18, 1981, 62.

248 **"I don't know what it is":** George Kiseda, "Philly Tops NBA—in 'Abusive' Fans," *Philadelphia Evening Bulletin*, November 27, 1969.

248 **"When I got audited":** Author interview with Robert Parish.

248 **"Tonight I felt":** Shirk, "At Midseason, Sixers Are Cream of the NBA Crop."

249 **"Where's the checks?":** Shirk, "Moses Malone."

249 **"like chasing Raquel Welch":** George Shirk, "Sixers' Numbers on Court Boost Team's TV Figures," *Philadelphia Inquirer*, March 27, 1983, 11-E.

249 **"It's gotten to where":** Bill Livingston, "Sizzling Sixers Brush Aside Bulls, 116–99," *Philadelphia Inquirer*, January 26, 1983, 1-F, 7-F.

250 **"It would be the crowning":** Bill Lyon, "Only a Players Strike Is Likely to Stop the Sixers," *Philadelphia Inquirer*, February 19, 1983, 1-C, 5-C. See also Mendelsohn, *The Cap*, 263.

250 **spiked by 85 percent:** Shirk, "Sixers' Numbers on Court."

250 **fans barraged him:** Mendelsohn, *The Cap*, 251.

251 **"Now, if I have to tape":** Author interview with Bobby Jones.

251 **headshots of all:** Earl Cureton and Jake Uitti, *Earl the Twirl: My Life in Basketball* (McFarland, 2024), 65.

251 **"things will go much":** Author interview with John Kilbourne.

252 **pricey travel agency:** Fowler, "Pulling the Old 'Wool-over-the-Eyes' Caper."

252 **"If I can help prevent":** Author interview with John Kilbourne.

252 **leaped, kicked, and:** Ray Didinger, "A Dance Fever Hits Sixers," *Philadelphia Daily News*, September 28, 1982, 72; Stan Hochman, "Ballet Coach Gives Sixers Jump on Others," *Philadelphia Daily News*, May 31, 1983, 99.

252 **wore a padded splint:** George Shirk, "Ailing Erving May Be Ready to Play Tonight," *Philadelphia Inquirer*, March 22, 1983, 1-C, 3-C.

253 **"But that's Andrew":** Phil Jasner, "Toney Declares Martial Law," *Philadelphia Daily News*, March 21, 1983, 88, 87.

253 **banged hard into:** George Shirk, "76ers Moan as the Stalwart Malone Is Benched Because He Has Tendinitis," *Philadelphia Inquirer*, April 12, 1983, 1-C, 5-C.

254 **"I've just gotta":** Ray Didinger, "Doc Is Back in the Office," *Philadelphia Daily News*, March 30, 1983, 87.

254 **"Seventy was just":** Didinger, "Doc Is Back in the Office."

254 **"least important thing":** Author interview with Billy Cunningham.

254 **held a meeting earlier:** Author interview with Franklin Edwards.

255 **"We set such a high":** Barreiro, "Moses Makes the Difference."

255 **"A player gets into":** Bill Livingston, "Knicks Stew over Timing of Malone's Time Off," *Philadelphia Inquirer*, April 11, 1983, 3-C.

255 **"He never says anything":** Phil Jasner, "Sixers' Malone Hurting Himself," *Philadelphia Daily News*, April 20, 1983, 75.

256 **"No matter what Moses":** Phil Jasner, "Worst of Times for Sixers," *Philadelphia Daily News*, April 14, 1983, 78.

256 **"stir-crazy":** Bill Lyon, "Malone Brings 76ers a Giant Sigh of Relief," *Philadelphia Inquirer*, April 25, 1983, 1-C, 4-C.

256 **"I don't mind the losing":** Jasner, "Worst of Times for Sixers."

257 **"Today, where he's normally":** George Shirk, "Malone Takes Things Slow and Easy After Layoff," *Philadelphia Inquirer*, April 21, 1983, 1-C, 7-C.

257 **"How far do you think":** Shirk, "Malone Takes Things Slow and Easy."

258 **"I mean, he just":** Lyon, "Malone Brings 76ers a Giant Sigh of Relief."

259 **"I was a little shocked":** George Shirk, "Malone Develops New Knee Problem," *Philadelphia Inquirer*, April 22, 1983, 1-C, 7-C.

Chapter 17: Role Reversal

261 **"I'd feel a lot":** George Shirk, "Malone Back in Action, but Only as Part-Timer," *Philadelphia Inquirer*, April 23, 1983, 1-D, 5-D.

261 **"You want us?":** Phil Jasner, "Series of Desire," *Philadelphia Daily News*, April 23, 1983, 44.

261 **declined ice bags:** Lyon, "Malone Brings 76ers a Giant Sigh of Relief."

261 **"I think I can go":** George Shirk, "Malone Is Up and Jumping Again," *Philadelphia Inquirer*, April 24, 1983, 1-E, 6-E.

262 **"We have got the best":** George Shirk, "For Sixers, the Court Has Become a Proving Ground," *Philadelphia Inquirer*, April 24, 1983, 7-E, 12-E.

262 **he heard nothing:** Lyon, "Malone Brings 76ers a Giant Sigh of Relief."

262 **"I just like to work":** Phil Pepe, "Malone's a Working-Class Millionaire," *Daily News*, April 25, 1983, 47.

262 **"You all make it sound":** Phil Jasner, "Malone Ticks Off Knicks," *Philadelphia Daily News*, April 25, 1983, 92.

262 **"Two days ago":** Jasner, "Malone Ticks Off Knicks."

263 **"Push it! Push it!":** Bill Lyon, "Reports of Sixers' Demise Premature," *Philadelphia Inquirer*, April 28, 1983, 1-D, 5-D.

263 **"He missed nine shots":** George Shirk, "Sixers Aren't Worried About Dr. J's Slow Start," *Philadelphia Inquirer*, April 30, 1983, 3-D.

264 **"like watching a rhino":** Stan Hochman, "Sixers Have a Giant of a Man," *Philadelphia Daily News*, May 2, 1983, 91.

264 **"That was such a big play":** Jayson Stark, "Neither Knicks nor Knee Could Conquer Malone," *Philadelphia Inquirer*, May 2, 1983, 4-C.

264 **"I couldn't stop him":** Author interview with Bill Cartwright.

264 **dubbing his performance:** George Shirk, "With Malone in Sixers' Middle, Knicks Are in Trouble," *Philadelphia Inquirer*, April 29, 1983, 1-D, 7-D.

264 **"Moses is the difference":** George Shirk, "Malone Knocks Out the Knicks," *Philadelphia Inquirer*, May 2, 1983, 1-C, 4-C.

265 **“I’m feeling like a stick”:** Phil Jasner, “Clean Sweep for 76ers,” *Philadelphia Daily News*, May 2, 1983, 92, 90.

266 **“That was the first time”:** Author interview with Robert Parish.

266 **“I always admired”:** Author interview with Robert Parish.

266 **“Our goal in 1983”:** As quoted in Bird and Johnson with MacMullen, *When the Game Was Ours*, 123.

266 **“I just wonder”:** Bill Livingston, “Just Where Did the Celts Go Wrong?,” *Philadelphia Inquirer*, May 4, 1983, 1-E.

266 **“There was no way”:** Author interview with Robert Parish.

266 **“That the 76ers and Boston”:** Bill Lyon, “Though Fans Long for the Celtics, the Bucks Are a Worthy Foe,” *Philadelphia Inquirer*, May 8, 1983, 1-E, 8-E.

267 **“a dead animal”:** George Shirk, “Key Call Infuriates the Bucks,” *Philadelphia Inquirer*, January 13, 1983, 1-C, 4-C.

267 **more than forty feet:** Bill Lyon, “Eating Cake, and Having It,” *Philadelphia Inquirer*, March 24, 1983.

268 **remove the contraption:** Stan Hochman, “Strong Cycle for Toney,” *Philadelphia Daily News*, May 9, 1983, 95.

268 **“I would play a guy”:** Author interview with Bobby Jones.

269 **“My expression for it”:** Phil Jasner, “Sore Knee Slows Down Doctor,” *Philadelphia Daily News*, May 10, 1983, 76, 74.

269 **stuck an ice bag:** George Shirk, “Defensive Sixers Take 2-0 Series Lead,” *Philadelphia Inquirer*, May 12, 1983, 1-C, 6-C.

269 **“tighter than the barnacles”:** Bill Lyon, “A Fiery Protest Springs Malone,” *Philadelphia Inquirer*, May 12, 1983, 1-C, 7-C.

270 **“angry, probing waves”:** Phil Jasner, “Even the Doctor Can Be Reduced to Mere Mortal,” *Philadelphia Daily News*, May 13, 1983, 106.

270 **“Winning is on my mind”:** Phil Jasner, “Moses Steals Sixers’ Show,” *Philadelphia Daily News*, May 12, 1983, 88, 86.

270 **“I’ll be back”:** Bill Lyon, “Erving’s Performance Must Speak for Itself,” *Philadelphia Inquirer*, May 15, 1983, 1-E, 10-E.

270 **“than most Presidents”:** Mike Littwin, “These Days He’s Dr. J, Elder Statesman in NBA,” *Los Angeles Times*, May 29, 1983, 3-1, 3-12.

271 **“all over me, saying”:** Mike Harris, “Moses’ Commandment: Anything but Retiring,” *Richmond Times-Dispatch*, December 22, 1996, D1, D8.

271 **“I’m just saying”:** Phil Jasner, “Moses Puts Sixers One Level Higher,” *Sporting News*, May 16, 1983, 29.

271 **“Gotta get to the airport”:** George Shirk, “Bucks Put Skid on Sixers Sweep,” *Philadelphia Inquirer*, May 16, 1983, 1-D, 6-D.

271 **"I saw Julius leave":** George Shirk, "Sixers' Vanishing Act Upsets NBA," *Philadelphia Inquirer*, May 17, 1983, 1-C, 7-C.

271 **"I needed to cool out":** Phil Jasner, "Dr. J Tries 'Heal Thyself' Cure," *Philadelphia Daily News*, May 16, 1983, 96.

272 **"Why must they make":** Peter Vecsey, "Dr. J Speaks His Piece," *New York Post*, May 17, 1983.

272 **"It was all B.S.":** Shirk, "Sixers' Vanishing Act."

272 **"If I owned a farm":** Phil Jasner, "Sixers Gallop by Bucks to East Winner's Circle," *Philadelphia Daily News*, May 19, 1983, 92, 90.

Chapter 18: The Final Fo'

273 **fire-melted record:** Bill Livingston, "Misfortune Helps Abdul-Jabbar Lift His Game to New Heights," *Philadelphia Inquirer*, May 22, 1983, 15-D.

273 **"my material world":** Abdul-Jabbar with McCarthy, *Kareem*, 54.

274 **"a horrific season":** Abdul-Jabbar with McCarthy, *Kareem*, 82.

274 **"James's injury had":** Bruce Newman, "The Force Ran Its Course," *Sports Illustrated*, May 9, 1983.

274 **laid down masking:** Randy Harvey, "A Confidence-Building Loss," *Los Angeles Times*, May 23, 1983, 3-1, 3-13.

275 **"Get the first":** Phil Jasner, "Sixers Open in Style," *Philadelphia Daily News*, May 23, 1983, 96, 94.

275 **"No rebounds, no rings":** Dick Weiss, "Abdul-Jabbar's Will to Win Remains," *Philadelphia Daily News*, May 26, 1983, 94.

276 **"a little gnawing machine":** Harvey, "A Confidence-Building Loss."

276 **"ticket line opened":** Jere Longman, "Malone: No 6-8 Man Can Check Me," *Philadelphia Inquirer*, May 27, 1983, 5-D.

276 **"How about a casket?":** Randy Harvey, "Nixon Says He'll Shoulder His Load," *Los Angeles Times*, May 24, 1983, 3-1, 3-8.

276 **"I don't want to lay":** Randy Harvey, "Is TV Running Pro Basketball?," *Los Angeles Times*, May 25, 1983, 3-6.

277 **Forcing Abdul-Jabbar to use:** Linderman, "*Playboy* Interview."

277 **off-balance just enough:** Abdul-Jabbar with McCarthy, *Kareem*, 175.

277 **"Cheap fouls":** Kevin Kernan, "Lakers to Get Down & Dirty," *New York Post*, May 28, 1983.

277 **deceptive practices:** Barkley, *Outrageous!*, 212.

277 **clutching his jersey:** Frank Dolson, "Sixers' Power Cut Abdul-Jabbar Down to Size," *Philadelphia Inquirer*, May 27, 1983, 4-D.

277 **Johnson glowered:** Mike Littwin, "Lakers Yell Foul After They Go 3 of 5 for Game," *Los Angeles Times*, May 27, 1983, 3-1, 3-14.

277 **"four-letter words":** Randy Harvey, "76ers Send Lakers Home Crying," *Los Angeles Times*, May 27, 1983, 3-1, 3-14.

278 **"That's their problem":** Harvey, "76ers Send Lakers Home Crying."

278 **"got Rambis checking":** Phil Jasner, "Sixers Holding a Pair," *Philadelphia Daily News*, May 27, 1983, 120, 118.

278 **"we won't spend much":** Littwin, "Lakers Yell Foul."

278 **"How would I know":** Author interview with Steve Springer.

279 **"I cannot relax":** George Shirk, "In 1977, a 2–0 Lead Was Not Enough…," *Philadelphia Inquirer*, May 28, 1983, 1-D, 6-D.

279 **"Hey, I don't care":** Ostler, "Now It's Moses Doing Surgery."

280 **"I figured I might":** Ostler, "Now It's Moses Doing Surgery."

280 **"forces in nature":** Bill Livingston, "Frustration: Abdul-Jabbar Finds His Best Is Not Enough," *Philadelphia Inquirer*, May 30, 1983, 4-D.

280 **appeared weathered:** Ray Didinger, "Jones Not Tired of Winning," *Philadelphia Daily News*, May 27, 1983.

280 **"I may leave here":** Bruce Newman, "Better by Leaps and Bounds," *Sports Illustrated*, June 6, 1983.

281 **"We're going to win it":** Jere Longman, "Erving Finally Predicts, 'We're Going to Win It,'" *Philadelphia Inquirer*, May 30, 1983, 5-D.

281 **"wouldn't have to answer":** Longman, "Erving Finally Predicts."

281 **"Ain't no way":** Bill Lyon, "Sixers Are Playing for More Than a Title," *Philadelphia Inquirer*, May 31, 1983, 1-D, 7-D.

Chapter 19: The Alliance

283 **"We must not allow":** Frank Dolson, "Guy from Petersburg Was the Key for 76ers," *Philadelphia Inquirer*, May 1, 1983, 4-C.

284 **Bill Lyon dubbed:** Lyon, "Sixers Are Playing."

284 **"See us comin' again":** Randy Harvey, "76ers' Big Finish Finishes Lakers," *Los Angeles Times*, June 1, 1983, 3-1, 3-12.

285 **"All I was thinking":** Jasner, *On the Case*, 165.

285 **"If you get every":** Jasner, *On the Case*, 163.

287 **"He brought in being flamboyant":** Frank Brady, "Julius Erving: The Doctor Makes His Final House Call," *Basketball Digest*, April 1987, 14–24.

287 **"I didn't find that shot":** Phil Jasner, "The Promised Land," *Philadelphia Daily News*, June 1, 1983, 80.

288 **"It was Doc's game!":** Mike Littwin, "Dr. J Heals All That's Ailed Him," *Los Angeles Times*, June 1, 1983, 3-12.

288 **"more tired in my life":** Author interview with Bobby Jones.

288 **a "spiritual" moment":** Author interview with Bobby Jones.

289 **"I was totally consumed":** Author interview with Billy Cunningham.

289 **"You're stayin' and":** George Shirk, "A High-Flying Party Hits Town," *Philadelphia Inquirer*, June 2, 1983, 1-C, 4-C.

289 **"I've had three rings":** Bill Livingston, "Happy Feet," *Philadelphia Inquirer*, June 1, 1983, 5-C.

289 **"I guess I'm happier":** Bill Lyon, "In a Season of Change, the Doctor Finally Gets What He Is Owed," *Philadelphia Inquirer*, June 2, 1983, 10-11-S.

290 **"This was for the Doc":** Newman, "Thou Shalt Rejoice."

291 **"Next to the birth":** Bill Lyon, "76ers' Owner Pulled the Trigger and Hit the Target," *Philadelphia Inquirer*, June 1, 1983, 6-C.

291 **"I'm tired. I'm tired":** Jayson Stark, "Amid the Hoopla, the Middle Man Is Happy, Tired and Still Very Stoic," *Philadelphia Inquirer*, June 1, 1983, 5-C.

291 **"I'm gonna go":** Jasner, "The Promised Land."

292 **"This isn't the end":** George Shirk, "76ers Are Kings of NBA at Last; Lakers Fall in 4-Game Sweep," *Philadelphia Inquirer*, June 1, 1983, 1D, 4D.

292 **"if you don't back off":** Bill Lyon, "Malone's Energy Recharged a Team," *Philadelphia Inquirer*, June 2, 1983, 1-C, 4-C.

292 **"Wake me up":** George Shirk, "A High-Flying Party Hits Town," *Philadelphia Inquirer*, June 2, 1983, 1-C, 4-C.

292 **"Of course, we had no":** Author interview with Lee Fentress.

293 **1.5 million households:** Leen Winfrey, "The Eyes of Phila.," *Philadelphia Inquirer*, June 2, 1983, 1-D, 12-D.

293 **"Thou art the champs":** Edgar Williams, "The Zink, the Sun, the Party," *Philadelphia Inquirer*, June 3, 1983, 13-A.

293 **"they have rice marks":** Jeff Jacobs, "This Time Moses Will Take 76ers to Long-Sought Promised Land," *Courier-Post*, May 19, 1983, C-1.

293 **"titanic mound":** Chuck Stone, "And the Waters Parted, 115–108," *Philadelphia Daily News*, June 1, 1983, 22.

293 **"a real tear-jerker":** Roger Cohn and Walter F. Naedele, "5,000 Welcome the Kings of Basketball," *Philadelphia Inquirer*, June 2, 1983, 1-A, 10-A.

294 **"We have a group":** Bill Livingston and Jere Longman, "The Champions Return," *Philadelphia Inquirer*, June 2, 1983, 1-C, 4-C.

294 **A few intrepid:** Gene Seymour, "Broad Street Was Teaming with 76er Fans," *Philadelphia Daily News*, June 3, 1983, 5, 36.

294 **"seeing all these different":** As quoted in Platt, *New Jack Jocks*, 146.

294 **"Many observers":** Gene Seymour, "76ers Ignite Celebrations in Black and White," *Philadelphia Daily News*, June 2, 1983, 5, 23.

295 **"It tickled me":** Author interview with Pat Williams.

295 **"We have the world championship":** Stan Hochman, "Hard Hats Win Some Warm Hearts," *Philadelphia Daily News*, June 3, 1983, 127.

Epilogue: The Unraveling

297 **"the ring was forcing":** Author interview with Pat Williams.

297 **"Last summer has got":** Anthony Cotton, "Blood, Sweat and Cheers," *Sports Illustrated*, October 31, 1983.

298 **"Is Malone worth":** George Shirk, "Sixers Owner Criticizes Efforts of Malone and Team," *Philadelphia Inquirer*, March 3, 1984, 1-A, 12-A.

300 **"who made me dream":** Bill Lyon, "Think of a Dunk, and You Think of Doc," *Philadelphia Inquirer*, April 16, 1987, 5.

300 **"He's one of the nicest":** Anthony Cotton, "Malone Center of Washington Hopes for a Title," *Daily Oklahoman*, December 14, 1986.

301 **"creates a void":** Mark Perner, "Mortal Wounds Self-Inflicted at 1986 Draft," *Philadelphia Inquirer*, May 7, 2013, 48–49.

301 **"curse of Moses Malone":** Rich Hofmann, "The Curse of Moses Malone," *Philadelphia Daily News*, June 20, 2011, 82–83.

301 **"began treating people":** David Kahn, "Katz! He's a One-Man Show in Philadelphia," *Basketball Digest*, December 1987.

301 **"that big cigar":** Jere Longman, "Scrooge Malone Coming to Town," *Philadelphia Inquirer*, December 25, 1986, 1-D, 3-D.

302 **"Doc has done":** Bill Lyon, "One of a Kind, in Every Way," *Philadelphia Inquirer*, April 16, 1987, 2–3.

302 **"retire by telephone":** Stan Isle, "Contract Contrast: Like Father, Not Like Son," *Sporting News*, June 22, 1987, 5.

303 **"You name it":** Phil Taylor, "Moses Malone," *Sports Illustrated*, November 8, 1993.

303 **testified in court:** Patti Muck, "Malone Says He Is a Role Model, Not a Wife Abuser or Adulterer," *Houston Chronicle*, September 10, 1992, 25A, 31A.

304 **Moses Malone denied:** United Press International, "Moses Malone's Divorce Case Ends," October 13, 1992, www.upi.com/Archives/1992/10/13/Moses-Malones-divorce-case-ends/3941718948800/.

304 **"self-defense":** Erving with Greenfeld, *Dr. J*, 350.

304 **"There's no justification":** Shoshana Davis, "Dr. J on Womanizing and Having 'No Justification' for Hitting Ex-Wife," CBS News, November 5, 2013, www.cbsnews.com/news/dr-j-on-womanzing-and-having-no-justification-for-hitting-ex-wife.

305 **"Maybe one with":** Bill Lyon, "Spawning a New Breed of Player at Small Forward," *Philadelphia Inquirer*, April 16, 1987, 4.

INDEX

Index

Index

Index

Index

Index

Index

Index

Index

Index

ABOUT THE AUTHOR

Luke Epplin is the author of *Our Team: The Epic Story of Four Men and the World Series That Changed Baseball*. His writing has appeared online in *The Atlantic*, *The New Yorker*, *GQ*, *Slate*, *The Washington Post*, *Los Angeles Review of Books*, and *The Paris Review Daily*. Born and raised in rural Illinois, Epplin lives outside New York City with his wife and daughter.